DATE DUE

Colorado

The Highest State

Colorado

The Highest State

Thomas J. Noel and Duane A. Smith

University Press of Colorado

© 1995 by the University Press of Colorado

Published by the University Press of Colorado
P.O. Box 849, Niwot, CO 80544
All rights reserved. Printed in the United States of America.

The University Press of Colorado is a cooperative publishing enterprise supported, in part, by Adams State College, Colorado State University, Fort Lewis College, Mesa State College, Metropolitan State College of Denver, University of Colorado, University of Northern Colorado, University of Southern Colorado, and Western State College of Colorado.

Chapter 1: "Two Rivers" by Thomas Hornsby Ferril originally appeared in *New and Selected Poems,* New York: Harper & Brothers Publishers, 1927. Reprinted with permission of the Thomas Hornsby Ferril Literary Trust.

Maps by Professor Richard E. Stevens, University of Colorado at Denver Geography Department. Maps are reprinted courtesy of the University of Oklahoma Press.

Library of Congress Cataloging-in-Publication Data

Noel, Thomas J. (Thomas Jacob)
    Colorado: the highest state / Thomas J. Noel, Duane A. Smith.
        p.   cm.
    Includes bibliographical references and index.
    ISBN 0-87081-373-0 (cloth : alk. paper)
    1. Colorado—History—Juvenile literature. 2. Colorado—Geography—Juvenile literature. I. Smith, Duane A. II. Title.
F776.3.N64   1995
978.8—dc20
                                      95-2813
                                      CIP
                                      AC

10   9   8   7   6   5   4

Contents

Maps

Preface

Colorado's history, like the state itself, has had many ups and downs. Booms and busts in farming and ranching, in mining and railroading, in water and oil have made Colorado's past a cycle of ups and downs as high as the state's peaks and as low as its canyons.

Our state's fascinating history is made up of interesting characters. Fathers Domínguez and Escalante, two Spanish priests, first explored, wrote about, and mapped much of Colorado. Ouray, the Ute Chief, fought for peace. Clara Brown, a former enslaved African American, made enough money washing miners' jeans to help her people build churches and become successful pioneers. Elizabeth Iliff came to Colorado selling sewing machines and wound up running the state's most famous ranch.

Charles Boettcher, a German immigrant who stepped off the train with only a few cents in his pocket, worked tirelessly until he became Colorado's richest tycoon. Josephine Roche, a pioneer policewoman, became a mine owner and ran for governor. Horace Tabor took millions out of his mines, only to lose his fortune.

Mayor Speer transformed Colorado's capital city from a dusty, drab, treeless town into a City Beautiful. His work was continued in recent years by mayors Federico Peña and Wellington Webb, who made Denver a big league city with the nation's newest airport and a National League baseball team, the Colorado Rockies. While Colorado's high plains communities produced wheat and beef, mountain mining towns recycled themselves as ski resorts and summer playgrounds for all Americans.

In each chapter of this book, you will find some questions, activities, and suggested readings to help you learn more of Colorado's story than we can present here. We hope you will enjoy these pages. You will discover a high, dry state with rugged natural beauty and an awesome history.

Acknowledgments

Teachers and students from all over Colorado have helped us with this book. Among others, we especially thank Chuck Woodward and Art Cordova of Gateway High School in Aurora, David Smith of Samuels School in Denver, Nancy Gregory and Ray Jenkins of Hinkley High School, Jerry Fabyanic and Pat Heist Ward of Aurora Hills Middle School, Andy Aiken of Boulder High School, and the Education Department of the Colorado History Museum.

Brent Brown, Lynn Brown, Michael Breunig, Aaron Bell, Doug Katie, Julie Potter, Kelly Hester, Elizabeth Watts, and Ward Lee of Smiley, Escalante, and Miller Middle Schools in Durango and Colorado history students Leslie Burger, Mike Ferguson, Rosemary Fetter, Marcia Goldstein, Katie Hartenbach, Judy Morley, Virginia Shannon, and Laralee Smith all helped make this a better book. James Hartmann, president of the Colorado History Museum, offered many helpful suggestions.

Thanks to Professor Richard E. Stevens of the University of Colorado, Denver Geography Department, who drew the maps. Many of these maps first appeared in *Historical Atlas of Colorado* (1994), by Thomas J. Noel, Paul F. Mahoney, and Richard E. Stevens. Maps are reprinted courtesy of the University of Oklahoma Press.

We also thank Governor Roy Romer, Senator Ben Nighthorse Campbell, and Denver mayors Federico Peña and Wellington Webb for interviews and their suggestions about what should be passed on to Colorado history classes.

We, like so many other fans of Colorado history, found the resources in both the Western History Department of the Denver Public Library and the Colorado Historical Society especially helpful. Between them, these Denver gold mines have a million illustrations of Colorado. For other photos, as well as printed research material, we are indebted to Colorado College and the

Pioneer Museum in Colorado Springs. The Pueblo District Library, the Museum of Western Colorado in Grand Junction, and the Southwest Studies Center at Fort Lewis College in Durango were also extremely helpful. To these institutions and their staffs, as well as to many other museums and libraries in the sixty-three counties of Colorado, our hats are off in gratitude.

This book for middle and high school students replaces our now out-of-print book (written with Fay Metcalf), *Colorado: Heritage of the Highest State* (Boulder: Pruett Publishing Company, 1984). We are indebted to the classic texts of LeRoy and Ann Hafen, who in four different editions refined the idea of what a Colorado history text should be.

Both authors and the University Press of Colorado welcome suggestions from students, teachers, and other interested readers about how we can make this a better and more useful book.

Colorado

The Highest State

PART I

From Dinosaurs to Denver

United States		Colorado	
15,000 – 25,000 B.C.E.	Indians arrive in North America from Asia	**11,000 B.C.E.**	Indians occupy eastern plains
1000 B.C.E.	Native Americans develop agriculture	**2000 B.C.E.**	Anasazi Indians settle Mesa Verde area
1598	Spanish begin to settle in New Mexico	**1600s**	Utes hear of Spanish settlers
1607	English settle Jamestown, Virginia	**1620s**	Utes meet Spaniards
1776	Declaration of Independence	**1776**	Domínguez-Escalante expedition
1803	Louisiana Purchase (includes eastern Colorado)	**1806**	Zebulon Pike explores Colorado
1848	U.S. defeats Mexico and takes northern third of Mexico; gold discovered in California	**1848**	Remainder of Colorado becomes U.S. territory; Fremont gets lost in San Juan mountains
1858	First stagecoach from St. Louis to San Francisco	**1858**	Rumors of gold in the Pikes Peak region
1859	First producing oil well	**1859**	Pikes Peak gold rush
1860	Population 31,443,321	**1860**	Population 34,277
1861	Civil War begins	**1861**	Colorado Territory established
1876	U.S. centennial	**1876**	Statehood
1877	Telephone patented	**1878**	Leadville silver boom
1880	U.S. population 50,155,783	**1880**	Population reaches 194,327
1884	*Adventures of Huckleberry Finn* published	**1881–1882**	Ute removal; Western Slope opened to settlement
1891	Bicycling craze begins	**1891**	Cripple Creek gold rush
1893	Chicago World's Fair; economic crash	**1893**	Colorado women get the vote
1898	Spanish-American War	**1899**	First automobile in Denver
1890	U.S. population 75,994,575	**1900**	Population 539,700

CHAPTER ONE
The Highest State

The young college professor hoped to see the Colorado prairies and mountains from the top of Pikes Peak. In 1893, for a young woman that trip would be quite an adventure. So Katherine Lee Bates and some friends hired a wagon and driver and started up America's most famous mountain.

The trip was worth all the planning and worry, Professor Bates decided. "I was looking out over the sea-like expanse of fertile country" when the opening lines of a poem "floated into my mind":

> O beautiful for spacious skies,
> For amber waves of grain,
> For purple mountain majesties
> Above the fruited plain!

You might recognize these opening lines from her poem, which became the song "America the Beautiful."

Years later, Denver poet Thomas Hornsby Ferril wrote a poem about the community where he lived for over ninety years. "Two Rivers" describes the South Platte River and Cherry Creek and the people who came to settle along their banks in Denver:

> Two rivers that were here before there was
> A city here still come together: one
> Is a mountain river flowing into the prairie;
> One is a prairie river flowing toward
> The mountains but feeling them and turning back
> The way some of the people who came here did.

Ferril wrote about the mountains, prairies, water, and people — the major factors in Colorado's history.

Like millions of other people, Katherine Lee Bates and Thomas Hornsby Ferril were impressed when they saw the wonders of Colorado. The high mountains have astonished visitors and Coloradans alike. "The Highest State" is what writers over a hundred years ago called the state. You will be amazed, too, when you read about and travel around Colorado.

Colorado is the only state that is an almost perfect rectangle. At its widest, Colorado is 387 miles from the Kansas border to Utah. It is 276 miles from the Wyoming border on the north to the New Mexico border on the south. It is the eighth-largest state, with a total area of 104,247 square miles.

Colorado became a state in 1876, the same year the United States of America celebrated its centennial, or one-hundredth birthday. That is how Colorado got one nickname, "the Centennial State." The state is divided into sixty-three counties, with Las Animas and Moffat the largest in area and Denver and Gilpin the smallest. In each county one town is designated the county seat. Denver is the state capital and Colorado's largest city.

Colorado is the highest state in the union. The average elevation is 6,800 feet above sea level. If we leveled out Colorado to an average elevation of 1,000 feet, what do you think would happen? Colorado would be the biggest state in the United States — larger than Texas or Alaska!

Mount Elbert (14,431 feet) is the highest point in Colorado and the fourteenth-tallest mountain in the nation. Alaska has twelve taller mountains and California has one. Colorado, however, has fifty-four peaks that are 14,000 feet or higher. The lowest point in the state is in the Arkansas Valley near Holly; it is 3,350 feet.

Snow falls somewhere in Colorado every month of the year. Leadville has had several snowfalls on July 4. You may have been picnicking in the mountains on a summer day when it snowed.

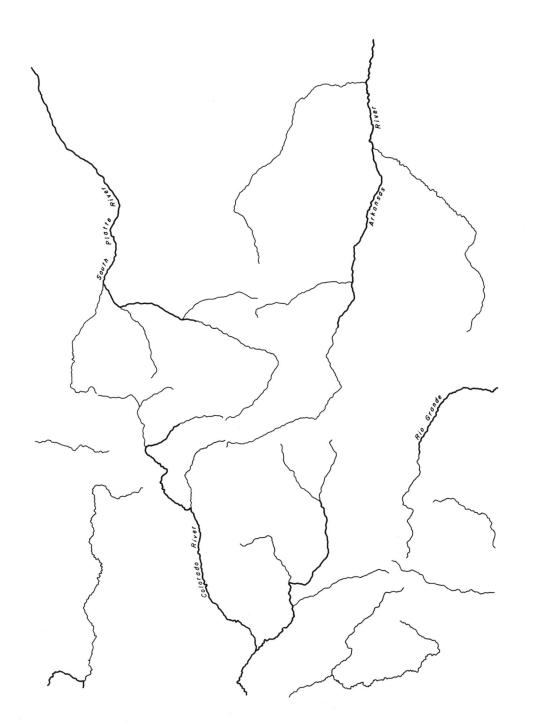

Rivers

Colorado holds the world's record for the most snowfall in twenty-four hours: seventy-six inches at Silver Lake, in April 1921.

Colorado is called the "mother of rivers" because so many waterways start in our mountains. Rivers radiate out of the state like the spokes of a wheel. The mighty Colorado River begins here and flows 1,450 miles to reach the Gulf of California and the Pacific Ocean. The Rio Grande (which means "Grand River" in Spanish) is even longer — 1,885 miles — and flows into the Gulf of Mexico.

Near Poncha Pass, something very unusual occurs. From starting points that are within a few feet of each other, water rolls in three different directions toward the sea. Part of it flows into the Colorado River, some flows into the Rio Grande, and the rest runs into the Arkansas River, which eventually ends up in the Mississippi River. Water that is only a stone's throw apart at the start will be separated by thousands of miles when it finally reaches its destination. The South Platte rises in South Park and flows northeast, while the Arkansas drains the southeast part of the state. Rivers, as we shall see, have played a very important role in Colorado's history. Settlers, animals, plants, and industry all need water.

Because Colorado has such a variety of climates and elevations, it has recorded some very unusual temperatures. The coldest was 61 degrees below zero in Moffat County. The hottest was 118 degrees at Bennett in Adams County. In addition, the Eastern Slope of Colorado often has weather completely different from the weather on the Western Slope. Rapidly changing climate conditions can raise or lower the temperature as much as 50 degrees in one day. Colorado's geography has shaped the history and development of the state. Farming, mining, ranching, tourism, townbuilding, industry, and transportation all have been changed by geography. Few other states can offer such breathtaking scenery, varied animal and plant life, and variety of climates.

Eastern Plains

Look at Colorado's geographic regions. The state divides itself naturally into three parts. The first region that visitors from the

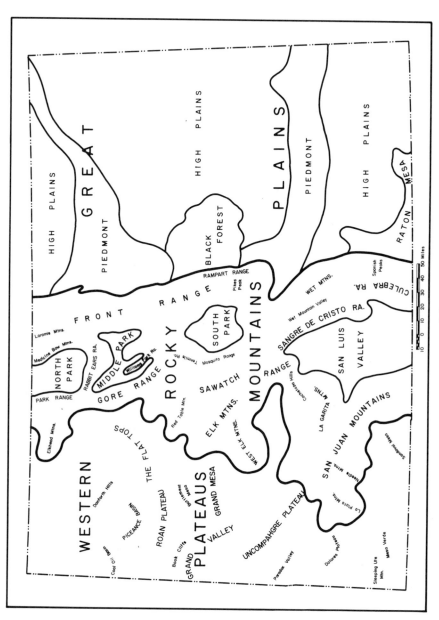

Landforms

eastern states saw was the eastern plains. They are part of the region called the Great Plains, which stretch eastward from the Rockies through North Dakota, South Dakota, Nebraska, Kansas, Oklahoma, and Texas.

The plains slope gently upward from Colorado's eastern border to the foothills of the Front Range, or the Eastern Slope of the Rocky Mountains. The Front Range stretches south from Fort Collins to Boulder, Denver, Colorado Springs, Pueblo, and Trinidad. Rainfall is scant in this region. These eastern plains are also windy in the spring and well known for their dust storms, heat, hail, and summer droughts, or dry spells. Because of these conditions and the sparse summer vegetation, early visitors were fooled into calling the plains the "Great American Desert." The region is not a desert at all, but it seemed that way to people who were used to the lush green forests of the eastern United States.

Native grasses grow abundantly on this prairie land. Buffalo, antelope, and other animals have thrived on these grasses, and numerous Indian peoples settled on the plains to hunt these animals. Because of the rich grasslands, Colorado's eastern plains became an important cattle ranching region. When the farmers came, they first settled along the rivers, then moved onto the drier land. The eastern plains, because they are at a lower elevation than the rest of Colorado, have a longer growing season (the number of days between the last frost of spring and the first frost of fall). The region is also well known for its abundant sunshine and its special beauty.

Mountains

Colorado has always been famous for its mountains, especially Pikes Peak, the state's first mountain to be named on maps. Tourists have been climbing it or riding to the top of 14,110-foot-high Pikes Peak for many years. Colorado has more than 1,000 peaks above 10,000 feet and 54 peaks that top 14,000 feet in "the Highest State."

The mountains stretch from the rolling foothills along the Front Range to the high Continental Divide and then westward. The Continental Divide is the "backbone" of the Rocky Mountains. It is a ridge of mountains that separates the water flow between east and west. On the Eastern Slope, water runs east to the Mississippi River and the Gulf of Mexico. Water running off the Western Slope eventually reaches the Pacific Ocean via the Colorado River.

The Rocky Mountains, which cut across central Colorado from north to south, are part of a larger chain of mountains. These mountains run from Canada into Mexico. The Rocky Mountains reach their highest elevation and greatest width in Colorado. Within the Rockies are other smaller ranges. Colorado has the Sangre de Cristo Range (the Spanish named it "Blood of Christ" for the red evening glow), the La Platas (or "silver" in Spanish), the San Juans, the Front Range, the Sawatch Mountains, and others.

In the Rocky Mountains of Colorado are found four great "parks," or high mountain valleys. They are North Park, Middle Park, South Park, and the San Luis Valley (originally San Luis Park). The San Luis Valley and South Park are the largest.

Old mine ruins recall the gold and silver booms of the San Juan Mountains, where this Yankee Girl Mine shaft house still stands south of Ouray near Red Mountain Pass. (Photo by Glen Crandall.)

Once buffalo, elk, deer, and antelope roamed these parks. They were the favorite hunting grounds for Indians and fur trappers. Settlement, especially ranching, came to them very early. In the mountains around these valleys, discoveries of gold, silver, and other valuable minerals later triggered mining rushes.

Rivers have cut some impressive canyons as they break out of the vast mountains. The Royal Gorge of the Arkansas River and the Black Canyon of the Gunnison River are the most famous canyons in Colorado. Royal Gorge narrows to 30 feet wide, with cliffs rising 1,200 feet above the river.

Beavers first drew Anglo and French Americans into the mountains. Fur trappers worked all through this region in search of the furry rodent whose fur hide was prized for hats. Grizzly bears, black and brown bears, deer, mountain sheep, mountain lions, and buffalo were once plentiful as well. Many of them were hunted until they were nearly gone before people realized what was happening. To European Americans of the 1800s, the buffalo, deer, and beaver were most important; their skins could be sold to make hats, blankets, and clothes. Buffalo and deer were also a source of meat, and beaver tail was a special food treat.

Western Slope

The part of Colorado that lies west of the Continental Divide is known as the Western Slope. It also has mountains — for instance, the very rugged San Juans surrounding Ouray, Silverton, and Telluride, and the Elk Mountains near Crested Butte and Aspen. Western Colorado has some large river valleys as well. Because they were protected from the worst winter storms and cold, these valleys attracted farmers and ranchers. The Gunnison Valley and the Grand Valley near Grand Junction are two of the best known. The Western Slope was the last of the three Colorado regions to be settled, since it was all by itself west of the mountains.

The climate, rainfall, and growing seasons of the Western Slope vary greatly. The far western and northwestern parts are semiarid, or almost a desert. This is a hard land for both animals and people because rainfall is very light. On the other hand, it is much wetter in the mountains. Some mountains receive up to 300 inches of snowfall each winter.

The Western Slope is a scenic land. It has high mountains and deserts, wide river valleys, and huge mesas (or "tables" in Spanish). Early Spanish explorers gave that name to these landforms. The largest one is Grand Mesa, which rises to 10,000 feet and towers over Grand Junction. Mesa Verde ("green tableland") in southwestern Colorado is the site of the famous cliff dwellings and thousand-year-old Indian villages.

Rivers carved awesome canyons into western Colorado. The Black Canyon of the Gunnison, not far from Montrose, is a national monument. At its deepest point, the canyon walls are 2,425 feet high.

Pioneers coming to Colorado had trouble finding water when they left the river routes. They found this to be a dry state, averaging only 16.6 inches of precipitation a year. (Denver Public Library.)

The northwestern part of the Western Slope is wild, lonely country. It was so isolated that it was the very last area of the state to be settled. The far southwestern corner of Colorado is the only place in the United States where four states — New Mexico, Utah, Arizona, and Colorado — come together at one point. Imagine being able to stand in four states at one time!

Geography and Settlement

Two geographic features dominate the history of Colorado: the Rocky Mountains and the rivers. In the mountains, the abundant beaver pelts and veins of gold and silver attracted newcomers to the future state of Colorado. People believed they could become fabulously rich in a few short years by trapping beavers or mining gold or silver.

Mining was the most important industry in Colorado for forty years after the 1859 Pikes Peak gold rush. Mining brought permanent settlement: first camps and then towns. To reach the mining settlements, people built wagon roads and railroads. Farmers and ranchers from the plains moved to the mountains to furnish food for the miners.

The rivers were equally important. Without water, people could not stay. This is true of all three regions of Colorado. The ranchers and farmers settled in the river valleys of the mountains and plains. It is no accident that Colorado's largest cities are found along the eastern foothills, where the rivers break out of the mountains. Colorado's commerce and industry are concentrated here, as well. These well-watered river valleys were the most popular places in which to settle. Likewise, on the Western Slope, the cities of Grand Junction, Durango, Gunnison, and Montrose were established along rivers.

Settlement, then, followed several basic geographic patterns:

1. towns and cities on waterways leading into the mountains (for example, Denver, on the banks of Cherry Creek and the South Platte River)
2. settlements along the rivers that cross the eastern plains (for example, Greeley, on the South Platte)
3. camps and towns near the mineral outcroppings of gold, silver, and coal (for example, the gold-strike town of Central City and the coal-mining town of Erie)
4. towns on agricultural sites and transportation routes (for example, Sterling, on the Union Pacific Railroad route and the South Platte River)
5. health or tourist resorts near scenic or unique geographic features (for example, Glenwood Springs, at the site of mineral hot springs, and Estes Park, the eastern gateway to Rocky Mountain National Park)

Think about the towns in your county. Did they follow one or more of these patterns?

Water

Colorado averages 16.6 inches of precipitation (rain, snow, and hail) yearly. However, this amount can change greatly from year to year. Fortunately, the mountain snowpack and runoff can be used for irrigating farms and ranches during the spring and summer. All the water in the state comes from precipitation and from the rivers that have their headwaters in Colorado. Neighboring states can get their water from rivers flowing into them; Colorado cannot. Hardly any water enters

As this 1900 view of Silverton shows, mountains have always shaped Colorado settlement and history. (San Juan County Historical Society.)

Colorado from other states. In this respect the Highest State is unique.

Water is Colorado's most valuable natural resource. Although many great rivers begin in the state's mountains, Colorado does not have the right to use all that water. It must share its water with neighboring states.

Seasons

People like to live in Colorado, as its growth over the years shows. Colorado's temperatures are usually mild — it is rarely too hot or too cold for very long. The air is very dry most of the time; the humidity, or moisture in the air, is rarely high enough to make you feel uncomfortable. Colorado is famous for its climate, and the lack of humidity is the main reason it is so pleasant. (Humidity makes cold air seem colder and hot air seem hotter.)

Colorado's changing seasons give variety to its climate. There are really only three seasons — fall, winter, and summer. James Grafton Rogers, in his book *My Rocky Mountain Valley,* explains why: "The four seasons, spring, summer, autumn and winter, are terms that belong to the language of Europe and of

Eastern North America. . . . There is, in the Rocky Mountains, no gentle spring, no gradual awakening of life, no slow emergence of vegetation. Summer comes suddenly, some day in early June, on the heels of winter."

Summer is the season in which the plants flourish and the animals are most active. They have to gather much of their food for the rest of the year. Fall turns the aspen yellow and brings the first snows.

Winter snows bury spring. As Rogers wrote, "Our winter is not gloomy or snowbound. It takes turns with sunshine and snow storms." Then summer arrives and the cycle begins again.

These seasons are important to Colorado. In "spring" and summer the crops must be planted and nurtured. The growing season — the number of days when the weather is warm enough to grow vegetables and fruits — ranges from 76 days in the mountains to nearly 200 days on the eastern plains. Farmers must be careful that what they plant has time to grow to maturity.

Fall is a good season to tour Colorado because there are fewer tourists and the weather is usually dry. Fall is the time when the crops are harvested (and winter wheat is planted) and the wild animals are preparing for the oncoming winter.

During Colorado's winters, rural communities often were isolated by severe storms and heavy snows. Winter still can shut down Colorado. In 1982, a Christmas Eve blizzard paralyzed Denver when 2 feet of snow fell. Yet this was not the biggest of all Denver blizzards. That one came in December 1913, when the city received 47.7 inches of snow, with drifts up to 20 feet high. Digging out was a tough job. Schools and businesses closed. Hundreds of men were paid $2.50 per day to shovel snow and load it into horse-drawn wagons. Some of the snow piles did not melt until summer.

Today people do not feel as lonely as they did in those earlier blizzards. Telephones, radios, and television keep them in touch with one another. In fact, winter has actually helped the state. It has become one of the biggest tourist seasons, now that Colorado skiing is world famous.

State Emblems

Like other states, Colorado has an official flower, tree, bird, and nickname. Colorado even has a state dinosaur. You will find these emblems listed in this chapter in a special section.

In a state as large and varied as this one, selecting these emblems was difficult. James Grafton Rogers tells why: "The Blue columbine is called the Colorado State flower but a single symbol is hard to find for a region so varied as ours, so full of wet and dry, high and low, hot and cold extremes. The columbine grows only in the mountains, less than half the state." The columbine was chosen in 1891 by Colorado schoolchildren as the state flower.

State Emblems

Colorado: *state named for the Colorado River; Colorado is Spanish for "red" or "ruddy"*

Nicknames: *the Highest State; the Centennial State*

Motto: Nil Sine Numine: *Nothing Without Providence (God)*

Flower: *blue/lavender columbine*

Bird: *lark bunting*

Animal: *bighorn sheep*

Tree: *Colorado blue spruce*

Fossil: *stegosaurus*

Song: *"Where the Columbines Grow"*

Flag: *three equal horizontal stripes, two blue and a white; a red letter "c" encircling a golden disk is at the left*

Fish: *cutthroat trout, green back trout*

The state flower and the state tree are mountain dwellers, but the state bird lives on the plains and is scarcely known to mountain people. It is the lark bunting, a little black and white

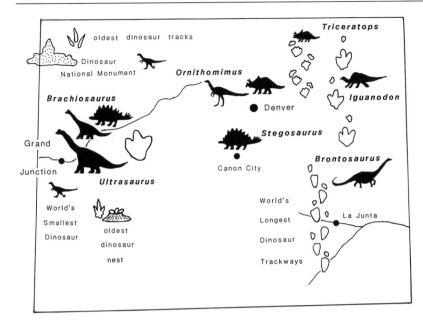

oldest dinosaur tracks

Dinosaur National Monument

Ornithomimus

Triceratops

Brachiosaurus

Denver

Iguanodon

Grand Junction

Stegosaurus

Ultrasaurus

Canon City

Brontosaurus

World's Smallest Dinosaur

oldest dinosaur nest

World's Longest Dinosaur Trackways

La Junta

Dinosaur bones and tracks found throughout Colorado point to a time when our state had tropical jungles crawling with prehistoric monsters. (Drawing by Martin Lockley.)

bird with a brilliant song. Students of your age and younger helped to select the lark bunting.

In 1981 and 1982 two groups of fourth graders from the McElwain Elementary School in Thornton worked hard to have a state fossil named. In 1982 they persuaded Governor Richard Lamm to choose the stegosaurus ("Steggy"). "Steggy" is the heavyweight of all the state emblems.

Millions of years ago, the stegosaurus and other dinosaurs roamed over the land that would become Colorado. The climate, landforms, vegetation, and rivers were different back then. Colorado had many volcanoes, inland seas, and lush jungles where dinosaurs roamed. No one living today ever saw dinosaurs, but we know they existed because dinosaur bones have been found throughout the state. The first complete stegosaurus skeleton was discovered in Colorado. That discovery is a major reason the stegosaurus was selected to be the state fossil.

Colorado, a Land to Behold

Colorado is a wondrous, fascinating land, a land to be explored. Its geography has played a major role in its history, from the days of the Mesa Verde Indians until today. In the words of our state song, "Where the Columbines Grow":

'Tis the land where the columbines grow,
Overlooking the plains far below,
While the cool summer breeze in the evergreen trees
Softly sings where the columbines grow.

Colorado has to be seen, felt, studied, and explored to be understood. The following chapters will give you a start.

QUESTIONS

1. Why is "mother of rivers" a good nickname for Colorado?
2. Explain how the mountains have influenced the course of Colorado history. Think about the people who came to Colorado, why they came, and what they did.
3. If you traveled from east to west across Colorado, what differences would you see between the eastern plains and the Western Slope?
4. Why is water Colorado's most important natural resource?
5. What pattern of development did your town, city, or county follow?
6. Do you think Colorado should have other state symbols, or emblems? What would they be? Why? Choose something that you think should be a state emblem. Draw a picture of it and explain why it should be an emblem.

ACTIVITIES

1. Make a map of your county. Show the waterways, mountains, and towns. Use symbols to show the ways most of the people make their living.
2. Find out the sources of water your town or school uses. Then make a map or chart showing how the water moves from its source to the water faucets you use.
3. Where can you find dinosaur bones or tracks in Colorado? Have any signs of the stegosaurus been found in your area?
4. Write a poem or song that reflects the Colorado you know best.
5. Take a walking field trip to see what plants and trees you find in your neighborhood. How many are native, and how many were brought by settlers?

6.   Find out how many of the state emblems can be found in your county or region. Make a drawing or take a photo of them.

Books You and Your Teacher Might Enjoy

Maxine Benson. *1001 Colorado Place Names.* Lawrence: University Press of Kansas, 1993. Find out how your town or county was named.

Dougal Dixon. *Dinosaurs.* Honesdale, PA: Bell Books, 1993. This book will introduce you to the prehistoric giants that once lived in Colorado.

Thomas J. Noel, Paul F. Mahoney, and Richard E. Stevens. *Historical Atlas of Colorado.* Norman: University of Oklahoma Press, 1993. This book of maps shows how geography has affected Colorado's history.

James Grafton Rogers. *My Rocky Mountain Valley.* Boulder: Pruett Publishing, 1968. This volume is one of the best books ever written about Colorado's environment.

The WPA Guide to 1930s Colorado. Lawrence: University Press of Kansas, 1987 (reprint of 1941 edition). Learn fascinating facts and stories about an important period in Colorado's past.

Did You Know?

Colorado once was covered by seas.

Colorado was the home of many dinosaurs.

Colorado is the starting point of five major rivers: North Platte, South Platte, Arkansas, Colorado, and Rio Grande.

Colorado is the home of four of the earth's major vegetation types: grasslands, desert shrub and brushlands, evergreen forest, and alpine tundra.

Colorado has more than forty large hot springs.

You can clearly see these dinosaur tracks along West Alameda Avenue at Dinosaur Ridge near Morrison. (Photo by Thomas J. Noel.)

CHAPTER TWO
The First Coloradans

Thousands of years ago — about 15,000 B.C.E. — the first human beings came to Colorado. These first arrivals were hunters and food gatherers who had migrated to North America from Asia. They are called Paleo-Indian, which means "ancient people who made stone tools."

Paleo-Indians

The Paleo-Indian people had no written language. We know about them because they left behind drawings on rocks, campsites, stone tools, and skeletons of some of the large animals they killed to eat. They hunted huge bison or buffalo, ground sloths, and mammoth elephants. These early people also hunted animals that you would recognize: rabbits, deer, and coyotes.

At the time of the Paleo-Indians, mammoths, camels, and horses roamed all over Colorado. Mammoth bones have been found at various sites in Colorado. These giant animals eventually all became extinct in Colorado.

Because there are no written records, scholars call this the prehistoric period. Women and men who study prehistoric peoples are archaeologists. When they find evidence of early people, they carefully explore the area and record their findings: bones, tools, drawings, and other signs of daily life. These archaeological sites are called "digs" because the scientists dig and sift through the dirt. The objects they find are called artifacts.

Not until the twentieth century was serious study made of these first Coloradans. In 1924, a group of artifact collectors found the Lindenmeier site northeast of Fort Collins. It became one of the most famous digs in the state. Archaeologists worked at this site for years. Knives, scrapers, engraved bone pieces, bone needles, and Folsom spear points were found. Archaeologists

Folsom points were hand-carved, stone spearheads that some of the first Coloradans used to kill rabbits, deer, buffalo, and other wild game. (Denver Museum of Natural History.)

called them Folsom points because they first were found at a site near Folsom, New Mexico. People who used these points were called Folsom people.

George Jenkins, an African American cowboy, made the first discovery of Folsom points. He found them amid some buffalo bones on a ranch. He told the Denver Museum of Natural History about the spear points, and the museum sent archaeologists to the site to study the Folsom people.

Folsom people are the first Coloradans we know much about because they left their tools behind. Many of these tools were found at kill sites, where Folsom families killed an animal and feasted. Evidence of the Folsom culture disappeared about 10,000 years ago.

Plano Culture

The Folsom people were followed by a group called the Plano culture. They lived on the Great Plains between 8000 and 5000 B.C. Plano people made fine projectile points for hunting animals and grinding slabs for crushing nuts and seeds, which they gathered along with fruits and berries.

Robert Jones, Jr., a rancher near Wray in eastern Colorado, found Plano spear points with the bones of bison and with the butchered remains of a dog. This and other discoveries show that Plano people lived in Colorado for several thousand years. Because the Plano people were both hunters and gatherers, they used almost everything edible to improve their diets.

Archaic People

Archaic (old) people occupied Colorado from around 5000 B.C. to the year 2000 B.C. After several thousand years of hunting big game — mammoths — a change came to these early Coloradans. Their primary food source became extinct, so they shifted more attention to plants and smaller animals.

As the years passed, the Archaic people started to live in rock shelters. This change was a great step forward. Shelters meant that people stayed in one place hunting and gathering, instead of following game. A site excavated near Granby in 1981 suggested that the Archaic people may have done more than simply look for a suitable rock shelter. These people may have built houses. Other house sites were found near Parachute and Curecanti.

Slab-covered fire hearths, baskets, and flax and yucca cords show that the Archaic people had advanced over their Paleo ancestors. Another sign is the more careful crafting of their projectile points. To find out more about these people, archaeologists continue to excavate their sites and study the relics they find. We do not even know what the Colorado climate was like during their time.

Anasazi: The Ancient Ones

About 2,000 years ago another change came to the people living in Colorado. New influences came from the south, from as far away as the land that would become Mexico. As a result, the hunter-gatherer people evolved into the culture we today know as Anasazi. *Anasazi* is a Navajo word meaning "Ancient Ones." We do not know what they called themselves because they had no written language.

We know much about the Anasazi because of their many village sites and cliff dwellings and the materials they left behind. The Anasazi period is roughly from 100 B.C. to A.D. 1300. Archaeologists know this because of tree-ring dating, or dendrochronology. Each year of a tree's growth creates a ring in its trunk. A tree-ring calendar has been devised that stretches back several thousand years. By taking a sample from a log at a site, archaeologists can match it against the calendar. That way they find the date the tree was cut. A tree ring also shows wet and dry cycles. A wide ring means a wet year and a narrow one, a dry year.

The Anasazi initially were hunters and gatherers. They lived primarily in the four corners region, where New Mexico, Colorado, Utah, and Arizona all meet. Hundreds of Anasazi sites have been found in all four states. The greatest concentration of their population seems to have been in the Cortez area in southwestern Colorado.

We can learn a great deal about the past from archaeological digs of sites where prehistoric Coloradans lived. This Anasazi ruin is being excavated by Fort Lewis College students in southwestern Colorado. (Fort Lewis College, Southwestern Studies Center.)

The Basketmakers

The Anasazi used yucca leaves to make sandals and baskets. Thus, archaeologists called these people Basketmakers. They also buried their dead, which showed a belief in life after death. Most of what we know about the Basketmakers comes from their grave sites. Archaeologists have found baskets, food, weapons, sandals, and other personal possessions in the graves. Mummies of dogs also have been found. Probably they were pets of Basketmaker families and children.

Because of Colorado's dry climate, some bodies found in the grave sites became mummified. These mummified bodies let us know what the people looked like. The Basketmakers were short. Their hair was thick and black and their skins were brown.

Example of Anasazi rock art survives in Yellow Jacket Canyon. (Denver Public Library.)

They had jewelry made of polished stones and feathers and sea-shells. The shells could have come only by trade, some from as far away as the Pacific coast.

Rattles made of deer hoofs and bones were used for ceremonial dances. What would you guess the Anasazi did with their whistles made of hollow bird bones? Interestingly, sticks and bones, similar to those used by modern Indians for games, have been found.

Basketmakers lived first in brush shelters, and then started to build homes. Eventually the pit house, part underground and part above, became very popular. They also built storage houses for their extra corn.

One important change came when the Basketmakers began to grow corn and squash. By planting and harvesting these crops, they gained some freedom from hunting and gathering. They ground the corn with a flat stone called a *metate* over which they pounded and rolled another stone, a *mano*. Archaeologists commonly find metates and manos in Basketmaker sites.

Pueblo Period

Toward the end of the Basketmaker era (about A.D. 750), the people started to live in small villages. This community life marked the next era of Anasazi culture, the Pueblo period. These people lived in villages down in the valleys and up on the mesas. *Pueblo* is a Spanish word for "village" or "town." The Spanish, who found Indian villages in the Rio Grande Valley, called them pueblos.

The Anasazi eventually abandoned their pit houses to live aboveground, sometimes in two-story structures. The Pueblo peoples used their pit-house idea to develop the kiva, an underground circular room. Kivas were used for religious ceremonies and were places for the men and young boys to meet. The Anasazi kivas were similar to those found in today's New Mexico pueblos.

During this period, the Anasazi began to make beautiful pottery. Pots, unlike baskets, were waterproof, so the Anasazi gradually stopped making baskets. They also made fur and feather blankets and clothing to help them keep warm. Stone axes helped them cut down trees and shape logs for roof beams for their homes. The homes were made with stone walls.

Corn was the main food of the Anasazi during this period. They also hunted deer, buffalo, rabbits, and bears. Dogs and turkeys were their only domesticated animals. They did not have the wheel or any large animals to help them carry things.

From the 700s to the 1200s, the Anasazi lived in their villages and worked their nearby fields. They were farmers who also hunted and gathered other things to eat. Life had become more stable and easier than in earlier centuries. As their population increased, they built more villages and planted more land with crops. Their land stretched from Chimney Rock, near Pagosa Springs in Colorado, to southern Arizona. They built large villages in Chaco Canyon, New Mexico, and also moved into Utah. The Anasazi culture was more advanced than other Native American cultures.

The Cliff-Dwelling Era

Around A.D. 1050 some of the Anasazi in the Mesa Verde region of southwestern Colorado began moving off the mesa tops and valley floors and into caves. The caves were in the sides of the many canyons cutting deep into Mesa Verde. Why did the Anasazi move into these spectacular sites? We do not know. They

*Cliff Palace is
the largest of the
stone cities now
preserved
in Mesa Verde
National Park.
(Mesa Verde
National Park.)*

may have wanted protection from enemies. They constructed large multistoried pueblos in their caves. Some of these "apartment" houses were five stories high. The Anasazi cliff dwellings were a great achievement in architecture. You can see and walk through some of them today: the Cliff Palace, Step House, and Balcony House at Mesa Verde National Park.

Living in a cave was not as easy as living on the open, sunny mesa tops. To reach their fields and the springs, where the Anasazi got their water, often meant a dangerous climb. Large trash dumps in front of their caves must have smelled awful and attracted all kinds of little creatures. The caves were dark and damp some days. Mothers and fathers must have worried about their little children falling off the ledges.

The farmers relied solely on rainfall to water their crops. They learned to build small dams to save water. Large dam sites and evidence of water ditches also have been found. These means of water storage helped the Anasazi survive dry spells. As before, the Anasazi continued to survive with a combination of farming and hunting and gathering. Their population increased, and they dominated a large area.

The Anasazi traded with distant peoples to acquire cotton and parrot feathers from Mexico or Texas and seashells from California. Roads from the Mesa Verde region stretched southeast to Anasazi pueblos in Chaco Canyon, New Mexico, now a national park. Was Chaco Canyon a religious center? We do not know.

The Anasazi started to leave the Mesa Verde area about 1270. After that time, no trees were cut. Within a generation (thirty-three years), their villages and fields were deserted. It was almost as if they expected to come back. They left behind many things that most of us would have taken if we knew we were making a permanent move — for example, cooking pots, clothing and jewelry, and religious objects. Why did the Anasazi leave? Where did they go? We do not know.

Archaeologists and historians believe that several factors caused the Anasazi to leave. The Anasazi may have moved into the caves as protection from enemy tribes. It would be easy to defend Balcony House, for example. There is no evidence of fighting, however, such as burned buildings or skeletons of people who were killed. Nor had any enemies moved into Anasazi land. Furthermore, it does not seem that a civil war exploded among the Anasazi. Other possible reasons for their disappearance include loss of topsoil from cutting forests and overpopulation.

Tree-ring dating tells us that a severe drought, or dry period, started in 1272 and lasted until 1299. The Anasazi had survived droughts before, however. Only a century before, a drought had lasted for thirty years.

The climate was gradually changing, becoming drier and colder. This change would have affected crop production. In addition, the Anasazi had used the same fields for hundreds of years. The soil probably was wearing out. They had cut trees for a long time in the same area, and they may have run out of wood. Perhaps the supply of game animals had dwindled, and hunters were forced to look elsewhere.

Over the years, the Anasazi population in southwestern Colorado had steadily increased, putting more pressure on the environment. Overcrowding made the people more vulnerable to disease and other pressures. In the end, the 1272 drought might have been the final blow. With the climate changing, agricultural production going down, trees and animals disappearing, and water becoming scarce, the Anasazi may have decided to abandon their longtime homeland. Does this tell us something about environment and population? Could it happen to your town?

The Anasazi did not all leave at once. They slowly trickled out of the canyons and river valleys and probably headed south toward warmer lands in New Mexico with more rivers and springs. Gradually their cliff dwellings became ghost towns. Quiet returned to southwestern Colorado — until the nineteenth century, when the Anasazi ruins were "rediscovered."

Mesa Verde National Park

For centuries, the abandoned Anasazi villages lay untouched. The later-arriving Utes knew the villages existed, but did not live in the Anasazi pit houses and cliff dwellings. When Spanish explorers arrived in the eighteenth century, they found the Anasazi villages were deserted ruins. The Escalante Ruin near Dolores is one that the Domínguez-Escalante party saw in 1776. Later explorers who came across Anasazi sites did not make public what they saw or collected.

In 1874, the famous photographer William Henry Jackson took photographs of ruins in Mancos Canyon. He showed and sold these photos all over the United States. Jackson's photographs drew attention to the ruins, and people became curious.

The Wetherills, a ranching family from nearby Mancos, finally called the world's attention to these fascinating ruins. The Wetherills wintered their cattle in the warm canyon. The Utes owned this land, but the Wetherills got along well with their Indian neighbors. The Utes told them about the many houses of "the ancient ones" that could be found deep in the canyons of Mesa Verde. The Utes did not go there, fearing to disturb the spirits of the dead.

On a cold December day in 1888, Richard Wetherill and his brother-in-law, Charlie Mason, saw Cliff Palace. They had been

*Two cowboys, Richard and John Wetherill, discovered Cliff Palace
and many other ruins while rounding up their cattle. To keep people from
vandalizing or taking home artifacts, the federal government set
up Mesa Verde National Park in 1906. (Mesa Verde National Park.)*

looking for stray cattle; now a new interest seized their attention. Charlie recalled, "We rode around the head of the canon [canyon] and found a way down over the cliffs to the level of the building. We spent several hours going from room to room and picked up several articles of interest, among them a stone axe with the handle still on it."

The Wetherills made a collection of pots, jewelry, and other artifacts. They exhibited them in Durango, Pueblo, and Denver. In 1889, a group of Denverites purchased the Wetherill collection and gave it to the Colorado Historical Society. You can see the collection today in the Society's Colorado History Museum.

The Wetherills started guiding visitors into Mesa Verde. They took a three-day round-trip from their ranch near Mancos, with one day to see the ruins and two riding to and from the site on horseback. One visitor in 1891 was a twenty-two-year-old Swedish writer and scientist named Gustaf Nordenskiold. He took photographs, helped name the sites, and wrote a book about what he had seen, *The Cliff Dwellers of Mesa Verde.* He found the Indian ruins exciting, but complained about the heat, dust, and steep climbs into some cliff dwellings. He reported one incident when skunks threw one of his camps into confusion.

These early visitors believed the Aztecs from Mexico had built the ancient villages. The nearby town of Cortez was named for the conqueror of the Aztecs, and Montezuma County, in which Mesa Verde is located, was named after an Aztec leader. The name "Anasazi" would not come into use until the 1920s.

The new interest in the ruins meant that more people visited the cliff dwellings. Many visitors took home souvenirs and damaged the remaining buildings. A group of concerned women, led by Virginia McClurg, began a long campaign to save the ruins. The area and its ancient sites had fascinated McClurg ever since she had visited there in the early 1880s.

McClurg was joined by Lucy Peabody and others in Colorado and throughout the United States in the fight to save Mesa Verde. They wrote to President William McKinley and Congress, asking that the site be made a national park. When the Washington officials did not act, the group raised money and hired men to do a survey, dig wells, and improve the trails. These measures were necessary for conserving scarce water supplies and preserving the historic structures. The determined women wrote letters and articles and gave programs. They talked to anyone who would listen about the exciting story told by the ruins and the importance of preserving that history.

McClurg, Peabody, and their supporters created the Colorado Cliff Dwellings Association. They invited leading archaeologists, scientists, and writers to visit Mesa Verde. The women went so far as to sign a treaty with the Utes to give them the cliff dwellings.

Finally, on June 29, 1906, President Theodore Roosevelt signed the bill creating Mesa Verde National Park. The Anasazi ruins would be protected from damage, theft, and destruction, and preserved so that future generations could visit and enjoy them. The canyons of Mesa Verde, silent for so many centuries, would never be the same again.

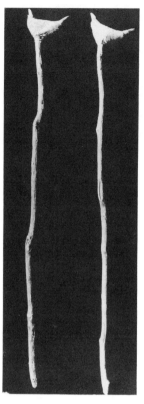

Crutches found in an Anasazi cliff dwelling suggest this culture took care of the elderly and the disabled. (Colorado Historical Society.)

QUESTIONS

1. Who were the first known human residents of what is now Colorado? Where did they live?
2. How did the building of shelters and contact with other cultures influence the lives of these early people?
3. What does *Anasazi* mean?
4. How was the day-to-day life of the Basketmakers different from that of the cliff dwellers of Mesa Verde?
5. Why did the Anasazi leave Mesa Verde?
6. Who was Richard Wetherill, and what did he do?
7. How was Mesa Verde National Park created?

ACTIVITIES

1. Obtain some books about Mesa Verde. Study the photographs and illustrations, and then draw or paint pictures of some of the artifacts. Make a model of a cliff dwelling.
2. Study the way an archaeologist excavates a site. Draw a diagram or cartoon that describes the process.
3. Invite an archaeologist or park ranger to speak to your class about Mesa Verde or other ancient sites. If possible, take a class field trip to an ancient site.
4. Write a skit or play about life at Mesa Verde. There are many good books for you to read.
5. Ask your teacher to show you one of the many videos about Mesa Verde. Would you like to have lived there? Write a paper telling why or why not.
6. Make a time line showing when the different prehistoric peoples lived in Colorado.
7. Form research teams to study the Anasazi. In your team, develop a hypothesis (theory) about why the Anasazi left Mesa Verde. Use actual research and visual aids such as maps and models to support and present your theory to your classmates.
8. Pretend you are a newspaper reporter covering the "discovery" of the Mesa Verde ruins in the 1880s. Write a news article about it, including quotes from key people and descriptions of the sites.

Books You and Your Teacher Might Enjoy

Deric Nusbaum. *Deric in Mesa Verde.* New York: Lippincott, 1926. Deric lived at the park with his father, who was superintendent. The book is out of print at the moment, but you may be able to find it in the library.

Gustaf Nordenskiold. *The Cliff Dwellers of Mesa Verde.* Stockholm: P. A. Norstedt & Söner, 1893 (reprinted 1979 by Rio Grande Press, Glorietta, NM). This Scandinavian scientist describes his investigation of Mesa Verde.

Duane A. Smith. *Mesa Verde National Park.* Topeka: University Press of Kansas, 1988. This book explains how the cliff cities of the Anasazi became a national park.

Scott Warren. *Cities in the Sand.* San Francisco: Chronicle Books, 1992. This book contains pictures and interesting stories about the Anasazi and other Indians in the Southwest.

Don Watson. *Cliff Dwellings of the Mesa Verde.* Mesa Verde: Mesa Verde Association, 1961. This volume provides a wonderful look at the park and its people. Linda Wommack. *Colorado History for Kids.* Van Nuys, CA: Valley Press, 1992. Here is an easy-to-read look at Colorado.

Did You Know?

Corn originated in Mexico, where it was so important as food that it became an object of worship.

Dogs were pets of Native Americans 2,000 years ago during the Basketmaker era.

The Anasazi built multistoried "apartment" houses at Mesa Verde during the period 1070–1270; America would not see taller ones until the 1880s.

In 1906, 27 people visited Mesa Verde National Park; in 1994, 699,000 people visited.

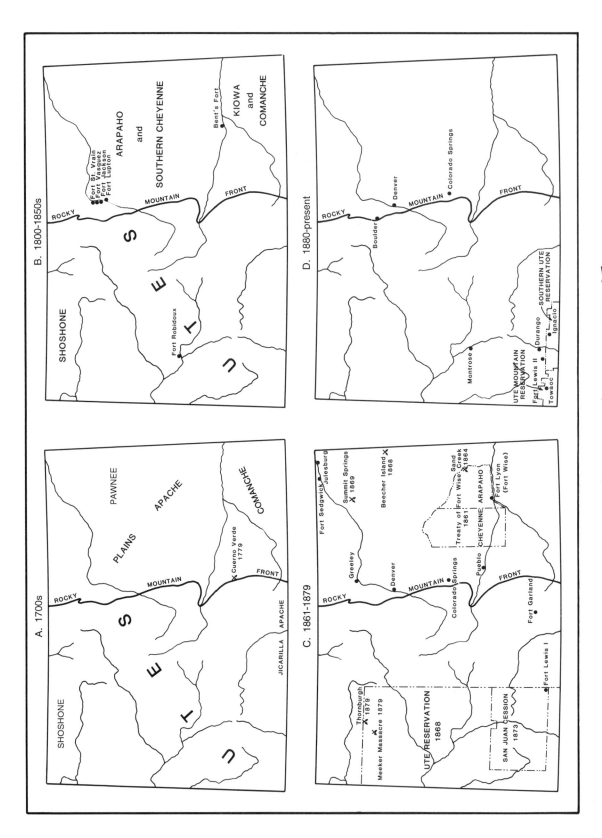

Native American Tribes

A. 1700s

SHOSHONE

U T E S

PAWNEE

PLAINS APACHE

COMANCHE

ROCKY MOUNTAIN FRONT

X Cuerno Verde 1779

JICARILLA APACHE

B. 1800-1850s

SHOSHONE

U T E S

Fort St. Vrain
Fort Vasquez
Fort Jackson
Fort Lupton

ARAPAHO and SOUTHERN CHEYENNE

Bent's Fort

KIOWA and COMANCHE

ROCKY MOUNTAIN FRONT

Fort Robidoux

C. 1861-1879

Fort Sedgwick
Julesburg
Summit Springs X 1869
Beecher Island 1868 X

Greeley
Denver
Colorado Springs
Pueblo

Sand Creek X 1864

Treaty of Fort Wise 1861

CHEYENNE ARAPAHO

Fort Lyon (Fort Wise)

ROCKY MOUNTAIN FRONT

Fort Garland

Thornburgh X 1879
Meeker Massacre X 1879

UTE RESERVATION 1868

SAN JUAN CESSION 1873

Fort Lewis I

D. 1880-present

Denver
Colorado Springs

Boulder

ROCKY MOUNTAIN FRONT

Montrose

Durango
Ignacio

SOUTHERN UTE RESERVATION

UTE MOUNTAIN RESERVATION
Fort Lewis II
Towaoc

CHAPTER THREE
Indians of Colorado

While the Anasazi were building and farming in southwestern Colorado, other Native Americans explored the eastern plains. Archaeologists have found sites of camps, storage pits, houses, and other artifacts. They also have excavated burial sites. Like the Anasazi, these other groups were hunters and gatherers at first and then became farmers. They were related to Indian cultures to the east, perhaps even the famous Mound Builders of the Midwest, who, like the Anasazi, built cities and farmed.

These ancient tribes may have made contact with the Anasazi. Undoubtedly they migrated into eastern Colorado from several directions. When the first Europeans reached this area these people, like the Anasazi, were gone. In their place were the Plains Indians, the most famous Indians in American history.

The Apache

Normally we think of the Apache as feared warriors of the Southwest. Long before that time, however, some of them lived as hunters and farmers on the Great Plains. The Plains Apache migrated from the north. We do not know when they arrived in the Great Plains. It may have been in the early 1400s. Perhaps the Spanish explorer Francisco Coronado met them on the plains during his expedition in the 1540s. The Spanish definitely mentioned the Jicarilla Apache in southern Colorado in 1706. The Jicarilla, who eventually moved to northern New Mexico, often fought with the Spanish over land, horses, and stolen goods.

Europeans made a huge change in Apache life. Before the arrival of the Europeans, the Apache and other Native Americans had no horses. With the horse, the roving Apache became even more independent. Iron pots, knives, spoons, and guns were other European items that changed the lives of the Apache.

The Comanche

Warfare and raiding were a part of Native American life that encouraged the fighting spirit. In some ways these activities were a game and a way to gain fame, wealth, and manhood. To a warrior, touching a live enemy was a braver act than killing one. They called it "counting coup." Warfare also was a way to seize enemy land and prisoners. The Indian people lived this way for generations, sometimes taking over an enemy's territory completely. The Comanche came late to Colorado and joined their allies the Utes to make war on the Apache.

The Comanche did not stay long before moving farther south and east into what today is Oklahoma and Kansas. By the time the mountain men came with the fur trade in the 1820s and 1830s, the Arapaho and Cheyenne had replaced the Comanche on Colorado's eastern plains.

The Arapaho and the Cheyenne

The Arapaho and Cheyenne were allies. Their languages were similar, and they often camped together for long periods. Both had migrated onto the plains from other areas — the Cheyenne from Minnesota, the Arapaho from the Red River Valley on the Canada-Minnesota border. Around 1760 they obtained horses, which changed them from farmers to mounted hunters and warriors. The horse gave them freedom.

The stories of the Arapaho and Cheyenne have come down to us by oral tradition, or storytelling, as these people did not have a written language. According to the stories, the people were terrified the first time they heard guns and saw their dreadful power. Eventually, by trade the tribes acquired guns and other items, although few had ever seen white men. They hunted buffalo and moved with the herds, lived in tepees, fought their enemies, and performed religious ceremonies, including the Sun Dance.

Religious ceremonies were important to the Cheyenne. The buffalo cap (sacred hat) and medicine arrows were the most

The buffalo, food for Indians and whites alike, has fascinated western visitors for over a century. (Photo by Jerry Hanes.)

sacred possessions of the Cheyenne. Occasionally when the whole tribe made war on an enemy, they carried these holy objects along. When the Pawnee captured the medicine arrows in battle in 1830 the Cheyenne were horrified. It was seven years before they recovered their sacred arrows.

The buffalo was the center of Plains Indian life. After the hunt, the people ate the fresh meat raw, roasted, or boiled. Some meat was dried, and some was cooked, shredded, and mixed with wild berries and fat. Hunters highly prized this "pemmican" for its nutritive value. The Indians used nearly all of the buffalo. The hide was used to make tepees, the tail as a fly-swatter.

The Arapaho and Cheyenne lived in villages, their tepees made of tanned buffalo hides soaring twenty feet or more in height. Dogs overran their camps. Dogs had once been beasts of burden, but now the horse did much of that work. Women were the lodge, or tepee, makers. Cleaning, tanning, and turning buffalo hides into lodge covers was hard work that required great skill and long hours. The women also cooked, took care of the children, made clothes, and helped move the village. They also joined the men in some dances and held dances just for women. Cheyenne women had the reputation of being the neatest

Freckled Face, an Arapaho woman, posed for Denver photographer Frank A. Rinehard in 1893. (Denver Public Library.)

housekeepers in the West. Their beadwork on their dresses was beautiful.

The men hunted and protected their village from enemy attacks. They became masters at using the bow and arrow and the lance. Their prize warhorse was staked right next to their

Do you think these Arapaho youngsters enjoyed going to the white man's school?
(Denver Public Library.)

lodge. Cheyenne and Arapaho men joined tribal clubs, such as the warrior society. The Cheyenne called their warrier societies names like Elk Horn Scrapers, Bow Strings, Kit Foxes, Red Shields, and Dog Soldiers. These clubs held dances and conducted religious ceremonies.

Cheyenne and Arapaho youngsters coasted on sleds made from buffalo ribs, wood, or pieces of rawhide. They might go a short distance from their village and make a play camp. Girls helped their mothers gather firewood, played with their friends, and did chores around the village. Boys rode stick horses, played war, helped their fathers, and hunted small animals.

In the summer of 1846, a New Englander, Francis Parkman, journeyed along the Oregon Trail. He left this fascinating account of how quickly Plains Indians could move their villages.

*Arapaho young-
sters learned to
hunt for food at
an early age.
(Denver Public
Library.)*

One by one the lodges were sinking down in rapid succession, and where the great circle of the village had been only a moment before, nothing now remained but a ring of horses and Indians, crowded in confusion together. The ruins of the lodges were spread over the ground, together with kettles, stone mallets, great ladles of horn, buffalo robes, and cases of painted hide, filled with dried meat.

Stephen Long's 1820 expedition visited a Cheyenne and Arapaho camp. Shy and quiet before visitors, the Plains people tried to talk to these Americans, but no one spoke a common language. Dr. Edwin James explained in the expedition's journal how they managed to communicate.

[The English] was translated into French, then into Pawnee, and afterwards into Kiawa [Kiowa] and other languages, by their respective interpreters. In reply a chief expressed his surprise that we had travelled so far, and assured us that they were happy to see us, and hoped that as a road was now open to our nation, traders would be sent amongst them.

The Cheyenne and Arapaho wanted goods that the Americans would trade for furs and hides. Later some of the Cheyenne moved to the Bent's Fort region to be nearer to this American trading post and its goods.

By the 1840s the life of the Plains Indians had begun to change. Overland trails, such as the Oregon and Santa Fe Trails, went through the Indians' land, bringing more and more European-American settlers. Merchants on their way to Santa Fe, New Mexico, hurried past the Native American villages. To protect these trails and travelers, the U.S. government built forts and sent out soldiers on patrol. The Cheyenne and Arapaho and the government soldiers watched each other. Neither knew what to expect from the other. To try to keep peace, the United States and the various tribes signed treaties promising friendship and an end to fighting. Sadly, the plains were entering an era when peace and friendship proved rare.

Meanwhile, in the last days before the whites would come to stay, the old times continued a little longer. For decades the Cheyenne and Arapaho fought with the Utes, who lived on the Western Slope. Raiding parties went back and forth, although the Plains Indians did not like staying long in the cold, stormy mountains.

The Utes

The Spanish first wrote about the Utes in the 1620s. At that time they were living in western Colorado. Their relatives, the Paiutes, lived in Utah, which was named for them. The Utes came to Colorado centuries before the Spanish. They and the Spanish watched each other cautiously and went through periods of war and peace. They even signed a treaty in 1680. This contact changed Ute life as it had every other Indian tribe. When they acquired horses, for example, they became more mobile and more warlike.

The Utes played a major role in spreading horses throughout the Rocky Mountains. At one point, the Spanish had made slaves of some Ute captives, who learned to ride horses. When the Pueblo people revolted in 1680 and drove the Spanish out of New Mexico, the Ute captives were freed. They returned home, taking herds of horses with them. Through trade the horse spread northward.

The Ute riders mastered horsemanship as quickly as Americans today master cars. In a few generations they became superb riders. Their wiry, sure-footed, strong horses were the best in the region. Other tribes valued them highly. For the Utes, horses were a source of wealth and a highly treasured trade item. They traded horses northward and eventually the Crow, Blackfeet, Sioux, and Bannock all acquired this wonderful creature.

The Spanish returned in the 1690s, and seasons of trade and seasons of warfare continued for the next 130 years. The Utes even became involved in the slave business. They traded Indian women and children, captured from their enemies, to the Spanish for horses and other goods. The Spaniards hoped to convert their captives to Catholicism. They also taught the enslaved Indians a trade. When the children grew up, the Spanish usually set them free.

From 1765, if not before, Spaniards traded regularly in Ute territory. Frequently they bullied the Utes to get furs and slaves, and sometimes trouble resulted. Much to the Spaniards' dismay, the Utes resisted attempts to Christianize them or to start a Catholic mission in their land.

Two Catholic priests, Francisco Domínguez and Silvestre Escalante, traveled through western Colorado in 1776. In his diary, Father Escalante said the Ute people were "all of good features and very friendly." He added an account of a Ute town: "We met about eighty Utes all on good horses, most of them being from the rancheria [village] to which we were going. Through this valley we traveled a league to the east and arrived at the rancheria, which was populous and must have consisted of about thirty tents." The Spaniards then spent a day trying to teach the Utes about Christianity. Even with a Pueblo Indian translator, however, the language barrier proved too great.

The Utes were described as mostly short, dark, and stocky. A shy people, even by Indian standards, they tended to avoid contact with the strange white people probing around their land.

The Utes first lived in small family groups scattered over a vast expanse of the Colorado mountains and Utah plateau lands. Later, the horse allowed them to join larger bands. They formed seven major bands: Capote, Mouache, Tabeguache, Uinta, Weminuche, White River, and Yampa. Some of these names are now geographical place-names where these groups once lived. Most of the Utes lived on the Western Slope, but the Mouache band lived in the San Luis Valley and northern New Mexico.

Each of the seven Ute bands, or clans, had its own hunting territory. Various bands came together once or twice a year to trade, hold dances, exchange news, and allow the young people to court. In time of war several bands might come together to defend their homeland or to join for a Bear Dance. The Bear Dance was a favorite social dance of the Utes.

Buffalo hide tepees were found in Ute villages such as this one in the foothills.
(Colorado College Library.)

The Utes looked upon religion as a normal part of everyday life. They had deep respect for the earth, sky, plants, and animals. All living things had a spirit or soul, and the Utes respected them as people of the world. Worship for the Utes was a personal matter. They had no complex ritual or formalized priesthood. When people became sick their family called a medicine man to find a cure. The medicine man also was supposed to provide religious leadership during troubling times. An unlucky or unwise medicine man could find himself in serious trouble. Elders of the village might order him killed after too many failures.

Boys ready to become men were expected to travel by themselves away from the village to a remote spot. There the youth

This young Ute mother artistically made her own dress and her child's cradleboard. (Colorado Historical Society.)

prayed and hoped to have a vision from the spirit world. This vision would guide his adult life. The horse permitted the Utes to travel farther than ever before and with more speed and ease than they had ever known. They spent their summers high in the mountains and their winters in secluded mountain valleys, where the snow was lighter and the days were warmer, and the grass grew thick for their horses. The Utes hunted in all directions for deer, buffalo, and elk. The skins and furs of these animals were made into clothing. Wild plant foods and berries supplemented the hunters' diets.

The Utes traveled south into the lands of their old enemy, the Navajo. They boldly traveled east from the mountains across the Continental Divide and onto the Great Plains. Here they trespassed on the hunting grounds of the Cheyenne and Arapaho. The results were warfare and raiding back and forth. The two peoples also learned about each other's customs and lifestyles. The Utes at first were awed by the wealth of the Plains Indians, but they soon learned not to fear them. Ute warriors could shoot the bow and arrow faster than their Plains foes.

By the early 1800s the Utes, thanks to the horse, had become a hardy, aggressive, and stubbornly independent tribe. The neighboring Jicarilla Apache were their only allies. They traded, talked, feasted, and sometimes intermarried with this tribe, whom they considered to be distant cousins. Ouray, the great Ute leader, was the son of a Jicarilla father and a Tabeguache mother. Ute war parties raided their other neighbors, the Navajo and Pueblo tribes, now and then. Generally, however, the Utes were content to keep to themselves.

The Utes and other native groups were not consulted when France sold part of their land to the United States in 1803. Several fur trading posts were located in the Utes' home country, and trappers wandered around their land hunting beaver for nearly twenty years. The Utes liked the "Yankees" better than the Spaniards because they had better trade goods. One Ute reportedly told an American, "Come among us and you shall have as many beaver skins as you want." They came, but they did not settle permanently, which was fine with the Utes.

Although the Spanish and later the Mexican governments considered Ute territory their land, the Utes did not recognize the claim. When the entire region became part of the United States at the conclusion of the Mexican War in 1848, again no one asked the Utes about their wishes. Meanwhile, the fur trade had declined. Only a few outsiders, such as John C. Fremont,

*The Ute people, who have lived in Colorado for hundreds of years,
fought off many other tribes to keep their mountain land.
(Colorado Springs Pioneer Museum.)*

explored parts of the Utes' Rocky Mountain home. The Utes were to enjoy only a few more years of peace. Unknown to them, gold had been discovered far to the west in California. It set in motion a chain of events that would change Ute life and history forever. Their culture already had changed drastically since the Europeans and then the Americans had arrived. Many of the old ways were gone for them and for the Plains Indians as well. The white man's ways and possessions had made inroads into Ute life. Sadly, neither group really understood the other: A tragedy was in the making.

QUESTIONS

1. Who were the various Indian peoples who lived in Colorado after the Anasazi left?
2. How did the coming of Europeans change the lives of Colorado's Indians?
3. What was significant about the horse in the lives of Colorado's Indians?
4. What role did the Utes play in spreading horses throughout the Rocky Mountains?
5. What role did the buffalo play in the life of the Plains Indians?
6. Compare and contrast the life of the Plains Indian woman and man.
7. Locate Ute place-names on a map of Colorado.

ACTIVITIES

1. Imagine yourself living with a Ute or Cheyenne group. Write a story about your daily life.
2. Find out which Native American groups lived in your neighborhood. Study their life and, if possible, visit one of their campsites or places where they hunted.
3. On a Colorado map locate the areas where all the various Indian peoples lived. Make a small sketch to show their homes, hunting methods, or some other aspect of their lives that interests you.

4. Imagine you are a European explorer who visits an Indian village in Colorado. Write a report to send back east telling about these people and their lives.

5. Make a model of a Ute mountain village or a Plains Indian village.

6. Trace the history of the horse in North America. Make an illustrated time line.

Books You and Your Teacher Might Enjoy

H. Jackson Clark. *The Owl in Monument Canyon.* Salt Lake City: University of Utah Press, 1993. This book contains great stories about the Utes and the Navajo.

George Bird Grinnell. *The Fighting Cheyennes.* Norman: University of Oklahoma Press, 1985 (reprint). This volume tells the classic story of the Cheyenne.

Will Hobbs. *Beardance.* New York: Atheneum, 1993. This novel will keep your attention.

J. Donald Hughes. *American Indians in Colorado.* Boulder: Pruett Publishing, 1987. This book provides an overview of the various peoples who lived in our state.

Jan Pettit. *Utes.* Boulder: Johnson Books, 1990. This history takes you back in time to visit these people.

Louis Taylor. *The Story of America's Horse.* Cleveland: World Publishing, 1968. Here is everything you want to know about horses!

Did You Know?

The Plains Indians made yellow body paint from a mixture of bullberries, clay, moss, roots, and buffalo gallstones.

The straight and skinny lodgepole pine was preferred for tepee poles.

Buffalo chips (dried manure) were valued as a fuel.

Among the Utes, young men typically married at about eighteen or nineteen years of age; young girls at fourteen or fifteen.

CHAPTER FOUR
Explorers, Trappers, and Traders

As early as the seventeenth century, it was clear that the Cheyenne, Arapaho, Comanche, and Utes were not going to have this wonderful land to themselves. From the south came men riding strange beasts, worshiping a different god, and bringing tools and weapons the Indians had never seen. Neither the lives of these foreigners nor of the Indians would ever be the same again.

In 1598 the Spanish explorer Juan de Oñate commanded the expedition that brought European settlement to what the Spanish called New Mexico. Word quickly spread among the Native Americans that a new and unusual people had arrived. It would not be long before the two peoples made contact, each side curious about the other.

Spanish Explorers
The Spanish in the Rio Grande Valley did more than simply trade with the Utes and the Plains Indians. They were interested in exploring the land. The Spaniards dreamed of finding gold and silver in the mountains to the north. Farther east, the plains beckoned them with the possibility of gold deposits. The Catholic friars hoped to find converts among the native population.

We do not know about all of the Spanish expeditions to the land that would become Colorado. In 1650 Juan de Archuleta led a search party to recapture some Pueblo Indians who, seeking freedom, had fled from the Spanish. Archuleta's party traveled to the eastern plains along the Arkansas River. Juan de Ulibarri captured some runaway Pueblo Indians in the same area in 1706.

Meanwhile, other Spaniards from New Mexico traveled northward to look for gold and silver. They explored southwestern Colorado and left place-names to mark their journey. The San Juan and La Plata mountains, the Animas and Dolores Rivers, and Mesa Verde carry the names of the Spaniards. These explorers prospected and found gold, but left no records. They did not want to pay the king one-fifth of all they found, which was the Spanish law, so they secretly mined. Some of their mines became "lost mines"; people still are trying to find them.

When Juan Maria de Rivera's official expedition arrived in 1765, western Colorado already had been named, explored, and mined by earlier Spanish explorers and miners. Eleven years later, two priests, Fathers Francisco Atanasio Domínguez and Silvestre Veléz de Escalante led a small party through southwestern Colorado trying to find an overland route to California. It was 1776 — the same year American colonists were signing the Declaration of Independence in Philadelphia.

One of the priests, Father Escalante, wrote in his journal about the La Plata River and the La Plata Mountains:

> [The river] flows through the canyon in which they say there are veins and outcroppings of metal. But, although years ago several persons came from New Mexico to examine them by the order of the Governor, . . . and carried away ore, it was not learned with certainty what metal it was. The opinion formed previously by some persons from the accounts of various Indians and of some citizens of this kingdom [said] that they were silver mines, [that] caused the mountains to be called Sierra de la Plata.

The Spanish explored, mined, traded, and sent out military expeditions, but did not settle in future Colorado at this time. Legends, geographic names, and historical sites first reported by the Spanish linger to this day.

Padres Domínguez and Escalante explored Colorado in 1776 and produced the first written report and map of the Highest State. The town of Paonia in Delta County celebrated the Franciscan friars with this mural. (Photo by Thomas J. Noel.)

American Explorers

While the Spanish were exploring Colorado, far to the east Americans won their independence from England, established their government, and began to move steadily westward. The West fascinated President Thomas Jefferson. Under his leadership, the United States purchased the vast Louisiana Territory from France in 1803. The cost was $15 million — about three cents per acre — for an area that would double the size of the United States. The Louisiana Purchase stretched from the Mississippi River west to the Rocky Mountains. Would you like to buy an acre of downtown Pueblo or Denver for that price?

President Jefferson wanted to learn more about the mysterious western lands he had purchased. In 1804 he sent Meriwether Lewis and William Clark to explore the Missouri River, which flows across the northern part of the purchase from present-day Montana to St. Louis.

Two years later Jefferson ordered Lieutenant Zebulon Pike to explore the southern portion of the purchase. Pike traveled across the plains and then along the Arkansas River. Pike was fooled by the plains; he thought they looked like a desert. One can understand how this happened. He came from the wooded, green, well-watered eastern United States. The plains were hot and dry as his expedition slowly rode across them.

His party reached the future site of the city of Pueblo in November 1806 and camped there along the Arkansas River. Pike became fascinated by a large mountain to the northwest and decided to climb it. A simple hike, he thought. Pike was fooled by the clear, dry air into thinking the high peak stood nearby. Others who came after him would make the same mistake.

Pike and his men never reached the top of the mountain now known as Pikes Peak. He wrote in his journal November 26: "The summit of the Grand Peak, which was entirely bare of vegetation and covered with snow, now appeared at the distance of 15 or 16 miles from us, and as high again as what we had ascended, . . . I believe no human being could have ascended to its pinnacle."

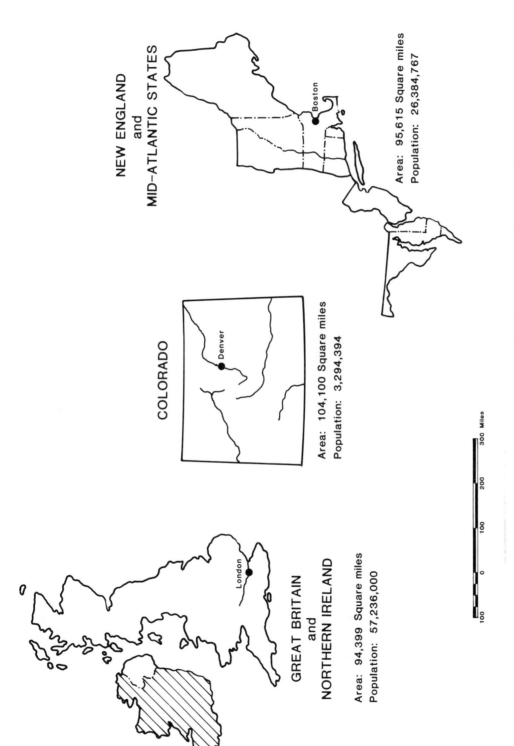

NEW ENGLAND
and
MID-ATLANTIC STATES

Boston

Area: 95,615 Square miles
Population: 26,384,767

COLORADO

Denver

Area: 104,100 Square miles
Population: 3,294,394

GREAT BRITAIN
and
NORTHERN IRELAND

London

Area: 94,399 Square miles
Population: 57,236,000

100   0   100   200   300 Miles

New England, Old England & Colorado

Zebulon M. Pike explored Colorado in 1806 to map the boundary between Spanish territory and U.S. territory along the Arkansas River. (Denver Public Library.)

Pike then led his men up the Arkansas River, past the Royal Gorge, to a place near today's Leadville. They made a winter crossing of the Sangre de Cristo mountains, passed the Great Sand Dunes, and into the San Luis Valley. He and his men suffered terribly from cold and hunger, but they continued southward. Eventually, exhausted and nearly out of supplies, they built a log fort south of Alamosa along the Rio Grande. In the spring of 1807, a Spanish patrol found them at their fort. Pike and his party were trespassing on Spanish territory. The Spanish soldiers arrested them and took them to Santa Fe as prisoners. Eventually the Pike party was sent back to the United States.

Pikes Peak is the most famous mountain in the United States. It has fascinated tourists ever since Pike wrote about it in his 1806 expedition report.

In spite of their misfortunes, Pike's party had been the first American tourists to see and write about Colorado! Considering all they went through, they probably did not appreciate the honor. Pike later wrote about his experiences, and the American public read about the land and his adventures. It was an exciting story about a region so different from the eastern states, a land of dry, high plains and snowy mountains almost three miles high.

The U.S. government sent many expeditions westward in the decades that followed. In 1820 Major Stephen Long and his expedition traveled along the South Platte Valley. It was from that valley that he first saw the mountain that would be named after him — Longs Peak. They journeyed southward past the future sites of Greeley and Denver and on to Pikes Peak. Despite Pike's belief that the mountain was unclimbable, several members of the Long party reached the top.

Compared to the Pike expedition, Long and his men enjoyed a pleasant summer excursion. Like Pike, Long was fooled by the bleak plains and labeled them "the Great American

Desert." If you had studied geography back then, future Colorado would have been identified on maps by Pikes and Longs Peaks and the Great American Desert. For many years people did not want to move to eastern Colorado because they thought it was a desert.

Western animals fascinated these eastern travelers, none more so than the buffalo. Botanist Edwin James, who with two other men climbed Pikes Peak, wrote this description of this large animal:

> On the following day [June 24, 1820], we saw immense herds of bisons, blackening the whole surface of the country through which we passed. At this time they were in their summer coat. From the shoulders backward, all the hinder parts of the animal are covered with a growth of very short and fine hair, as smooth and soft to the touch as a piece of velvet. The tail is very short and tufted at the end, and its services, as a fly-brush, are confined to a very limited surface.

How would you describe a buffalo to someone who had never seen one?

The most famous of the American explorers was John Charles Fremont. He made five expeditions to the West, the first in 1842, the last in 1853. The handsome, dashing Fremont explored much of Colorado, guided by such mountain men as Kit Carson, Thomas Fitzpatrick, and Bill Williams. Fremont's reports of the region were fascinating reading for many people who thought Colorado too remote and dangerous a place to visit. Through his writing, Americans became quite familiar with the region. His smart, talented wife, Jessie Fremont, aided in writing and editing his reports. The Fremonts made an excellent team in promoting future Colorado.

Fremont's reports on Colorado and his accurate maps guided many people who came after him. Even he made mistakes, however. In 1848 his party, led by Bill Williams, tried to cross the San Juan mountains in the winter. Eleven of this thirty-three-man party died as howling blizzards and deep snow trapped them. The survivors ended up eating their mules and barely getting out alive. Would you like mule steak or mule pie?

Other explorers also came to Colorado during these years. John Gunnison arrived in 1853. Like Fremont, he was looking for a route through the Rockies. At that time, Americans already were dreaming of building a railroad across the continent. Gunnison found a route and left his name on a river, a county, and a town of the Western Slope.

The explorers, both Spanish and American, made the land that would become Colorado known to the world. They found passes through the mountains, named geographical sites, drew maps, and wrote reports and journals. The Americans collected flowers, birds, and animals and made drawings and, later, photographs. For their readers they made the West seem a romantic, larger-than-life land. The readers were very interested, but they wanted to know something else: Could you make a living on the plains and in the mountains?

Fur Trappers

Fremont's reports said there was profit to be made in the lands of the West. He wrote about mountain men like Kit Carson, who had earned a living trapping beaver in the 1820s and 1830s. Carson and other mountain men had found a way to turn one of Colorado's natural resources into money.

The trappers, or mountain men, generally were young, strong outdoorsmen who were looking for adventure. Kit Carson became the best known. Seventeen-year-old Carson had traveled west from Missouri in 1826 and learned the fur trade. For the next ten years he trapped furs throughout the Rocky Mountains and the West. He had a home in Taos, New Mexico, where he lived with his beautiful Mexican wife.

Some of Carson's friends described him in the colorful language of the fur trade:

> Kit wasn't afraid of hell or high water.
> Kit Carson's word was as sure as the sun comin' up.
> Kit never cussed more'n was necessary.

Kit Carson, the famed mountain man, became one of the most trusted guides for those tackling the Colorado Rockies. (Denver Public Library.)

A writer in the 1850s described Carson's quiet manner: "There is nothing like the fire-eater in his manners, but to the contrary, in all his actions he is quiet and unassuming. He has endured all imaginable hardships with steady perseverance and unflinching courage."

After the trapping era ended (in the late 1830s), Carson guided several of John C. Fremont's expeditions. Later he served as an Indian agent and army officer and commanded Fort Garland in the San Luis Valley. He became a bitter enemy of the Navajo after driving them out of their homeland in Canyon de Chelly, Arizona, in the 1860s. For a while he was a rancher and in 1853 drove a large flock of sheep from New Mexico to the gold fields of California. Carson died at Fort Lyon, Colorado, on May 23, 1868.

Kit Carson lived longer than most of the mountain men who trapped beaver in Colorado. Being a fur trapper was very hard work. They spent long hours setting traps in cold rivers, streams, and ponds. Then the beaver skins, or "plew," had to be dried, cleaned, wrapped in packs, and shipped to eastern markets. Trappers often married Indian women, who helped with this hard work. Trappers had to keep moving, often after a couple of days, to find as many beaver skins as possible. The short spring and fall trapping seasons offered little time for play and relaxation.

In the spring the trapper worked his way up the streams into the high mountains. In the fall, as the water began to freeze, he went back downstream. The winter season was spent in a sheltered valley as far as possible from the chilly, snowy high country. It was a lonely life, unless a trapper found an Indian wife and perhaps a few friends. Some trappers were killed and others were driven out of the area by Indians who did not like these intruders.

Once a year, at the end of the "spring hunt," the trappers met at a prearranged spot for their annual rendezvous, or gathering. Merchants came from as far away as St. Louis with the goods the mountain men needed. It was a time for business and trading, but also for relaxation and partying — horse racing, wrestling, shooting matches, buffalo chases, and fighting. The mountain men had fun, as one visitor observed:

> The rendezvous is one continued scene of drunkenness, gambling, and brawling and fighting, as long as the money and credit of the trappers last. Seated, Indian fashion, round the fires, with a blanket spread before them, groups are seen with their "decks" of

> cards, playing at "euker," "poker" and "seven-up"
> the regular mountain games. . . . There goes "hos
> and beaver!" is the mountain expression when any
> great loss is sustained; and, sooner or later, "hos and
> beaver" invariably find their way into the insatiable
> pockets of the traders.

The mountain man era passed quickly. By the mid-1830s the market for beaver skins had declined, and by the 1840s the era had faded into history. Trapping might have seemed like a rugged, independent life, but in fact the fur trade was dominated by companies in St. Louis, New York, and Europe. Even the "free trappers" who did not work for the companies were not truly independent. They sold their pelts for low company prices and purchased goods — at high prices — from company merchants.

These faraway companies and their owners made most of the profit from beaver skins — just as they would profit again and again from other western natural resources in the future. The market had been based on fashion — beaver hats and coats — and fashions change. When silk hats replaced beaver hats as the style in New York and other eastern cities, western fur trappers were thrown out of work. By that time, the beaver had been trapped out in some regions. Throughout the mountains the animals had become harder and harder to find.

Before they pass from the scene, the trappers must be given credit for opening and publicizing the region. Fur trapping represented the first large-scale business in Colorado. The mountain men brought the white man's goods — and his diseases — to the Indians. The Indian way of life would never be the same again.

The Traders

Merchants had made more money than the trappers in the fur trade. Some of them had established forts or trading posts in Colorado and elsewhere to trade with trappers and Indians.

The first trade in the region was between American merchants and residents of the Mexican town of Santa Fe (in present-day New Mexico). In the 1820s traders from St. Louis, Missouri, opened the Santa Fe Trail, which crossed 900 miles of prairie and desert. The trail was busy with a constant stream of travelers into the 1840s.

Americans brought guns, pans, clothes, and other goods from the states. They returned home with gold, silver, furs, and mules. Some of them settled in New Mexico and began talking about making it part of the United States. For those still trading between the two countries, the trip from St. Louis to Santa Fe was long and dangerous. One branch of the trail, the Cimarron Cutoff, crossed present-day southwestern Kansas and northeastern New Mexico. On this dry, open stretch, travelers risked thirst and raids by Indians. The longer and more difficult Mountain Branch headed westward up the Arkansas River valley and then south over Raton Pass.

The brothers Charles and William Bent and their friend Ceran St. Vrain were involved in both the fur trade and the Santa Fe trade. They built a fort along the Arkansas River on the Mountain Branch of the Santa Fe Trail where trappers, traders, and wagon trains could stop for repairs and rest.

Charles drew a plan for the fort and William and Ceran hired laborers from New Mexico to build it. Constructed of mud bricks, called *adobe*, it covered an area larger than a football field. Bent, St. Vrain and Company opened for business in the fall of 1833. The fur trade was starting to decline, but the partners energetically traded with the Cheyenne and other Plains Indians. William married Owl Woman, a Cheyenne. When she died, he followed the Cheyenne custom and married her sister, Yellow Woman.

Bent's Fort became the urban center of future Colorado. The cultured, observant Kentuckian Susan Magoffin visited Bent's Fort in 1846. She came west with her husband Samuel, a veteran Santa Fe trader. Magoffin described the fort:

> Well the outside exactly fills my idea of an ancient castle. It is built of adobes, unburnt brick, and Mexican style so far. The walls are very high [fourteen feet] and very thick with rounding corners. . . .
>
> Now for our room; it is quite roomy. Like the others it has a dirt floor, which I keep sprinkling

Bent's Fort, the most famous fort in Colorado, was rebuilt by the National Park Service using adobe, which was used in the 1830s original. (Photo by Glenn Cuerden.)

constantly during the day; we have two windows one looking out on the plain, the other is on the *patio* or yard. We have our own furniture, such as bed, chairs, wash basin, table furniture, and we eat in our own room.

The Magoffins were only two of many visitors to Bent's Fort before it was destroyed in 1849. William Bent then moved farther down the Arkansas River and built another post. It never proved to be as important as the earlier one.

The era of Bent's Fort was over by the time the gold seekers appeared in 1859. The Bents and St. Vrain had carved an empire out of the plains and mountains of Colorado. They were Colorado's first U.S. entrepreneurs — men who organized and operated a business, in spite of the risks. Unlike many easterners who followed them, they usually made friends with the Native Americans. Years later, William's children joined the Cheyenne in their fight against the flood of settlement that threatened their land and way of life.

Bent's Fort was not the only one in Colorado. Bent, St. Vrain and Company had done so well that other men believed they also could make money. Lancaster Lupton built Fort Lupton, near the present town of that name. Fort Jackson appeared nearby in the mid-1830s. Fort Vasquez, built in 1837 by Louis Vasquez, also challenged the Bents' business. They responded by building Fort St. Vrain, northwest of present Platteville.

On the Western Slope, traders built a couple of smaller posts. Fort Davy Crockett and Fort Robidoux lasted only a very short time. None of these forts was as significant as Bent's Fort.

During these years Colorado became an important trading and trapping center of the Rocky Mountains. When the fur trade declined, all of these posts, except Bent's Fort, were abandoned. They all are gone now, except Bent's Fort near La Junta and Fort Vasquez in Platteville. These two have been rebuilt so you can visit them and see how the fur trappers and traders lived.

By the 1850s the fur trade era was over and calm appeared to have returned to Colorado. The Cheyenne, Utes, Arapaho, and other Indians' lives had been changed forever, but for a while it seemed that they might keep their homelands. Through most of the 1850s, the small Mexican settlements in the southern end of the San Luis Valley, the U.S. military post of Fort Garland, and a couple of villages of retired fur trappers (El Pueblo, for one) and Mexican farmers along the Arkansas River were the only European-American toeholds of settlement.

The explorers, fur trappers, and traders did not leave many permanent marks on the land, but Colorado was better known because they had been here. They proved that they could live and make a living in Colorado. Other people would remember that. These tough, adventurous men would not be forgotten.

QUESTIONS

1. What did Spanish explorers of the 1700s hope to find in Colorado?
2. What places did Zebulon Pike visit on his Colorado tour?
3. Why did Pike and Long think eastern Colorado looked like a desert?
4. Discuss the importance of the mountain men to Colorado history.
5. Why was Bent's Fort important in the development of future Colorado?
6. Compare and contrast the expeditions of the Spanish explorers of the 1700s and 1800s, Zebulon Pike, and John Charles Fremont. Use factors such as weather, discoveries, and results in your comparison.

ACTIVITIES

1. You are a friend of Kit Carson. Write a letter telling about this man and his activities.
2. Write a short essay about the importance of the buffalo and the beaver in Colorado history.
3. You have traveled down the Santa Fe Trail and are staying at Bent's Fort. Write a newspaper article about your visit.
4. On a Colorado map trace the various American exploring expeditions that traveled through the region in the 1806–1848 era.
5. Find pictures and descriptions of Bent's Fort — or, if possible, visit the restored fort in southeastern Colorado. Build a clay model of the entire fort or construct one room of the fort, complete with furniture.
6. Read one of the books on the fur trade or the Santa Fe Trail and tell the class something special you learned.

Books You and Your Teacher Might Enjoy

M. Morgan Estergreen. *Kit Carson: A Portrait in Courage.* Norman: University of Oklahoma Press, 1962. This book gives an interesting account of Carson's life.

Edward Harris. *John Charles Fremont.* New York: Chelsea House, 1992. In this book, a fascinating man comes to life.

David Lavender. *Bent's Fort.* Lincoln: Bison Press, 1972. This book is an entertaining account of the Bents and their fort.

————. *The Trail to Santa Fe.* Santa Fe: Trails West, 1988. The dust, excitement, and danger are all here.

Susan Magoffin. *Down the Santa Fe Trail and into Mexico.* Lincoln: Bison Press, 1982 (reprint). Travel with this spirited woman and learn about the West firsthand.

Jared Stallones. *Zebulon M. Pike.* New York: Chelsea House, 1992. Follow Pike up the peak and across the mountains.

Did You Know?

It took Edwin James two days to climb Pikes Peak, July 13–14, 1820.

Santa Fe wagons carried five tons of freight.

A Hawken rifle could kill a "griz or buffler" at 200 yards.

Susan Magoffin traveled six weeks in a wagon to reach Bent's Fort from Independence, Missouri.

The albino beavers's fur was the rarest and most valuable fur of all.

Charles Bent was the first territorial governor of New Mexico.

Spanish settlers coming up the Rio Grande built adobe churches like this one in San Luis, the oldest town in Colorado. (Photo by Thomas J. Noel.)

CHAPTER FIVE
Up the Rio Grande

Before the gold rush and the arrival of English-speaking settlers, Spanish Americans had already settled in Colorado. These pioneers came up the Rio Grande from New Mexico. The Rio Grande, the third-longest river in the United States, became the pioneer route from old Mexico and New Mexico into what is now southern Colorado.

San Luis Valley

Hispanics found a wide mountain valley on the upper Rio Grande, where they started the first permanent towns in Colorado. They built their villages with adobe — a mixture of clay and water with grass or straw mixed in to help hold the brick together. On top of adobe walls, they built log and dirt roofs. To help keep out Indians and keep in their children and animals, these Hispanics made their towns into *plazas*, or town squares. A plaza was created by lining up the buildings to form four walls around a central square.

The Plaza de los Manzanares was the first of many plaza villages in the San Luis Valley. Manuel and Pedro Manzanares brought their families to settle in 1849. This tiny town, now called Garcia, is on the Colorado–New Mexico state line.

The first big town was San Luis, founded on the Culebra ("Snake") River in 1851. San Luis was a plaza town with a large public pasture, or *vega*, where all townspeople could graze their cattle and sheep. The people of San Luis also built an irrigation ditch so they could grow beans, corn, wheat, and other crops. The farmers let water from the ditch drain into their fields and provide much-needed moisture for the crops. This San Luis People's Ditch (1852) is the oldest still-working irrigation canal in Colorado.

Mexican Americans soon started other towns in the San Luis Valley. Most of these people were farmers, and their farms spread out from the village, usually in long, narrow strips. Everyone lived in the village and went to work in the fields during the day. To grind the wheat and corn they grew into flour, mills were built in several San Luis Valley towns. This flour was sold or used to make tortillas. Some mills shipped their flour to the northern Colorado gold fields after 1858 to feed gold miners.

Life was not easy for people who hoped to make their homes in the San Luis Valley. They were 100 miles away from the nearest city — Santa Fe. The San Luis Valley is about 8,000 feet high and has a cold, dry climate. Growing food was difficult, and sometimes people were attacked by Ute Indians while working in their fields. The San Luis Valley and all the land south of the Arkansas River had belonged to Mexico before the Mexican American War of 1846–1848. At the end of that war, the United States acquired southern and western Colorado. To help protect settlers in the San Luis Valley, the U.S. government built Fort Garland, the first U.S. fort in Colorado. Commander Kit Carson and the troops at Fort Garland fought the Ute and Apache warriors who had been raiding the region. Peace finally came to the San Luis Valley when the Utes agreed in 1862 to move to western Colorado. The Apache moved south to New Mexico and Arizona.

Hispanic Life and Culture

After the Utes left the area, Hispanic settlement spread northward. The newcomers from New Mexico brought sheep and used their wool to spin yarn and weave fabric for clothing and rugs. They made their own plows and grew their own food. They raised cattle, sheep, pigs, and chickens.

Hispanic women worked beside their husbands and children in the fields to grow food for the family. Mothers taught their daughters to grind wheat into flour to make soft, white, delicious tortillas. When men were away hunting, fishing, irrigating their fields, tending livestock, or looking for gold, women often ran the family *hacienda* (ranch or farm house).

Like their parents in New Mexico, the people of the valley were mostly Catholics. The church and its festivals were the center of their life. At first, priests came from New Mexico to conduct services and perform necessary duties. In 1858, the settlers built a permanent church, Our Lady of Guadalupe, in Conejos. Other Catholic churches, many of them tiny adobe chapels, were built throughout the San Luis Valley.

The church provided not only religious services, but also colorful festivals. Everyone, young and old, took part in these fiestas to celebrate Christmas, Easter, saints' days, weddings, and anniversaries. Celebrations included parades, plays, and dances. St. Isidro, the patron saint of farmers, was especially popular. Many people believed he sent angels to earth from heaven to

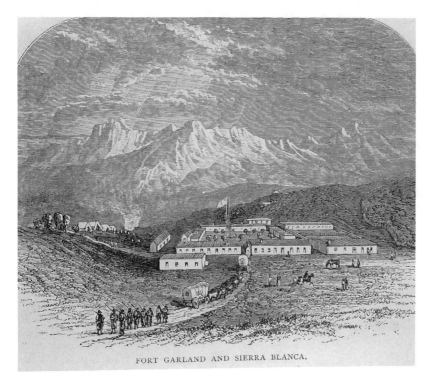

FORT GARLAND AND SIERRA BLANCA.

Fort Garland in the San Luis Valley is now a museum of the Colorado Historical Society. (Thomas J. Noel Collection.)

Nuestra Señora de Guadalupe in Conejos is Colorado's oldest church.
(Photo by Tim H. O'Sullivan.)

help with the hard work of plowing fields and protecting crops from bugs, drought, and hail.

By the 1860s, these hardworking settlers had transformed their valley into a place very much like their New Mexican homeland. Small plazas dotted the land, and irrigation ditches spread out from the rivers to provide water for fields of corn, beans, squash, and wheat.

A similar pattern of settlement took place east of the Sangre de Cristo mountains. Along the Purgatoire River Valley, other plaza towns were started. Settlement began in the 1860s, and was different from the San Luis Valley because both New Mexicans and Anglos took part. Trinidad became the best known of the towns, but San Miguel Plaza and others made attempts to attract people. Although many of these smaller settlements failed, their efforts helped other towns take hold and survive. By the 1860s, Trinidad had become the largest town in southern Colorado.

Arkansas Valley

Settlers also came early to the Arkansas River Valley in central and southeastern Colorado. Bent's Fort, the scene of so much history during the fur-trading days, was the first important non-Indian settlement on the Arkansas. Another early gathering place for trappers and traders was established in 1842 at the junction of Fountain Creek and the Arkansas River. This post, named El Pueblo, would one day become the city of Pueblo; the name came from the trading post there. *Pueblo* means "town" in Spanish. Trader Rufus Sage described it:

> This post is owned by a company of independent traders, on the common property system, and from its situation can command a profitable trade with both Mexicans and Indians. Its occupants number ten or twelve Americans, most of whom are married to Mexican women, while everything about the establishment wears the aspect of neatness and comfort.

A Christmas Day massacre of the settlers by a Ute raiding party in 1854 ended the first period of Pueblo's history. All inhabitants were killed or chased off, and the town was abandoned.

Thirty miles west of Pueblo, the farming settlement of San Buenaventura de los Tres Arrollos, better known as Hardscrabble, had begun in 1844. Of Hardscrabble, Rufus Sage said, "The land indicates a fitness for agricultural purposes, and holds out strong inducements [attractions] to emigrants. A small settlement of whites and half-breeds, numbering fifteen or twenty families, has

Trinidad, located on the Las Animas River at the foot of Raton Pass, became the gateway to southern Colorado. (Denver Public Library.)

already commenced. . . . The only fears entertained for its success are on account of the Indians."

With the fur trade declining, this settlement was populated almost entirely by former trappers and hunters and their families. The farms did well in wet years, but too many dry years soon caused Hardscrabble to disappear. Many other small farm and ranch communities had even shorter lives than Hardscrabble.

By the time the 1859 gold rush began, the settlements on the Arkansas River were gone, except for a few ranches. The little settlements had been too weak and isolated to become permanent. Poor judgment, poor timing, hostile Indians, and bad weather ended their hopes of survival.

Hispanic towns often preceded later Yankee railroad towns. This Mexican settlement at El Pueblo preceded the modern city of Pueblo. (Pueblo Library District.)

Growth of the San Luis Valley

In the San Luis Valley, people hung on despite hardships that killed many other settlements. The wealth-seeking hordes of the gold rush bypassed the valley almost entirely. Several groups of prospectors tried, but did not find enough gold to look further or stay long. For the farmers, life went on much as it had earlier, with several exceptions. Once the roads were improved, the mining camps to the north of the valley gave the San Luis farmers a new market for their crops.

Another important change in this valley was the coming of Anglo, or English-speaking, settlers during the 1880s. Most of these Yankees spread out into the middle and northern parts of the valley, where more land was to be found. They were farmers, too, but their settlements, like Saguache, did not look like the plazas to the south. They were more like eastern farming communities — like those red brick and white frame towns started later in eastern Colorado.

The railroad chugged into the San Luis Valley in the 1870s, ending forever the frontier way of life. The Denver and Rio Grande Railroad climbed over La Veta Pass and down to the Rio Grande. In 1878 the railroad established the town of Alamosa and made it the hub of the valley.

A letter writer from the new town of Alamosa proudly wrote to the *Rocky Mountain News* (March 26, 1879): ". . . not more than twenty-five miles from the city, mines are being opened that from indications promise to rival the best in this great mineral state. . . . The business houses of Alamosa are among the largest and best in the south. Alamosa has two newspapers, both spicy sheets."

Such pride was common for newborn towns. Nearly every young community claimed that it had the best stores, the best newspapers, and the brightest future. Denver's *Rocky Mountain News,* for example, was the state's first newspaper and promoted Denver as Colorado's queen city.

From its huge Alamosa railyards, the D&RG built a line to New Mexico. Another branch went to Durango and Silverton in the San Juans. Along the D&RG tracks grew such towns as Antonito and Monte Vista. Some older settlements like Del Norte prospered when the tracks reached them.

Alamosa residents not only built railroads but began looking for valuable minerals. They found gold at Summitville in the San Juan Mountains on the western edge of the San Luis Valley. In 1879 this San Luis Valley strike looked as if it might become one of Colorado's great gold mines. Like many other gold strikes, however, this one was not as rich as prospectors hoped.

Bonanza, another San Juan mining district, sprang up at the north end of the valley. Anne Ellis recalled Bonanza, located to the north of Saguache, in her book, *The Life of an Ordinary Woman*:

> Bonanza was not as rough and tough as most new camps, because in the very beginning it was incorporated as a city, and always had all the town officials. In speaking of the population, you didn't count people, anyway, you counted saloons and dance-halls. There were thirty-six saloons and seven dance-halls.

One of the richer mining districts was Orient, on the east side of the valley. Iron ore was mined there for nearly forty years, beginning in 1880, and was used to make steel at the big plant in Pueblo.

The Denver and Rio Grande's narrow-gauge line from Antonito, Colorado, to Chama,
New Mexico, reopened in the 1970s as the Cumbres and Toltec Scenic Railroad.
(Cumbres and Toltec Scenic Railroad.)

Mining helped settle and develop the San Luis Valley, but the region was and still is primarily agricultural. More typical than Bonanza or Orient is Monte Vista, founded in 1884. This community took pride in having no "gambling dens or liquor saloons." Around it developed farms and ranches that are still the heart of the San Luis Valley's economy. Monte Vista celebrates its rich ranches and croplands with its Sky High Rodeo.

Hispanic Colorado

Because English-speaking peoples later became more numerous and politically powerful, Coloradans sometimes overlook the pioneering role and contributions of Mexican Americans. Most people like at least one contribution, because it is so tasty — Mexican food. With hot salsa and plenty of fresh lettuce and tomatoes, Mexican food spices up the Colorado diet.

Another Mexican contribution — beef — originated in Spain. The Spanish first introduced cattle to the Americas. Spanish *vaqueros* (changed by English speakers to become "buckaroos") were the first cowboys. The words *bronco*, *lasso*, *bandana*, and *rodeo* are reminders that the first cowboys spoke Spanish. Hispanics also developed irrigation dams, ditches, and canals. Since Colorado averages only 16.6 inches of rain each year, irrigation is necessary to keep farm crops alive.

Mexican buildings were sometimes criticized by Anglos as "mud" huts. Not until the 1920s did many other cultures come to appreciate the adobe bricks, which are easy to make and fit well into the natural landscape. In addition, the thick adobe walls keep buildings cool in summer and warm in winter. Mexican-style adobe and stucco began to be used not only on houses but also on hotels, restaurants, and even gas stations. Stucco is a plaster coating applied over adobe or brick walls. Some of Colorado's finest neighborhoods and fanciest houses are Spanish style, made with adobe and stucco walls. These buildings may have flat roofs with *vigas* (beams) or fancier red-tile sloped roofs.

Mexican Americans, as the largest single ethnic group in Colorado, have given the state not only its name but also many of its leaders. For example, Casimiro Barela of Trinidad served in the territorial and state legislature from 1861 until 1916. Senator

Barela helped make sure that the Colorado Constitution and state laws were printed in Spanish as well as English. Barela and other Hispanic leaders sometimes had to remind everyone that Hispanics were the first European Americans to settle in Colorado.

Mexican Americans contributed many of the state's place-names, beginning with Colorado, or "red," for the red canyons of the Colorado River. Many Spanish place-names have been lost, and many were changed to English. Pikes Peak, for instance, was known to early Hispanic explorers as El Capitan. Still, the early Spanish and Mexican settlers left behind many names that remind us today of our state's Hispanic legacy — for example, Monte Vista ("mountain view"), Sangre de Cristo ("blood of Christ"), and Pueblo ("town"). Because Hispanic as well as

The first cowboys were Hispanic, as the words bronco, lasso, bandana, *and* rodeo *suggest. This outfit near Pueblo has stopped for lunch around the chuck wagon. (Pueblo Library District.)*

Anglo Americans created Colorado, it is a richer and more colorful place.

Casimiro Barela, longtime state senator from Trinidad, promoted Spanish culture, language, and heritage in the Colorado legislature. (Denver Public Library.)

QUESTIONS

1. What is the oldest permanent town in Colorado?
2. Which large Colorado city began as a trading post on the Arkansas River?
3. What factors caused the fast rise and fall of the town of Hardscrabble?
4. Describe family life in the San Luis Valley in the 1850s.
5. What role did the Catholic Church play in the lives of San Luis Valley residents during the 1850s–1870s?
6. Why did the San Luis Valley start to grow faster after the 1870s?

ACTIVITIES

1. Draw a map of the Rio Grande and label the Spanish-named towns that grew up beside it. If you don't know the English meanings of the names, use a Spanish-English dictionary or ask a Spanish-speaking person to help you translate.
2. Draw a map of the Arkansas River showing the biggest riverside towns.
3. Draw or build a model of a small plaza.
4. See if there is a church near you with services in Spanish. Organize a field trip to one of the church's ceremonies.
5. How many Spanish names of towns, cities, water bodies, or landforms can you find on a map of Colorado? What do the words mean in English?
6. Look up the history of traditional Mexican foods — tacos, enchiladas, tortillas, and others. Create a classroom display of these foods. Have your classmates explain the origins of these foods before they eat the samples.

Books You and Your Teacher Might Enjoy

Samuel P. Arnold. *Eating Up the Santa Fe Trail.* Niwot: University of Colorado Press, 1990. This cookbook is stuffed with historical recipes.

Maxine Benson. *1001 Colorado Place Names.* Lawrence: University of Kansas Press, 1994. This guide is the best source of place-names in the Highest State.

Anne Ellis. *Life of an Ordinary Woman.* Lincoln: University of Nebraska Press, 1980 (paperback reprint). This book is a young woman's account of life in the rough San Luis Valley mining town of Bonanza.

Janet LeCompte. *Pueblo, Hardscrabble, Greenhorn.* Norman: University of Oklahoma Press, 1978. This book tells the story of Pueblo and two of its short-lived neighbors in the Arkansas River valley.

Jose de Oñis, ed. *The Hispanic Contribution to the State of Colorado.* Boulder: Westview Press, 1976. Various experts write about Hispanic exploration, land grants, heroes, folklore, religion, art, and language.

Virginia M. Simmons. *The San Luis Valley.* Boulder: Pruett Publishing, 1979. This book is a well-illustrated overview of the area.

Olibama López Tushar. *The People of "El Valle."* Pueblo: El Escritorio, 1992. This fine introduction to the San Luis Valley is by a descendant of a pioneer family.

Did You Know?

Adobe bricks like those used by Hispanic Coloradans have been made for thousands of years.

Ancient Egyptians used similar bricks to build some of the pyramids.

The San Luis Valley is the largest and lowest of Colorado's four mountain parks.

Spanish-surnamed people are the fastest-growing major ethnic group in the United States.

The first cowboys were Hispanic.

INDIAN VILLAGE IN DENVER, IN 1860.

Arapaho Indians camped in and around Denver. (Thomas J. Noel Collection.)

CHAPTER SIX
The Longest Civil War

It was a civil war — a battle between two peoples who wished to live their own lives in their own land. Both called North America home. Sadly, neither group ever completely understood the other. Neither the Indians nor the whites were all bad or all good; they were just human beings trying to do their best for themselves, their families, and their friends. Their disagreement had started centuries earlier on the Atlantic coast of the North American continent, where the struggling English colonists and the local Indians had engaged in a series of bitter attacks and counterattacks. As European, then American, settlement moved west, the conflict continued. This long civil war lasted nearly 270 years.

During the 1700s, the Spanish in New Mexico had campaigned against the Utes and the Comanche from Colorado. The Indians had raided Spanish lands, and the governor of New Mexico sent troops northward to punish the raiders and show them the might of Spain. The Spanish, however, never were able to establish a permanent settlement in this part of the Rocky Mountains. This struggle, therefore, proved a minor one compared to what happened later.

By the time permanent settlement by European Americans took hold in Colorado in the early 1850s, the civil war had been going on for over 230 years. The causes were as old as the struggle itself, and the result for the Native Americans would be the same as it had been during Virginia's troubles — they would lose their lands no matter how hard they fought to keep them.

Treaties and Troubles
When all of Colorado became American territory in 1848, the Utes, Cheyenne, and Arapaho found themselves governed by the

United States. They had not asked for this to happen, nor had they been asked if they wanted it. Like the land, the Indians simply were traded as part of the 1848 peace treaty with Mexico.

Ever since the United States of America had declared its independence in 1776, the government had been signing treaties with various Indian peoples. These treaties promised land for the Indians to live on and peace between the two peoples. Unfortunately, one side or the other had broken nearly all of the treaties. The pattern would continue in Colorado and throughout the West.

In 1849 the United States made its first treaty with the Ute people. The Utes promised to settle down, recognize the authority of the United States government, and remain at peace. In return the Utes received gifts and a promise of $5,000 per year. Two years later the Cheyenne and Arapaho joined with other Plains tribes to sign the Fort Laramie Treaty. The land in eastern Colorado between the Arkansas and Platte Rivers was given to the Cheyenne and Arapaho. This had become their homeland, a fact the United States recognized.

Meanwhile, the Utes in the San Luis Valley had threatened the small Mexican settlements located there. These Hispanics were now American citizens, and the United States needed to protect them and maintain the peace. To do so, the U.S. government built Fort Massachusetts in 1852 and stationed troops there. Such incidents had happened often before in American history, but they were new to the Utes.

The trouble that developed between the Utes and the settlers in the southern San Luis Valley should have been expected. The intruders were living and farming on land the Utes considered theirs, land where they had hunted for years. Sometimes when they could not find deer or buffalo, the Utes stole the farmers' cattle and sheep to feed their families. The settlers feared the Utes and did not consider themselves trespassers. The stage was set for something bad to happen.

In late 1854 and early 1855, some Ute people attacked some ranches and farms. The worried settlers quickly asked for help from the U.S. government. Troops marched north from Fort

The Utes moved around in search of buffalo and better campsites. Women, like the two shown here, made and moved the buffalo hide tepees. (Fort Lewis College, Southwest Studies Center.)

Union, New Mexico, guided by Kit Carson. After a series of battles in March and April 1855, the defeated Utes asked for peace. They signed another treaty, this time agreeing to leave the area and move to western Colorado. After that peace returned to the San Luis Valley.

Trouble on the Plains

During the 1850s, more and more Americans from the East crossed the Great Plains on their way to Oregon, California, and Utah. More than 200,000 people joined this mass migration. They trespassed on Indian land, killed buffalo, and, worst of all, brought white people's illnesses with them. Smallpox, cholera, and other diseases swept through the Indians' villages.

The pioneers moving west believed they had a God-given right to the land. They often feared meeting hostile Plains Indians along the way.

The U.S. government, caught in the middle, faced a difficult decision. The Plains tribes had signed treaties that whites often broke. The pioneers were taxpayers and voters, whereas Indians paid no taxes and were not allowed to vote. Whites felt they had rights to these "new" western lands. To protect these rights, they wanted more forts, more troops, and more patrols along the trails. The basic question — Who owns the land? — remained unanswered.

In 1857, the government army accidently started a chain of events that led to a solution. It was not a solution that pleased the Plains Indians, however. Colonel Edwin Sumner led troops onto the plains to punish Indians for raiding pioneer wagon trains along the Oregon Trail. A Delaware Indian guide, Fall Leaf, returned from this campaign with a "bunch of gold nuggets tied up in a rag." Fall Leaf said he had bent over a mountain stream to get a drink and had seen the nuggets lying in the streambed. Some of his neighbors from Lawrence, Kansas, decided to go west the next spring to find more gold. Along with another party from present-day Oklahoma, they started west. The central Rockies were about to undergo a big change as thousands of Americans rushed in looking for gold.

The Road to War

These pioneer prospectors did find a little gold that summer, and the news quickly spread throughout the states back east. By 1859 the cry was "Pikes Peak or Bust" because Pikes Peak was the only known landmark to most of them. Thousands of people rushed west along the Arkansas and South Platte Rivers to the new gold discoveries.

The Cheyenne and Arapaho could not believe so many whites existed. They watched a never-ending stream of pale faces moving westward. These newcomers scared away the buffalo and generally believed the Indians to be in the way. They denied that they were trespassing on Indian land or that the

Cheyenne and Arapaho had any real claim to this country. In their rush for riches, the eager gold seekers would not tolerate anything or anyone that stood in their way. Tragically, neither side trusted or understood the other.

Mollie Sanford saw the Plains Indians while traveling to Colorado in the spring of 1860. Among the comments found in her diary are these:

> A band of Indians rushed into camp today and stampeded our cattle. They were either drunk or bent on mischief. The men will keep watch tonight.

The Arapaho, who initially welcomed miners, grew more suspicious and warlike as whites took their land and killed their buffalo. (Denver Public Library.)

> We passed through a camp or Indian village of 200
> wigwams. Mercy! I almost fear we will be taken
> scalps and all, yet before we get through. The Indi-
> ans are peaceable, I suppose, but are too treacherous
> to trust out alone.

Susan Ashley, who came to Denver as a bride in 1861, agreed with Mollie. The sight of Cheyenne and Arapaho Indians on Denver's streets disturbed her. She especially worried about them walking unannounced into her home. A friend told her they would not open a gate, so she insisted a fence be built around her house. It did not work; the curious Indians looked in her windows and one day wandered in. "With assumed bravery I cried out 'Puck-a-chee' (which I had been told was the Indian way of saying be gone!) and I put my hands against the nearest Indian as if to push him out." They left, but the incident left Ashley very scared.

These two women's comments were much milder than the comments of others from these years. The *Daily Mining Journal,* published in Black Hawk, told its readers on January 15, 1864, that "every white man in every part of the West should consider them [Indians] as his deadly enemies, — more vengeful and dangerous than the scorpion or the panther." Such comments did nothing to cause understanding or peace between the two peoples. They only made worse prejudices that already existed.

In this climate of fear and mistrust, any event or threat could bring about armed conflict. It was not long in happening. Neither side was entirely to blame. Good people on both sides hoped to avoid killing and warfare, but, sadly, that would not happen.

Sand Creek

In 1862 the Sioux living in Minnesota attacked the white settlers who were taking over their land. Quickly troops arrived, and many Indians fled to their relatives on the plains. They were angry and upset, and they wanted revenge. The next spring the Sioux and other Plains Indians attacked wagon trains and stage stations along the pioneer trails. Travel and shipping of goods to

Denver, the supply center for white settlers, spearheaded efforts to conquer the Arapaho and Southern Cheyenne during the Indian War of 1862–1868. (Thomas J. Noel Collection.)

Colorado stopped because people were afraid of the Indians. Mail had to be shipped all the way to San Francisco, then east to Denver. The miners and settlers in Colorado felt isolated and angry. With no supplies coming in, they feared food shortages. They wanted the U.S. government to send troops, but it had none to spare. The United States was fighting the Civil War (1861–1865), and every soldier was needed.

In the fall of 1863 the Indians finally left the overland trails, and pioneers once again traveled west. The next spring, however, trouble started again. The Hungate family — father, mother, and two daughters — was killed and mutilated within a few miles of Denver. Raiding parties of Sioux, Cheyenne, and Arapaho closed the trails and tore down telegraph lines. As a result, once again the mail had to be rerouted, shortages of food and mining equipment occurred, and prices went up.

Furious Coloradans demanded action, but the government in Washington could not help as long as the Civil War continued. Left to their own resources, Coloradans raised a regiment of troops, the Third Colorado, and prepared to handle the crisis on their own. Some people and newspaper writers wanted to wipe out all of the Indians.

Sadly, little attention was paid to the Indians' point of view. They had ample reason to be angry. For years white people had broken treaties and the government had failed to keep promises that it would help the Indians. The pushing and shoving of Indians by whites had grown worse after the Pikes Peak gold rush. Harassment had mounted as more settlers had arrived. From past experience, the Indians feared that they would have to give way.

On November 29, 1864, the Third Colorado volunteers attacked Black Kettle's Cheyenne village on Sand Creek in southeastern Colorado. Black Kettle was a good man who truly wanted peace with the whites. But members of his tribe had raided and caused trouble, and Coloradans were in no mood to separate "good Indians" from "bad Indians."

The bugles sounded, and the troops charged. Fear, intolerance, and hatred rode in with the soldiers; lies, accusations, and controversy rode out. The controversy, or dispute over what happened, outlived everyone who was there that day. George Bent, son of William Bent and Owl Woman, was in the camp. Though wounded, he survived and remembered:

> At dawn on the morning of November 29 I was still in bed when I heard shots and the noise of people running about the camp. I jumped up and ran out of my lodge. From down the creek a large body of troops was advancing at a rapid trot, some to the east of the camps, and others on the opposite side of the creek, to the west. More soldiers could be seen making for the Indian pony herds to the south of the camps; in the camps themselves all was confusion and noise — men, women, and children rushing out of the lodges partly dressed.

Bent and other Cheyenne men made a stand, but they were outnumbered and out-gunned. His letters later continued with the tragic result:

> We ran up the creek. . . . Many of the people preceded us up the creek, and the dry bed of the stream was now a terrible sight: men, women, and children lying thickly scattered in the sand, some dead and the rest too badly wounded to move [on] the terrible march, most of us being on foot, without food, ill-clad and encumbered with wounded and women and children.

Bent was right; it was terrible. The officers lost control of their men. The soldiers killed men, women, and children and scalped and mutilated many bodies.

Ever since the bugles went silent at Sand Creek, people have argued about the event. Were warriors in the camp? How many women and children died? What was the total number of people killed? How much mutilation occurred? All the facts will never be known, and the dispute echoes down the decades.

Perhaps today we can learn something from this tragic event. Why did it happen? Should fear, misunderstanding, and intolerance be allowed to poison relations among human beings?

After Sand Creek, an Indian war broke out that would continue for a decade. The Sand Creek attack had solved very little, and the enraged Indians fought even harder to preserve their homes. This ongoing war finally left the Indians huddled on reservations, their way of life gone.

Beecher Island and Summit Springs

Two other skirmishes took place on Colorado's high plains. On September 16, 1868, a party of army scouts was camped near Wray. Suddenly, at daybreak, a large force of Cheyenne and Sioux warriors led by the famous warrior Roman Nose swept in and attacked them. Realizing the Indians had trapped them, the soldiers sent two of the scouts for help in the dark of the night. The fight became a siege, and for nine days the troops held out on a sandy island in the Arikaree Fork of the Republican River.

Both sides fought bravely. Meanwhile, the soldiers started running out of food. The smell of dead horses rotting in the hot sun made it all the worse. Roman Nose was killed, but the siege continued until the cavalry from Fort Wallace, Kansas, arrived. The Sioux and Cheyenne, realizing their chance for victory was gone, disappeared back into the vastness of the prairie. The siege finally was over. Among those killed was Lieutenant Fred Beecher, and in his memory the site was named Beecher Island.

During the fall and winter after the Beecher Island siege, the army conducted a series of campaigns against the hostile Plains Indians camped in Kansas and Oklahoma. In response, the Indians raided farms and ranches in western Kansas and Nebraska during the summer of 1869. Pawnee army scouts and companies of the Fifth Cavalry were soon on their trail.

William "Buffalo Bill" Cody was chief of scouts for the cavalry. Between 1868 and 1872 he took part in sixteen Indian fights. He was praised for his "extraordinarily good services as a trailer and fighter." Cody later would reenact these battles and become a famous western showman. His Buffalo Bill's Wild West show toured this country and Europe. For the moment, however, he faced more pressing matters. He had to find the Indians who were doing the raiding.

Cody's troops found a band of Cheyenne led by Tall Bull camped near what is now Sterling. The troops attacked. Frank North, who had helped organize the Pawnee scouts, jotted down the day's events in his diary.

> Sunday, July 11, 1869. Marched this morn at 6 A.M. with fifty of my men and two hundred whites, with three days' rations. Follow trail until three P.M. and came up to the village. Made a grand charge and it was a complete victory. Took the whole village of about 85 lodges. Killed about sixty Indians. Took seventeen prisoners and about three hundred ponies and robes, etc.

The last fight for control of Colorado's eastern plains ended with a victory for the onrushing American settlers. Farmers and

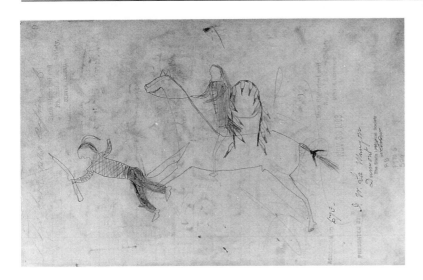

*A soldier found these drawings in a sketchbook he captured at the
Summit Springs battle site. They were drawn by Cheyenne warriors wanting
to tell their side of the Colorado Indian wars. (Colorado Historical Society.)*

ranchers could now safely reside where only a few years ago the Cheyenne and Arapaho roamed free.

The Ute Claim to Western Colorado

On the Western Slope the Utes still lived freely. By yet another treaty, in 1868, they received a reservation that included much of western Colorado. No whites, except necessary government officials, were "permitted to pass over, settle upon, or reside in this reservation." In return the Utes had given up their claim to the San Luis Valley, Middle Park, North Park, and the Yampa River Valley.

Both sides seemed satisfied — but would it last? Would the Utes keep their beloved Western Slope land? You have examined this long-running war between these two groups of people. Do you think peace would continue? In a later chapter, look for the story of the Utes and their famous leader, Ouray.

For the eastern portion of Colorado, the fight was over. It had been a tragic struggle involving good people on both sides. Many innocent people (especially women and children) had suffered. The Plains Indians' way of life was destroyed and their homeland taken away forever. Superior technology, greater firepower, and a larger population had carried the day — just as they had throughout American history. The Indians had fought courageously, but they could not stand long against the advancing white settlement.

QUESTIONS

1. What were the terms of the 1849, 1855, and 1868 treaties between the Utes and the U.S. government?
2. Why did conflicts develop between the Utes and the Hispanic settlers in the San Luis Valley?
3. Explain why the Cheyenne and Arapaho were upset with the coming of the whites.
4. Why did Mollie Sanford and Susan Ashley distrust the Indians they met?
5. Who were George Bent, Fall Leaf, and Buffalo Bill?

6. How did the attack at Sand Creek affect the Indians and the citizens of Denver?

7. Why is this chapter called "The Longest Civil War"?

ACTIVITIES

1. Imagine you are a Cheyenne at Sand Creek. Write a letter to a friend describing what happened there on November 29, 1864.

2. Find out if any Indian battles took place in your area. Research the battle and report the events to your class.

3. What if the Cheyenne, Utes, and Arapaho had won, and the white settlers were placed on reservations? Write a newspaper account about life on the reservation or in Colorado.

4. You have been asked to draw up a treaty between the U.S. government and the Ute people. Using everything you know about the different points of view, write a fair agreement.

5. Study the Cheyenne and Arapaho and draw some pictures of lives both before and after 1859.

Books You and Your Teacher Might Enjoy

Alfred Kroebe. *The Arapaho.* Lincoln: Bison Press, 1983. Meet the friends of the Cheyenne.

Pat Mendoza. *Song of Sorrow: Massacre at Sand Creek.* Denver: Willow Wind Publishing Company, 1993. Storyteller Pat Mendoza presents an Indian view of the 1864 tragedy.

Mollie: The Journal of Mollie Dorsey Sanford. Lincoln: Bison Press, 1976. Learn about early Colorado from this firsthand account.

John H. Monnett. *The Battle of Beecher Island and the Indian War of 1867–1869.* Niwot: University Press of Colorado, 1992. Both sides get fair treatment in this careful look at the clash between the U.S. Cavalry and the Cheyenne in eastern Colorado.

Duane A. Smith. *The Birth of Colorado.* Norman: University of Oklahoma, 1989. This book focuses on both civil wars: the War Between the States and the war between the Plains Indians and white settlers.

Did You Know?

In 1855 the United States purchased thirty-four camels for army use.

More white people died of accidents and disease in the 1849 California gold rush than were killed in all the Indian wars.

Some Indians figured the eastern United States must be deserted because so many whites were coming west.

An army private received $16 a month until 1870, when pay was reduced to $13.

CHAPTER SEVEN
Miners

"PIKES PEAK GOLD — A NEW CALIFORNIA." This headline greeted the reader of the *Leavenworth* [Kansas] *Times*, on September 11, 1858. In Kansas and elsewhere the news of a new gold discovery raced like the wind across the land.

Gold! Golden dreams excited many people beyond reason and drove them to go and get it, to leave behind everything and head for the mountains. Gold, people thought, would make them rich with little work. Unfortunately, most men and women who rushed to Colorado to find their pot of gold did not get rich. What they found was hard work under very difficult conditions. As one person said, "I never worked so hard in my life, to get rich without working."

Legends and Rumors

The first Europeans who traveled to what became Colorado were looking for gold or silver. The Spanish from New Mexico searched for minerals in this land to the north during the 1700s. They left behind names for places they had been (Animas River), names of minerals they had sought (La Plata — "Silver" — Mountains), and legends of lost mines. They did not stay very long and did not find great wealth.

When explorer Zebulon Pike was in Santa Fe in 1807, he heard interesting news from mountain man James Purcell. Purcell told Pike that he had found gold at the place where the South Platte River begins. In the following years other stories about gold in the mountains drifted into the American settlements back east. One story even claimed that Indians used gold bullets in their guns.

In 1821, Spain lost most of what is today Colorado to Mexico. Then Mexico lost Colorado to the United States in 1848 at the end of the Mexican-American War. A year later the California gold rush started. Gold seekers went north and south of Colorado to get to California, since Colorado's mountains were too high and difficult to cross. Some of these forty-niners, as they were called, did stop for a little while, however, to look for gold along the foothills of Colorado's Rocky Mountains.

A party of Cherokee Indians from what is now Oklahoma passed by the future site of Denver in June 1850. One of them wrote in his diary on June 22, "gold found." It was discovered in Ralston Creek on the future site of Arvada. There was not enough gold to tempt them to stay, and they went on to California. The Cherokee gold seekers did not have much luck there, and they eventually returned home. But they could not forget about the gold they had found along the Rockies on their trip. In the winter of 1857–1858, some of them decided to go back and search again.

The Cherokee did not know that another group of men from the town of Lawrence, Kansas, had the same idea. They were interested in the Rocky Mountains because of a story they had heard from a Delaware Indian, Fall Leaf. He had gone west with the army as a scout and had brought back some gold. His neighbors were very interested in it and made plans to find the place where it had been found.

That spring both groups started west. William Green Russell, who had mined in Georgia and California, led the Oklahoma group that included the Cherokee. This group was the first to arrive. After weeks of disappointment, they finally found several hundred dollars' worth of gold at the place that is now the Denver suburb of Englewood. The Lawrence party heard about the Russell party's success and hurried to join it. So did a trader named John Cantrell, who was on his way back east. Cantrell took a small amount of gold with him and became the Paul Revere of the Colorado gold rush. He told everyone he met about the discovery.

Because of Cantrell's story about the gold, a newspaper in Kansas City used this headline on August 26, 1858: "THE NEW ELDORADO!!! GOLD IN KANSAS TERRITORY." (Much of eastern Colorado was then part of Kansas.) More reports of gold came back, and Americans grew excited. Many wanted to go to the Pikes Peak country, as it was called then. They were sure that fortune awaited them, if only they could get there first.

Pikes Peak Gold Rush

The winter of 1858–1859 was exciting. Many, many people planned to go west as soon as they could. They were afraid that if they waited too long all the gold would be gone. They made plans and talked endlessly of gold. Each family purchased a wagon and horses, mules, or oxen to pull it, plus equipment, food, and a guidebook to tell them how to get there. Then they dreamed about how much gold they would find. They could hardly wait!

Spring finally came. It was like the firing of a gun to start a race — all at once, it seemed, 100,000 fifty-niners rushed west. Most of them rode in wagons or on horseback. A few walked, and some pushed handcarts all the way. One group purchased tickets to ride a "wind wagon." Its owner promised that his wagon with a sail would get them there faster and more comfortably than anything else could. Unfortunately for him and his passengers, the wagon "sank" by running into a gully. Their dreams ended right there on the prairie.

Meanwhile, out in the Pikes Peak country, not much gold was being mined. A few hardy souls arrived before the winter snows closed the overland trails. They organized towns that became Boulder and Denver and waited for the snow in the mountains to melt so they could go into the hills to prospect. A few brave men did go into the mountains west of Denver and Boulder that winter.

In January 1859, George Jackson discovered gold near the future town of Idaho Springs. The bitter cold, snow, and frozen ground drove him out. That same month a group of men found gold above Boulder at a place they called Gold Hill. In May, John Gregory, another experienced miner, made the biggest discovery yet, between soon-to-be Central City and Black Hawk.

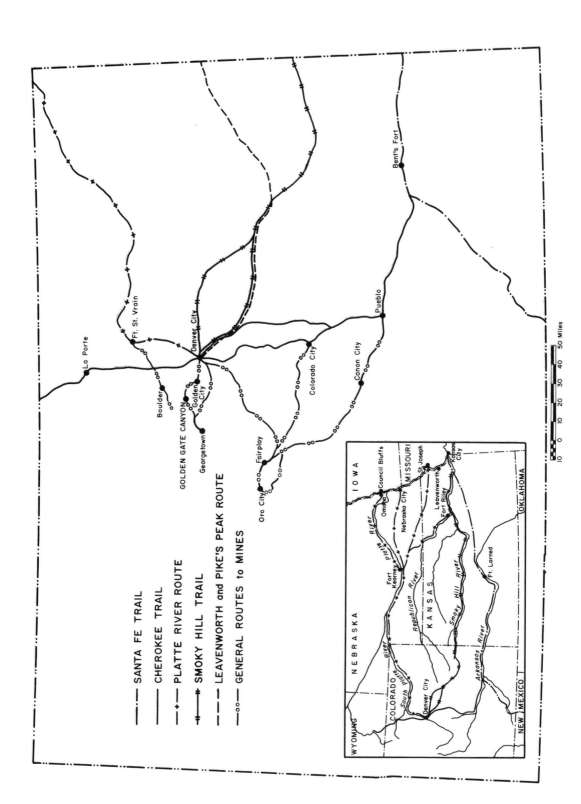

SANTA FE TRAIL
CHEROKEE TRAIL
PLATTE RIVER ROUTE
SMOKY HILL TRAIL
LEAVENWORTH and PIKE'S PEAK ROUTE
GENERAL ROUTES to MINES

Gold Rush Routes

All of these men tried to keep their finds a secret. Each one wanted to be the first person to mine the claim as soon as mountain snows melted.

Meanwhile, the fifty-niners began arriving in Denver. They soon learned that very little gold had been found there. Denver was only a collection of log cabins and stores, and living there was very expensive. Few people wanted to venture into the mountains until the weather was better. Disappointed by what they found, many people turned around and went home. Others on their way west heard of the troubles and turned around before they even reached Colorado. Newspapers, which had been praising the region only a few months before, now called it a failure — a "humbug."

Those who had discovered gold in the mountains could not keep it a secret. By May the news was out, and now people rushed into the mountains with their picks and pans. About 35,000 of the nearly 100,000 fifty-niners who started west stayed; the rest gave up and left.

Gold Mining

When the fifty-niners reached gold diggings, these would-be miners found the work hard, tiring, and long. Most of them had never mined before in their lives. They had to learn by watching the experienced miners or by trial and error. It looked easy enough: All you needed was a pick, a shovel, a pan, and a strong back. When you found a spot that looked good, you staked your claim to let everyone else know that it was yours.

Then the diggings could be worked. A miner placed gravel and sand in a pan with water. Swirling water around the pan and gently washing the gravel caused the lighter materials to float away. The gold, which is a very heavy mineral, would stay in the pan. If you were lucky, there would be some gold left at the bottom. The process seemed simple, but it took a lot of skill and hard work. The experienced miners soon built rockers and sluice boxes, which let them wash much more gold-bearing gravel in less time. This process was called placer mining, or the mining of free gold, which is gold found on the surface or in streambeds.

Miners used picks, shovels, and sluices to take gold from the earth. (U.S. Geological Survey.)

Hard-rock mining involves digging deeply into the earth and mining gold ore from a vein. Placer mining was much more common in Colorado during 1859.

The 1859 gold rush had happened so quickly that there was no time to organize local governments or courts. This did not bother the miners. They quickly formed their own mining districts, miners' laws, and miners' courts to file, record, and protect their claims. If someone "jumped" your claim (tried to take it from you and say it was his), you could take your case to a jury of your neighbors to decide who was right.

If enough gold was found in an area, mining districts and little mining camps sprang up almost overnight. Georgetown, Fairplay, Breckenridge, Oro City, and Nevadaville were just a few of these camps. Miners did not have the time to raise crops or make their own clothes. They wanted only to mine and make money. They figured they could buy whatever else they needed or wanted. As a result, storekeepers, blacksmiths, saloonkeepers, bootmakers, and carpenters came to the mining camps. Soon

they were joined by lawyers, doctors, and ministers. When families with children arrived, schoolteachers were needed. In this way, communities grew out of rough mining camps.

Denver became the largest town. Although little gold was ever found there, it was the destination of most newcomers. Once stagecoaches established regular service, in 1859, they stopped at Denver. Wagonloads of food, equipment, and other supplies also arrived in Denver. From there, the goods were shipped to the mountain districts. Denver became the main storage and supply town for the mountain mines. The Mile High City also hoped to become the capital of the new territory created by this rush of people.

The Wells Fargo stage stop in downtown Denver at Fifteenth and Market Streets was Colorado's first transportation hub. (Colorado Historical Society.)

A New Territory

Almost immediately, the fifty-niners sought a legal basis for their settlement to protect their claims. During the 1860s, eastern

Colorado was divided between New Mexico, Kansas, and Nebraska territories. Western Colorado was part of Utah territory. The territorial governments were too far away to govern the newly settled area very well. The Colorado pioneers, however, had created mining districts, and now they thought they could create their own territory. They called it Jefferson Territory and asked the United States Congress to approve their action. Congress refused because national lawmakers wanted to create the territory and establish the government under federal rules.

Congress was having a difficult time in 1860–1861 because of the problem of slavery. Northerners and Southerners were angry and divided over this question. The South wanted slave owning to be allowed; the North thought it should be abolished and the slaves freed. This was one of the disputes that led to the Civil War. What did the slavery issue have to do with the Pikes Peak mines? Before the outbreak of war, the creation of new territories in the West became tied to slavery. Lawmakers argued over the question: Should the new territory allow or not allow slavery? The South wanted new territories to allow slave owning. Northerners wanted new territories to be "free," which meant free of slavery. After some southern states left the United States to form their own government, the remaining northern congressmen organized a new territory and called it Colorado. Colorado Territory's birthdate was February 28, 1861.

President Abraham Lincoln selected the first governor for Colorado Territory. He chose a man who had long been interested in the West, William Gilpin, who arrived in Denver in May 1861.

Because Colorado was a U.S. territory, its governor, judges, and other officers were appointed by the president. The local voters could elect their own legislators and a territorial delegate to represent Colorado in Washington. When Colorado had enough settlers, it could apply for statehood. If accepted, it would become an equal partner in the union with the other states. This would take time, but many Coloradans wanted statehood right from the start.

By the summer of 1861, Colorado had a territorial government and had developed an economy based on mining. It had come a long way since those exciting days of 1859. The future would hold troubles as well as blessings, however.

Hard-Rock Mining

The placer mines were neither as rich nor as large as everyone had thought. The amounts of gold being found soon decreased, but the miners did not give up. Instead they began to dig into the mountains to look for more gold, using a different form of mining called hard-rock, deep, or quartz mining.

The gold they were looking for was locked in a vein. A vein is a deposit of mineral in another type of rock, usually granite. They had to pick and blast the gold out of this vein; it was rough, dangerous work. Next, the ore had to be taken to the surface and then crushed to separate the gold from other minerals. Hard-rock mining involves greater skills, more equipment, and much greater costs than placer mining. Most of Colorado's mining has been of the hard-rock kind.

As the miners began digging into the mountains, they had problems. Water flooded some of the mines, and pumps had to be installed to get rid of it. The underground workings needed to be timbered, using logs and wood beams, to keep the earth from falling onto the miners. To get the ore to the surface, eventually a hoist, or cage, was devised. It worked much like an elevator does. For hard-rock mining, skilled workers were needed. The fifty-niner miners usually did not have the experience or the money to do this type of mining.

The biggest problem was finding a way to separate the gold from the rock when it got to the surface. It was easy enough to crush the ore in a stamp mill, where heavy lead weights pounded the ore into small pieces. The gold was not being separated and saved, however. Sometimes more than half of it was lost with the waste rock and other materials that went out on the tailings pile. The miners and millmen tried many methods, but they could not solve the problem. By the mid-1860s, Colorado mining was in serious trouble. People began to leave Colorado.

Georgetown in 1867 already had a smelter (the smoky stack at left), one of the factors of a successful mining town. (Photo by William G. Chamberlain. Colorado Historical Society.)

At this point a young chemistry professor, Nathaniel Hill, arrived on the scene. He had traveled to Colorado in 1864 to check on some mining property. Fascinated by the milling problems, he became determined to solve them. Hill knew that a fortune awaited the person who could find the answer to separating out the gold. For three years he studied and experimented, even traveling to England to see how smelters there worked. A smelter is a factory that crushes, heats, and dissolves ore. Finally Hill developed a process, and in 1868 he opened a smelter in Black Hawk, near Central City. His solution worked, and Colorado mining made a comeback. Hill's smelter became the best known in the territory.

In 1870 the railroad came to Denver, allowing both cheaper and faster transportation. Now, instead of weeks or even months, people and goods could get to Denver in days. The railroad helped mining tremendously. Within ten years railroads had reached Central City, Georgetown, and Boulder, and plans were being made to lay tracks elsewhere.

Silver

One other factor helped put Colorado mining on the road to recovery. Silver was discovered, and Colorado then had two rich minerals to mine. Silver had been found near Georgetown in 1864 and across the mountains in Summit County in 1865. Unfortunately, silver proved to be even harder to separate than gold. Again, the miners had to wait for a smelting process. Lorenzo Bowman, an African American from Missouri, came up with a method that helped somewhat, but it did not provide the final answer. Thanks to Hill and others, however, silver smelting developed rapidly. By the 1870s Colorado smelters could handle many of the silver-bearing ores.

The successful silver-smelting process came just in time. Just as the 1860s had been the decade of gold, silver was queen of the 1870s and for twenty years afterward. In the 1870s silver was found all the way from Boulder County in the north to Dolores County in the southwest. Before these ten years were over, it seemed as though silver was being found under nearly every rock or on every mountain. Colorado, by the end of the 1870s, became the United States' greatest mining state. The dreams of 1859 had come true, not with gold, but with silver. As with gold, first came the discoveries, excitement, and rushes. The organization of mining districts followed, and then the start of mining camps and towns. One mining rush quickly followed another.

Caribou, in Boulder County, was the first of the silver booms. Silver was found there in 1869, and the rush came in 1870. The camp went through ups and downs for a decade before the rich silver played out. Caribou's days of glory ended, and it soon became a ghost town. This was the fate of most Colorado mining communities.

One exception was Georgetown. It came to be Colorado's first "silver queen," the district with the richest mines and the greatest population. Because it had richer mines than Caribou,

Georgetown attracted more publicity, investments, and eventually a railroad. Silver and gold were mined there for many years, and Georgetown became one of the state's major mining towns. It had churches, schools, railroad connections, a large business district, and smelters. Unlike many now-dead silver towns, Georgetown has survived.

Leadville

Nothing in Colorado mining was more thrilling than the Leadville silver discoveries of 1877–1878. Both Georgetown and Central City seemed dull in comparison. Not since 1858–1859 had mining fever run so high Colorado.

Mary Hallock Foote, a writer and artist, visited Leadville in 1879 at the height of the rush. She wrote a friend, "All Roads Lead to Leadville. Everybody was going there! Our fellow citizens as we saw them from the road were more picturesque than pleasing. I was absorbed by this curious exhibition of humanity all along the 70 mile long journey."

Leadville fascinated not only Mary Foote, but Americans throughout the country as well. Newspaper reporters flocked to Leadville to write about "the Magic City."

Leadville had not always attracted so much attention. Prospectors had come to the area in 1860 and found some rich placer diggings at what they called California Gulch. Within a few years these gold diggings were mined out, and the people drifted away. In the following years, the few who stayed continued to mine, but nobody thought much of the region. Why should anyone go there when richer districts beckoned? In the end, those who stayed were rewarded. In 1877, rich silver deposits were found, and Leadville was born. Almost overnight, Leadville and Colorado became familiar names in America and abroad. By 1880 the census takers counted nearly 15,000 people there, although some claimed the number went as high as 20,000. Leadville ranked second only to Denver in population.

Leadville's mines astonished the mining world. In 1879 over $9 million worth of silver was mined; the next year the total topped $11 million. When the figures for lead and gold were added to these, it was easy to see that Leadville was a mineral treasure box. Colorado had never seen anything like it before.

Leadville produced legends. None is better known today than that of Horace Tabor. Tabor had been a fifty-niner miner, without much success. He had mined at Idaho Springs and then, in 1860, had come to California Gulch, where he opened a store, while also mining. With the help of his hardworking wife, Augusta, Tabor managed to make a decent living. The Tabors moved across the mountains to Buckskin Joe and then back to Oro City at the head of California Gulch. The mining riches Tabor sought still eluded him. He continually grubstaked prospectors; that is, he gave them food and supplies from his store in return for a share of any mines they found. It appeared that Tabor was going to spend his life on the fringe of Colorado mining without ever becoming rich or famous.

Everything changed in 1877, when he moved to Leadville. Although he was the second merchant in the community, Tabor hoped that his opportunity for fortune had come at last. Tabor grubstaked two prospectors, who found the Little Pittsburg Mine, a silver bonanza. Other discoveries soon followed, and very quickly Augusta and Horace became millionaires.

Horace Tabor came to symbolize the story of Colorado mining. After twenty years of hard work, he had succeeded. To other hopeful miners, he was living proof that a miner's dreams could come true.

The Silver State

Prospectors found silver in the Gunnison country, in the San Juans, at Silver Cliff in the Wet Mountain Valley, and in other places. Many communities followed Caribou's path, booming and then quickly becoming ghost towns; a few lasted and became permanent.

The only town and district that rivaled Leadville for any period of time was Aspen. Today, Aspen is world famous for its skiing, but silver gave the town its start in 1880. Aspen soon had railroads and smelters and, by the 1890s, it had almost passed Leadville as Colorado's major silver mining district. By then

Augusta Tabor arrived in Colorado in 1859 with her husband, Horace. They lived in Denver, Colorado City, and Buckskin Joe before they struck a silver bonanza at Leadville. Augusta ran their store, served as postmistress, helped carry gold to Denver, cooked for miners, and nursed them when they were sick. (Colorado Historical Society.)

Colorado was mining over $20 million worth of silver per year and had begun to call itself the Silver State.

A very dark cloud was looming on the horizon, however: The price of silver was falling. Several factors caused this to happen. Many countries had stopped making silver coins. Only a few industrial uses for silver had been developed, so there were not many people who wanted to buy it. So much silver was being mined that it flooded the market. That made the price fall from $1.32 an ounce in 1870 to $.87 in 1892. Miners worried about this, but they hoped the problem would somehow be solved and the price would go up again.

In 1893, Colorado, along with the entire United States, suddenly plunged into a severe economic depression, or a sharp downturn in economic activity. Banks failed, businesses closed, and people lost their jobs. The mining industry was hurt by these events, especially when the price of silver dropped another 20 cents per ounce. Mining silver was no longer profitable, so the mines closed, miners were thrown out of work, and towns shrank or died. All of Colorado suffered, because silver had become the backbone of the state's economy.

Colorado had never seen anything like this before. It seemed to Coloradans that they suffered more than anyone else in the country. Colorado's people wondered if the state would ever regain the prosperity it had known for the past twenty years. Fortunately, it was saved again by its mineral treasures.

Cripple Creek

Back in 1859 Pikes Peak was the best-known geographic point in the central Rockies. Although it gave its name to the gold rush, no gold had been found there. In the 1890s, however, the story changed. Southwest of Pikes Peak, a place called Cripple Creek became Colorado's greatest gold district.

A wandering cowboy named Bob Womack found gold ore on Cripple Creek in the 1880s, but had a terrible time convincing others. Finally he did, and in the early 1890s the rush started. It came just in time to take some of the sting out of the collapse of silver and the 1890s depression. Many little camps were established, but the district was dominated by two communities, Cripple Creek and Victor.

Cripple Creek became a city quickly, as these two photos from the early 1890s show. Most mining towns did not graduate from the tent-and-wood stage to become solid cities of brick and stone. (Colorado College, top, and Colorado Springs Pioneer Museum, bottom.)

The Cripple Creek district produced many millionaires. The most famous was Winfield Scott Stratton. Like Tabor, Stratton had spent a long time in Colorado searching for a rich mine without great success. He had gone to Leadville and other mining districts, and he had studied mining techniques, but to no avail. When he went to Cripple Creek, however, Stratton finally was rewarded for his efforts. His Independence Mine, which he discovered on July 4, 1891, made him a millionaire many times over. He later sold it for $10 million, and there was no income tax in those days.

Cripple Creek was the last of the great nineteenth-century Colorado mining rushes. By this time, mining had become a big business. The mines were owned by large companies or stockholders who often lived far away. The chances for making big money at Cripple Creek were high, but so were the costs of mining.

Most of the men at Cripple Creek never owned a mine. They were miners who simply worked for someone else for a day's pay. Because of the low pay and the lack of opportunity for better jobs, the miners joined labor unions. They hoped that by banding together in their demands for better pay and conditions, they would have more power. In 1894, union members went on strike (refused to work) to protest their low wages and long working hours. The miners won this struggle and gained an eight-hour day and $3-per-day wages.

Colorado mining had come a long way since 1859 — from a lonely miner with his pick and pan to the large company and the hired miner. Colorado had been fortunate that it had both gold and silver and other metals and fuels. Many western mining states had not been so lucky, and their mining days were over.

In Colorado, mining was the single most important factor in the economy from the 1860s to 1900. It created jobs, encouraged railroad building, and attracted wealthy investors. Farms, ranches, businesses, and manufacturing all benefited. Camps and towns were established and grew because of mining. Most of Colorado's political leaders had mining backgrounds. In the years that followed the Pikes Peak rush, mining

Deep, dark, gassy, and wet mines were dangerous. Yet they were the most common
workplace for Coloradans between the 1860s and the 1910s.
(Duane A. Smith Collection.)

had done what people had expected it to do back in 1859.
Without it, Colorado's growth and development would have
been much slower and much different. Miners became a legend
in their own day — and our own.

QUESTIONS

1.   Where did the Spanish look for gold and silver in Colo-
     rado? What caused them to lose interest in Colorado?
2.   Who were John Gregory, Horace Tabor, and Bob Womack?
3.   How did Nathaniel Hill help Colorado mining?

4. What did it mean to "stake a claim"? What happened if someone "jumped" your claim?

5. How did Leadville and Cripple Creek change Colorado history?

6. What is the difference between placer and hard-rock mining?

7. Augusta Tabor came west in 1859. What was her life like?

ACTIVITIES

1. Imagine you were part of the Pikes Peak gold rush in 1859. Explain your trip and mining experiences.

2. Look at some of the mining histories and make a model of sluice box, mining tools, or a hard rock mine.

3. On a Colorado map, locate the major mining towns.

4. Are there any mining districts or ghost towns in your county? If so, study their history, talk to old-timers who might have lived there, and visit the site to get a feel for the mining days.

5. The whole class can participate in building a model mining town complete with stores, homes, mines, and maybe a railroad.

Books You and Your Teacher Might Enjoy

Edward Blair. *Leadville: Colorado's Magic City.* Boulder: Pruett Publishing, 1980. This two-mile-high town became Colorado's greatest silver city.

Anne Ellis. *Life of an Ordinary Woman.* Lincoln: University of Nebraska Press, 1980. A miner's wife recalls the heartaches of her Colorado.

Mabel B. Lee. *Cripple Creek Days.* Lincoln: University of Nebraska Press, 1984. A charming account of growing up in Cripple Creek.

John H. Monnett & Michael McCarthy. *Colorado Profiles.* Evergreen, CO: Cordillera, 1987. Interesting stories of a gallery of Coloradans.

Muriel S. Wolle. *Stampede to Timberline.* Athens: Ohio University, 1991 (reprint). This book was the first (and is still the best) guide to Colorado's mining ghost towns.

Did You Know?

In 1899 miners were paid the following wages:

Hard-rock miners: $3 for nine hours' work

Laborers on the surface: $2–$2.50 for ten hours' work

Coal miners: 60 cents per ton mined

Mule drivers: $2.50–$3 per day

CHAPTER EIGHT
Townspeople

The mining frontier was an urban frontier; that is, camps and towns were built at the same time the miners came. This was different from the cattle and farming frontiers, where towns usually came quite some time after the first settlers. The miners did not have time to raise crops, manufacture their equipment, or haul in their supplies. But they did have gold and silver to pay others to do those things for them. Therefore, people came and settled in communities along the foothills and in the mining districts.

Denver

Denver quickly stood out as the most important of Colorado's new communities. Although it was not near the mines, it had a good location close to two of the gateways to the mountains, Clear Creek Canyon and the South Platte River. It also had the advantage of being well known to the miners, since it was the point to which fifty-niners first traveled.

Denver grew rapidly and annexed the neighboring towns of Auraria and Highlands. Of Denver's early rivals, Golden proved hardest to overcome. Golden was closer to the mountains and Clear Creek Canyon. Both towns wanted to be the capital of the territory. They took turns serving as capital until Denver officially became the state capital in 1881.

Even with its advantages, Denver had problems during its early years. In April 1863 fire burned out the center of the city, destroying seventy buildings. Fire was always greatly feared in communities where most buildings were made of wood. Denver citizens rebuilt with brick and recovered just in time for a second disaster, on May 20, 1864. This time, Cherry Creek flooded, washing away the *Rocky Mountain News* office and other buildings. Eleven people were killed. When the town had started at

Stores such as Cornforth's, which opened at Fifteenth and Blake Streets in lower downtown in 1865, helped make Denver the state's main supply town. (Colorado Historical Society.)

the junction of Cherry Creek and the South Platte River, Indians had warned about flash floods, but the settlers ignored the warnings.

Nothing could stop Denver's town builders. The fire and flood damage was quickly repaired, and life went on as before. Then came more bad news: Mining was on the decline. Denver's future depended on mining, and the decline was hurting the town's businesses. The troubles with Indians during the years 1863–1865 slowed growth even more. By far the worst news, however, was that the new transcontinental railroad connecting the East and West Coasts would bypass Denver. Plans showed that it would go north through Julesburg and on to Cheyenne, Wyoming, instead of coming to Denver. The railroad was the cheapest, fastest, and most comfortable means of transportation. A town without a railroad had very little chance of growing into a city.

Denver's leaders tried without success to change the plans of the Union Pacific Railroad. They decided the only thing to do was to build their own railroad, if they wanted to keep their baby town from becoming a ghost town. Some of Golden's business-men decided to do the same thing, and the race was on.

It took courage for either town to start such a project. Railroad building was costly, and money was scarce in Colorado. But Denver's business leaders were determined to have a railroad. They built the Denver Pacific to connect Denver with the Union Pacific line at Cheyenne in 1870. Golden had lost again and would never again seriously challenge Denver, Colorado's Queen City.

Denver's ambitious leaders had looked into the future and planned well, overcoming many setbacks in the process. Several other railroads soon reached the town, and it became a major business and trading center. Before long, Denver had the best theaters, schools, and hospitals in Colorado and the richest banks. Industry also began on a small scale. In 1878 Nathaniel Hill moved his smelter from Black Hawk and made the capital city a smelting center. He came to Denver because of its transportation advantages, the lower cost of living, and the nearby coal fields. Coal supplied power for running the smelters.

Hill was not the only one who moved to the city. Others were attracted for similar reasons. Denver grew from 4,749 in 1870 to 106,713 in 1890. Besides being Colorado's largest city, it was larger than any other western city except San Francisco.

Denver's success caused jealousy in other communities, but none of them could match the "Queen City." For a short time Central City thought it was the best, but when gold mining declined, so did Central City. Leadville also challenged Denver briefly, at the same time that much of its silver wealth was going to help build Denver. For example, Horace Tabor built a lavish grand opera house in Denver that cost $850,000. There was none finer between Kansas City and San Francisco. Other communities, including Cripple Creek, tried, but none could rival Denver. By the 1890s, the Queen City was the biggest and the best, not only in Colorado, but in the Rocky Mountain West.

Other Communities

The mountain mining communities and the settlements along the foothills were the start of Colorado's urbanization — the growth of its cities and towns. They not only provided the core of permanent settlement, they also helped develop the economy and plans for the future. Every town hoped to become the county seat, the center of the county's government. Being chosen for this honor meant government offices and jobs would come to the town. Rivalry between towns often led to changes in county seats over time.

These towns were in some ways similar to the ones you know today, but in other ways they were quite different. In appearance they were certainly different. A visitor from England, Isabella Bird, found most Colorado towns ugly during her visit in 1873. She described Longmont as "a wide straggling street, in which glaring frame houses and a few shops stand opposite to each other. A two-story house, one of the whitest and most glaring, and without a veranda like all the others, is the 'St. Vrain Hotel,' called after the St. Vrain River, out of which the ditch is taken which enables Longmont to exist."

Isabella Bird did not care for Boulder, either: "Boulder is a hideous collection of frame houses on a burning plain, but it aspires to be a 'city' in virtue of being a 'distributing point' for the settlements up the Boulder Canyon, and of the discovery of a coal seam."

Writer Sara Jane Lippincott visited Black Hawk in September 1871 and described what she saw:

> Narrow and dingy as is this mining town, its people are making a brave effort to give it a look of comfort, in pleasant private dwellings, neat churches and

Isabella Bird, an Englishwoman, wrote one of the best books on early Colorado, A Lady's Life in the Rocky Mountains, *published in 1879 and still in print. (Denver Public Library.)*

fine school-buildings, perched up against the mountain-side, where it would seem no building larger than a miner's hut could find lodgement. Scarcely a tree or shrub is to be seen, or even a flower, except it be in some parlor window.

When you lived in the mountains, growing a garden or a lawn successfully was not easy. Many people wondered why they should go to the trouble when they would soon be moving on to some new mining district anyway. For the same reason, few people worried about painting their homes.

You might wonder why people moved frequently. Irving Howbert was a teenager when he lived in Hamilton (in South Park) in the summer of 1860. He commented that "two or three times that summer, there was what was known as a 'stampede' from Hamilton to reported new discoveries." What started it?

"These stampedes usually originated from a prospector coming to town and telling a friend, as a great secret, of rich placers he had discovered." As soon as they heard about a new discovery, people hurried off expecting to find a fortune.

Living in town meant that you had more of the "modern" conveniences and other advantages than your friends out in the rural areas. Towns offered a greater variety of stores. In May 1878, for instance, Leadville had two each of drugstores, banks, restaurants, dry goods stores, and bakeries. There were three meat markets, three livery stables, and three barber shops, plus four general stores. In the spring of 1879 the city boasted twenty meat markets, thirty-one restaurants, fifty-one groceries, seventeen barber shops, and four banks. Leadville was booming then because of its silver, but other towns also had the same kinds of businesses in smaller numbers.

At first the cost of living was sky-high. Horace Greeley visited Denver in 1859 and was shocked at the high prices. He wrote in his newspaper column:

Cities depended on farmers for food, like these farmers bringing their crops to the railroad in Berthoud. (University of Wyoming, American Heritage Center.)

To the bread, bacon, and beans, which formed the staple of every meal a short time ago, there have been several recent additions; milk, which was last week twenty-five cents per quart, is now down to ten, and I hear a rumor that eggs, owing to a recent increase in the number of hens, within five hundred miles, from four or five to twelve or fifteen, are about to fall from a dollar a dozen to fifty cents per dozen.

As soon as transportation improved, prices started going down.

Transportation

Transportation was important to the growth of any Colorado community. All goods had to be hauled by wagons in the beginning. Large wagons transported supplies to Denver, where the goods were put into smaller wagons to be hauled into the mountains. Sometimes mules and burros carried supplies to the more isolated districts. All these transportation costs added to the price of everything else. A town located on a main transportation route held an advantage over its rivals.

The fastest way to reach Colorado before the railroad came was by stagecoach. The stage crossed the plains in ten to twelve days, but the cost was high: $100 to $125 one way in 1859–1860. And they weren't much fun to ride. Mark Twain recalled his trip in 1861:

Our coach was a great swinging swaying stage, of the most sumptuous description — an imposing cradle on wheels. It was drawn by six handsome horses. . . . We changed horses every ten miles, all day long, and fairly flew over the hard, level road. We jumped out and stretched our legs every time the coach stopped. . . . As the sun went down and the evening chill came on, we made preparation for bed. We stirred up the hard leather letter-sacks, and the knotty canvas bags of printed matter. . . . We stirred them up and redisposed them in such a way as to make our bed as level as possible.

The stage rolled on through dust, rain, cold, and heat. The passengers ate and washed at stations along the way, while the horses were changed and a new driver took the reins.

It is easy to understand why the railroad was preferred over the slow, tiring trip by wagon or stagecoach. Even so, until the 1870s, Colorado depended on these wagons and stages to bring supplies and people to the territory. That was one reason the early settlers worried so much about the Indians. When trouble with Indians broke out and the overland trails were closed, Colorado could face food shortages, and travel back and forth to the states might be stopped.

The pioneers wanted news about what was happening in the rest of the United States, especially in their former homes. From the time of their first appearance in 1859, stagecoaches carried the mail. Faster service was supplied in 1860 by the Pony Express. Pony Express riders galloped at breakneck speed, changing horses every few hours. They could deliver mail from Missouri to California in ten days. The overland telegraph replaced the Pony Express in 1861 but did not reach Denver for two more years. Coloradans continued to rely on mail by stagecoach until 1863, when the clacking of the telegraph keys tied Colorado to the East Coast within minutes. Coloradans were no longer isolated.

Newspapers

Every town needed a newspaper to print local news and promote local events and businesses. To be without one was almost as bad as being bypassed by the railroad. Denver thrived partly because it had Colorado's first newspaper after William Byers started the *Rocky Mountain News* in April 1859. Byers sold his paper all over Colorado.

The newspaper editors of these years were often interesting characters, and sometimes they had to fight to protect freedom of the press. One remarkable editor was David Day of Ouray. He loved to poke fun at rival newspapers and towns, and his wit and clever writing made his *Solid Muldoon* just about the liveliest paper in Colorado during the 1880s. Day

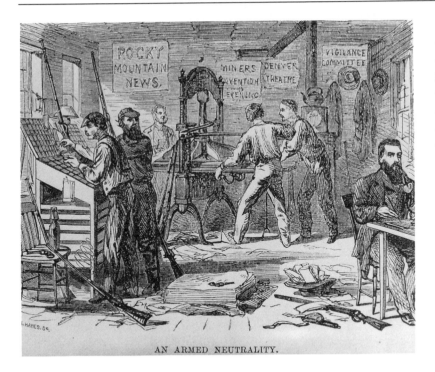

AN ARMED NEUTRALITY.

Editor William N. Byers, with a pipe poking out of his beard, began publishing the Rocky Mountain News *on April 23, 1859. (Denver Public Library.)*

This was the home of Colorado's first newspaper, the Rocky Mountain News. *The* News *promoted Denver as the Queen City of Colorado and the Rocky Mountain West. (Denver Public Library.)*

teased visiting politicians by lying down in the audience while they were speaking on stage. "I can lie down here," he told them, "as long as you lie up there!"

Caroline Romney edited the *Durango Record*. She pushed for reform in her community, defied outlaws, and encouraged women to come settle there to help make Durango a more civilized community. Caroline Romney proved to be a very good newspaper editor, and she helped her town get off to a fine start.

Women

Caroline Romney was right — Colorado needed more women. During the 1860s and 1870s many more men lived in Colorado than women. The few women who came found life full of hard work, trouble, and sorrows. Augusta Tabor remembered her first experience in Colorado in June 1859. While passing through Denver, her party stopped near future Golden. Her husband Horace and the other men then went on into the mountains to prospect, leaving Augusta behind. As she described her circumstances: "Leaving me and my sick child in the 7 x 9 tent, that my hands had made, the men took a supply of provisions on their backs, a few blankets, and bidding me be good to myself, left on the morning of the glorious Fourth. How sadly I felt, none but God, in whom I then firmly trusted, knew. Twelve miles from a human soul save my babe." Augusta lived through this experience and labored twenty years in Colorado before she and Horace made their fortune.

Most women and their families were not as fortunate as the Tabors. Anne Ellis's mother found neither fame nor fortune in Colorado, as Ellis wrote in her book, *The Life of an Ordinary Woman:*

> Mama never went to school a day in her life, and it was always a great sorrow to her that she could neither read nor write. . . . This is the summer before Frank is born (yes, I know I am having a baby in every chapter, but that is the way we had them!). Mama, keeping up her laundry work, still finds time to go after wild raspberries, four or five miles to the

nearest patch. Here she picks all day, coming home at night so tired. . . . In addition to the laundry, Mama sewed for the men.

Anne Ellis's mother worked hard all her life in a number of mining camps. Her family never escaped poverty.

Being a housewife and mother was a full-time job. Cooking took a lot of time, with only a wood or coal stove and no instant, prepared, or frozen foods. Clothes had to be made or mended, washed, and ironed. Homes needed to be cleaned and the shopping done. Larger families in those days meant that there were usually children to be tended and illnesses to be treated.

There were not many jobs or professions open to women. Caroline Romney, the newspaper editor, was an exception. So was former slave Aunt Clara Brown, who was hardworking and thrifty. She charged miners 5 cents a garment to wash their clothes, and she saved her money to help build Central City's St. James Methodist Church. She became a respected Central City citizen and businesswoman. Aunt Clara used some of her earnings to help other African Americans move to Colorado and the West.

Women dominated the teaching profession but also moved into other occupations. In those days, people did not think women should be in the business world. Politics was another area believed to be unsuitable for women's involvement. They were not even allowed to vote in Colorado elections until 1894. Even at that late date, Colorado was only the second state to give women the right to vote, and it would not be until 1920 that they could vote in a presidential election. Although women were respected and honored, they were not considered equal with men in either jobs or wages. Fortunately, they had access to education, and some women worked very hard to gain total equality for their sex.

Aunt Clara Brown, an African American pioneer, made money in the laundry business. She used it to start churches and to bring other blacks to Colorado. (Colorado Historical Society.)

Schools and Churches

Both young boys and girls went to school. Many only finished a few grades, and very few went beyond the eighth. Boys often went to work by the time they reached their mid-teens, and girls had by then reached an age when they were seriously thinking of getting married.

Edwina Fallis recalled vividly her first day at the Broadway School (now the site of the Colorado History Museum) in Denver in the 1880s: "Mama took me to school on the first day to tell the teacher who I was and to tell me what to do and what not to do. The do's were only two. 'Be good and mind the teacher.'" The Broadway School was a large building with a classroom for each grade. Many Colorado schools crowded everyone together in only one room, from youngsters aged six or seven to those of fifteen and sixteen. Elizabeth Amelia Lee, who was born in Caribou in 1876, went to a one-room school. The school year was sometimes three months, sometimes nine months, depending on whether a teacher could be found.

The teachers in these early schools stressed the three R's — reading, 'riting, and 'rithmetic. There were no "extras," just the basics. Elizabeth Lee thought she got a good education for the time. She fondly remembered her pioneer school days many years later.

The schoolhouse often became the center of community life. School programs, for example, brought people together. Schools also hosted town meetings and guest speakers, since they were the only places large enough to hold a crowd. They could also be converted into a theater, church, or dance hall when necessary. Citizens wanted schools to show that culture had arrived, even in the most isolated Colorado settlements.

Churches also showed that a community had become a solid one. Ministers came to Colorado almost on the heels of the original miners. The Reverend John Dyer's circuit in 1861 took him back and forth across the mountains from South Park to the Gunnison country. In his first four months of preaching he walked over 500 miles. During the winter, the energetic Dyer occasionally used skis (they were called snowshoes then) to reach some of his scattered Methodist congregations. He also carried U.S. mail to help support himself and his scattered missions.

In the early years of mining camps, when people were moving frequently, a camp might be abandoned before a church could be built. Presbyterian George Darley was a pioneer in the San Juan mining district in the mid-1870s. He explained why this kind of ministry required a special type of person. After traveling over steep mountain trails to reach a camp, he found that the only building large enough for a church service was the saloon!

Inside the saloon, clergymen tried to stop the drinking and gambling so they could hold religious services. It was not always an easy matter to stop the games. Winners were usually willing, but the losers were not. Soon, however, "roulette," "keno," "poker," and "faro" games gave way to the Gospel. A more con-

This horse-drawn school bus took children to St. Joseph's Catholic School in Longmont. (Denver Public Library.)

venient pulpit than a "faro-table" could not be found; nor a more respectful and intelligent audience.

Although the ministers were almost always men, women formed the real backbone of the local church. Here was an institution in which they could hold office, serve on committees, and play an active leadership role. They were very good at raising money by serving dinners and organizing fairs. The church was also one of the few acceptable social outlets for them. Often the congregation and minister also led the fight to reform the town's morals by closing the saloons and gambling "hells."

Leisure Time

Even though most men worked six days a week during the years before 1900, they still found time to relax. Most of the leisure activities involved masculine interests and tastes such as sports and drinking. Women and children had to create their own entertainment through the home, the school, or the church.

The saloons and gambling halls that the Reverend Darley mentioned were for men only. Any women seen in them were thought to be wicked. City ordinances prohibited youngsters from visiting such places. Young children also had to be home by the time the curfew bell rang in many communities, or the local policeman would take them to their parents' house.

Much of the entertainment for families took place in the home. Family members read to one another from books or newspapers, played games, or talked together. Picnics and fishing trips were popular in the summer, and in the winter a sled was great for coasting down a long hill. Church and school programs, plays, and musicals were family affairs. Only a few towns had opera houses, so traveling theater companies had to make do with a local hall or school.

Christmas, New Year's, and Fourth of July were the big holidays. The Christmas season featured special church and school activities, and Santa Claus always came to delight the youngsters. Santa was not a fat, jolly individual in those days; he was rather lean. Christmas trees gradually appeared in homes, but a community tree in the school or church was more common. For the

Bicycling has been popular with Coloradans since the 1880s, when these cyclists toured Golden on early bikes known as "bone shakers." (Colorado Historical Society.)

adults, fancy dinners and dances highlighted the season. The dances might go on until the early hours of the morning, with a dinner served at midnight.

The Fourth of July was a very patriotic celebration, with speeches, reading of the Declaration of Independence, and maybe a parade. Firecrackers banged all day, and a baseball game — America's favorite sport — might be the feature of the afternoon. A dinner and dance concluded the festivities.

July 4, 1876, was a noteworthy occasion: The people of Colorado had just overwhelmingly voted to become a state. Lake City's *Silver World,* July 8, hailed the outcome: "Three Cheers for the State of Colorado." Since the mid-1860s people had worked hard to gain this honor, and now it was at hand. On August 1, 1876, President Ulysses Grant issued the proclamation of statehood from the White House. Colorado became a state the year the United States celebrated its centennial, or its one hundredth anniversary. This is why it was nicknamed the Centennial State.

The Denver Fire Department entertained townsfolk with practice runs down Seventeenth Street. (Colorado Historical Society.)

Lawlessness

Law and order developed slowly in pioneer Colorado. The problem was particularly bad in a booming, wealthy community like Leadville. Newspaper editor Carlyle Davis wrote, "For a number of years nothing was so cheap in Leadville as human life. Nor was the murderous instinct confined to the lower and less cultivated element. . . . The [jail cell] bars were down and free rein was given to promiscuous [casual] bloodletting. The history of crime easily would fill a large volume."

Fictional accounts of frontier bandits, bank robberies, and shoot-outs have been the subjects of many books and movies.

The most common problem any lawman had to deal with, however, was controlling the dogs and drunks.

Before long, law and order came to every Colorado community and county. It was bad for a community's reputation to have drunken fights, murders, and hangings. Most people wanted a peaceful atmosphere, which would attract families and businesses and promote growth.

QUESTIONS

1. How did Denver become Colorado's most important city? What advantages did it have over other communities?
2. How did railroads and newspapers contribute to a community's growth?
3. What contributions did women make to the settlement of Colorado?
4. What activities did Coloradans do in their leisure time?
5. How did a nineteenth-century school differ from your school?

ACTIVITIES

1. Research and write a history of your community. Each student might select a different local person, place, or thing to study.
2. Interview old-timers in your town to find out what life was like fifty or more years ago.
3. Once Colorado had almost 100 different railroads. Only a few are left today. Draw a map of the former railroad that came closest to your school.
4. Take photographs of the oldest buildings in your county. Write a short history of each building. Find out how you can help preserve, or save, these old buildings.
5. Publish a newspaper with articles about your school's history.
6. Compare an evening or weekend at your house with the family entertainments described in this chapter. How are they different? How are they alike?

7. Research children's toys of the late nineteenth century (1870s–1900). Choose one toy and describe, with illustrations, how to play with it.

Books You and Your Teacher Might Enjoy

Isabella Bird. *A Lady's Life in the Rocky Mountains*. Norman: University of Oklahoma, 1960 (reprint). This book gives an exciting account of a climb up Longs Peak and other adventures in Colorado.

Sandra Dallas. *Colorado Homes*. Norman: University of Oklahoma Press, 1981. This volume contains many photos and great stories about Coloradans' homes.

Stephen J. Leonard and Thomas J. Noel. *Denver: Mining Camp to Metropolis*. Niwot: University Press of Colorado, 1990. Histories of Denver and its suburbs fill this book.

Muriel Wolle. *Timberline Tailings*. Chicago: Swallow, 1977. Firsthand accounts about living in mining communities.

Did You Know?

In 1899 working people earned the following wages:

Male teachers: $82.30 per month

Female teachers: $58.21 per month

Railroad engineers: $130 per month

Nurses: $3.25 per day

Newspaper reporters: $15 per week

Carpenters: $3 per day

CHAPTER NINE
Southern Coloradans

Often Denver dominated Colorado news. Some easterners were convinced that Denver *was* Colorado. Other parts of the state, however, were developing in their own ways and in ways that would benefit the state. In southern Colorado, towns and industries grew because of two important resources: coal and oil.

Colorado Springs

William Jackson Palmer was the organizer and president of the Denver & Rio Grande Railroad. He built the D&RG from Denver to the Rio Grande in southern Colorado. He believed Colorado's southern region had a great future. More than a railroad man, General Palmer was a town builder. He founded Colorado Springs in 1871 to greet his first train from Denver. Palmer hoped his new town at the base of Pikes Peak would become "the one spot in the West where nice people could gather together and live out their days in gentility and peace."

Tourists did come to hike in the mountains, climb Pikes Peak, visit Garden of the Gods, and drink the mineral waters at the nearby resort of Manitou Springs. The mild, dry climate also attracted sick people who came to try to regain their health. People with tuberculosis, a lung disease that was the country's main killer, flocked to Colorado Springs and other Colorado communities. Colorado's high, dry climate was a cure for various lung diseases. It brought more people to the state than all the gold and silver rushes combined.

Colorado Springs lived up to Palmer's dream. It had an opera house, a museum, parks, several grand resort hotels, fine homes, churches, and schools. It was the county seat; that is, the county government was located there. The famous author Helen Hunt Jackson moved to this city of culture and

William J. Palmer, shown here relaxing with his beloved dogs, founded the Denver & Rio Grande Railroad, as well as Colorado Springs and many other Colorado railroad towns. (Colorado College Library.)

recreation. General Palmer built his beautiful stone mansion nearby at Glen Eyrie. The Cripple Creek gold discoveries, on the other side of Pikes Peak, enriched Palmer's town. Mining millionaires such as Spencer Penrose and Winfield Scott Stratton invested their money in Colorado Springs.

Pueblo

Denver's other rival in southern Colorado was Pueblo. Pueblo became the second-largest city in the state and the leading town in southern Colorado. It emerged as the industrial center, the "Pittsburgh of the West." Like Pittsburgh, Pennsylvania, its mills turned out iron and steel products. Pueblo was older than Denver, but the early settlement had been burned by Ute Indians.

Colorado Springs, like many other Colorado communities from Alamosa to Westcliffe, was a creation of railroad developers. This early photo of Colorado Springs shows how the town grew up around the Denver & Rio Grande tracks. (Denver Public Library.)

Rebuilt in 1860, Pueblo grew slowly at first. During the 1870s it acquired two railroad connections — the Denver & Rio Grande and the Santa Fe. Along with the railroads came increased settlement and more industry. William Jackson Palmer and his fellow railroad investors played a major role in the community's economic development, just as they did in other towns that the Denver & Rio Grande reached.

Plentiful water, plenty of land, and good transportation helped Pueblo grow. In 1892 twenty-two passenger trains entered and left the city every day. The railroad could easily bring in raw materials such as coal and take the finished products out to many markets. The iron and steel mills produced railroad rails and barbed wire sold throughout the Rocky Mountain West.

The railroad men knew that once the mills got started, their railroads would make more money. Furthermore, the local land they owned would increase in value. Pueblo was a railroad center. Besides the Denver & Rio Grande, the Atchison, Topeka & Santa Fe, the Union Pacific, and several other railroads steamed into town.

Pueblo's railroads also helped make it a center for smelters. The huge factories crushed, roasted, and mixed ore with chemicals to extract silver, gold, lead, and other minerals. In 1891

Pueblo's mighty steel mills were originally fed by both railroads and horse-drawn wagons. (Pueblo Library District.)

Pueblo smelters refined over $12 million worth of minerals. Pleased with its smelters, Pueblo called itself the "Bullion City of the World" (bullion is gold or silver bricks). The industries helped Pueblo's population jump from 666 in 1870 to over 44,000 in 1910.

Even more important than the smelters was the Colorado Fuel & Iron Company (CF&I). General Palmer and his D&RG Railroad helped found the company to make railroad track. CF&I became the biggest steelmaker in the West. By 1900, Pueblo had become famous as Colorado's "Steel City."

Pueblo's citizens were proud of their city. By the 1890s it had excellent hotels, twenty-six churches, and twelve schools. To honor their community and the state's main industry, mining, Pueblo citizens built a "Mineral Palace" to showcase Colorado's mineral resources in July 1890. Such exhibits of Colorado resources helped attract tourists, and Pueblo did not want to be a step behind Denver or Colorado Springs.

James Owen grew up in Pueblo in the 1870s and 1880s, and he recalled another side of community life:

> After the steel works were built, on paydays we occasionally had a rough time. One of the best fights

Queen Silver and King Coal reigned in Pueblo's Mineral Palace, which showcased Colorado's mineral wealth. (Photo by Felix Bauer. Thomas J. Noel Collection.)

I ever saw was between the town marshal and a big husky steelworker. The steelworker was big and strong, but the marshal was gritty. . . . they fought rough and tumble for half an hour . . . [the marshal] finally knocked the steelworker out by bumping his head on the ground, and dragged him off to the calaboose [jail].

Coal Mining

One key to Pueblo's industrial might lay in the nearby coal mines. With Trinidad and Walsenburg at its heart, the southern coal field became the state's top producer. Its coal veins were bigger and richer than any others in the state — even the northern coal field in the Boulder-Louisville-Erie region. Coal mining played a very important role in nineteenth-century Colorado, even though it was overshadowed by the more glamorous gold and silver mining.

One of the desperate needs of early settlers was fuel. The obvious answer was wood, and the fifty-niners and their followers cut down trees recklessly. The price of wood quickly rose as the nearby forests disappeared. In the Denver-Boulder area, coal outcroppings were found as early as 1859. Settlers in need of fuel simply backed their wagons up to the outcroppings, chipped off enough coal for their use, and drove away. It was not long before some clever men claimed this coal for themselves and started to mine and sell it. Thus began Colorado's coal industry.

When coal had to be carried by wagon over long distances, the price became very high. To lower the price, the coal indus-

Coal cars at the Crested Butte depot shipped millions of tons of "black gold" from a place that boomed as a coal town a century before it became a ski resort. (Colorado Historical Society.)

try needed cheap shipping by railroads, which also relied on coal power for their locomotives. Not until the railroad came did "black gold" really pay off. In the 1870s and 1880s, prospectors found coal throughout much of the state. In addition to the well-known northern and southern coal fields along the Front Range, fields were located near Durango, Grand Junction, and Crested Butte on the Western Slope. The railroad companies eventually owned most of the coal mines. Due to their control of this source of fuel, they prospered. Colorado coal soon heated local homes and businesses and powered industry and smelters. It was shipped beyond the state to Kansas, Nebraska, Oklahoma, and Texas.

Coal mining differed from placer and hard-rock mining. First, there were no exciting "rushes" to open coal districts. They were developed by companies that quickly gained control of the coal mines. Unlike gold and silver, coal development had to wait for population and industrial growth and improved transportation. Furthermore, coal mining was much more dangerous. The mines often filled with gas and dust, which could explode or ignite and cause terrible accidents. A true hard-rock miner did not wish to work in a coal mine — it was dangerous, backbreaking work, and it paid poorly. Coal miners were paid by tons of coal they mined, rather than by the day.

What was work like for a coal miner? John McNeil, Colorado's state inspector of coal mines, told of a 1883 visit to a mine:

> When I looked into this close and dirty hole, I could hear the miner's pick striking the coal, but I failed to see the miner. When I arrived at the face of this place I found that the miner had his lamp hanging downward on his rib side to enable it to give more light. The air was almost stagnant to the feeling, and densely charged with coal dust, and in a few minutes I could feel the effect of carbonic acid gas, better known to the miners as black damp.

The mines were full of coal dust that eventually filled the miners' lungs causing an illness known as black lung. McNeil warned the governor, "The coal mines of the State, as a rule, have hitherto been worked in a rude, miserable and even reckless manner." Coal mining was hard, dirty, and dangerous, yet even teenagers were sent to work in these black holes.

Life in the Coal Camps

Families in coal camps lacked the freedom and individual effort seen in hard-rock communities. Coal mines and camps were company controlled almost from their birth. The company that owned the coal mines controlled the lives of the miners. It told them how much they were paid and where they could dig coal in the mine. The company also owned large pieces of land around the mines and ruled the area like a small kingdom.

Barron Beshoar, in his book *Out of the Depths*, described the coal camps and their people:

> They lived in wretched, isolated camps strung along the slopes of twisting canons [canyons] on either side of the coal mine with its unpainted shafthouse, breaker buildings and powerhouse. The single men lived in company-owned boarding houses and those with families in company-owned houses and shanties, barren little homes that reared their weather-beaten boards above piles of ashes and tins.

The company owned the store where miners bought supplies, the homes of the miners, and the boardinghouses. It furnished a company doctor and perhaps a hospital. The company often decided what churches would be allowed in the community and who would teach in the school. One miner said bitterly that "the company owned you from birth to grave." Some companies paid their miners in scrip, a form of paper money that could be spent only at the company store. Of course, everyone had to pay whatever prices the company charged. It was not a good situation for the miners. Labor unions tried to organize the workers and fight for better conditions, but they were often kept away by the mining companies.

Not all coal towns were company owned. Trinidad and Walsenburg were supply and railroad shipping points for miners,

Coal miners were almost enslaved by the coal companies and their company towns. At a coal camp near Trinidad, this couple was unable to leave the mine even for their wedding. (Photo by Glenn Aultman. Colorado Historical Society.)

ranchers, and farmers. They were county seats that prospered because of nearby mines. Trinidad, named for Trinidad Baca, daughter of pioneer settler Felipe Baca, had a population of 10,000 by 1910. Its factories manufactured bricks, mattresses, cheese, beer, macaroni, and brooms. Beautiful old homes and buildings remind today's visitor of those days, when Trinidad was one of Colorado's biggest and richest cities.

Who worked in the coal mines? Right from the start it was a different racial and cultural population from the gold and silver communities. Many of the miners came from an eastern European or Hispanic background; a few were Asians. Only a scattering came from northern Europe, where many of the hard-rock miners were born. Residents of southern Colorado coal communities such as Hastings, Berwind, Segundo, and Starkville came from many different backgrounds. These camps developed in isolation from the rest of Colorado. Most Coloradans had no idea of what was happening in them or how the coal companies controlled people's lives. Coloradans wanted the coal to keep coming, and it did. By 1889, 2.5 million tons were being mined each year, fueling an economic boom for Colorado. Coloradans did not notice that same year that twenty miners lost their lives in the state's coal mines. In January 1884, a gas and dust explosion at Crested Butte had killed fifty-four miners. Coloradans were shocked, but little or nothing was done to improve safety conditions in the coal mines. To make safety improvements would complicate mining and raise the price of coal. Conditions got worse instead of better. Colorado would pay a terrible price for its neglect.

A mine explosion in 1910 at Primero, about eighteen miles west of Trinidad, killed seventy-five miners. Superintendent William Kilpatrick was walking toward the mine when he saw a terrible sight:

> Great volumes of flame, smoke and dust issuing with terrific force from the mouth of the Main North [mine entrance], followed by reports of heavy concussions. The entrance to the haulage-way was caved and was nearly filled with debris for a distance of 75 feet. The first rescue party found Leonardo Virgen, the only one to survive the explosion, lying unconscious . . . closely surrounded by fourteen dead bodies.

These men were only part of the horrifying total of 319 killed in 1910 while mining Colorado coal.

The Trinidad area was the center of this slaughter. Besides the seventy-five dead at Primero, seventy-nine died at Delagua and fifty-six at Starkville. The men killed in 1910 in these coal disasters left behind 163 widows and 303 children. The worst single mine disaster occurred in April 1917. Northwest of Trinidad, a lonely marker at the site of Hastings honors the 121 miners killed in a coal mine explosion and fire.

Excuses and blaming could not cover up the obvious fact that coal mining was dangerous. These miners, many of them immigrants from such countries as Mexico, Japan, Poland, Russia, Italy, and Austria, paid a terrible price in sickness and death. Colorado's coal miners worked and died in the dark, dangerous, dusty silence of the mines. They had little political voice or power to stand up for their rights.

Oil

Southern Colorado offered another major natural resource — oil. Oil is a liquid found in deposits under the earth's surface. It is processed into gasoline and other fuels as well as other products such as petroleum. During all the gold excitement of the early 1860s, an oil well had been drilled successfully near Canon City in 1862. This was only three years after the first American oil field had opened in Pennsylvania. Early well operators used buckets to take oil out by hand. Unfortunately, poor transportation, few buyers, lack of money, and isolation almost killed the oil industry before it got started.

Meanwhile, the oil interested local people. Oil could be burned for light or as fuel. Some people also thought it would cure dandruff if you put it in your hair. Others drank oil to cure upset stomachs. Some rubbed it on their horses to cure saddle sores or on themselves for relief from aches and pains.

The Florence Oil Field, a short way down the Arkansas River from Canon City, proved more lasting and was the only producing Colorado oil field in the 1880s and 1890s. Kerosene and fuel oil were the principal products. One Florence well drilled in 1889 produced a million barrels of oil during its life.

The town of Florence became the center of a small boom, complete with oil refineries. It also had one of the first apple orchards in Colorado. Both Florence and Canon City grew

Canon City had a key location at the eastern edge of the mountains and at the mouth of the Royal Gorge of the Arkansas River. It emerged as a trade center for farmers, miners, and oil men. (Amon Carter Museum.)

quickly after the Denver & Rio Grande reached them in the early 1870s. Agriculture and oil gave these towns life, but what the oil business really needed was the invention of the automobile!

Proud citizens once had called Canon City the "gateway" to the faraway San Juan mines of southwestern Colorado. Once they had thought of Canon City as a rival of Denver. Nearby rich farmland and coal mines held out a much more promising future, however. Canon City hoped to become the state capital, but in 1868 received a consolation prize — the state prison.

QUESTIONS

1. Match the items that go together from the left and right columns.

coal mines	Colorado Springs
William J. Palmer	company control
"Mineral Palace"	Florence
oil	Pueblo

2. How did the Denver & Rio Grande change life in southern Colorado?
3. Why did people come to Colorado Springs? List three reasons.
4. How did Pueblo earn the nicknames "Bullion City" and "Steel City"?
5. Name three dangers faced by a coal miner.
6. What did people do with some of the oil when they first found it?

ACTIVITIES

1. Draw a map of southern Colorado and put on it the railroad lines, towns, and rivers.
2. Is there a mineral spring in your area? If possible, visit it and taste the water. Was it ever a health resort? Write an illustrated history of the resort.
3. Read some books about coal mining. Make a model of a coal mine and a coal mining town.
4. Imagine you live in a coal mining town. Write a short story about a day in your life.
5. If there were coal mines in your county, study their history. Your class might want to visit the site — but be very careful, as mine sites can be very dangerous.
6. Research the locations of oil and coal deposits in Colorado, in the western United States, or in the entire United States. As a class or team project, prepare a report about oil drilling or coal mining. Use diagrams, illustrations, and working models to explain how some of the processes worked.

Books You and Your Teacher Might Enjoy

Jane Valentine Barker and Sybil Downing. *Wagons and Rails*. Boulder: Pruett Publishing, 1980.

Barron B. Beshoar. *Hippocrates in a Red Vest*. Palo Alto, CA: American West, 1973. The story of a doctor in southern Colorado.

———— . *Out of the Depths*. Denver: Golden Bell Press, 1942. Do you want to be a coal miner? Read this first.

Joseph Gordon and Judith Pickle (eds). *Helen Hunt Jackson's Colorado*. Colorado Springs: Colorado College, 1989. This book describes some of the favorite places of a famous Colorado author.

Marshall Sprague. *Newport of the Rockies*. Athens, OH: Swallow, 1987 (reprint). Colorado Springs comes to life in this urban biography by that town's leading author.

Did You Know?

One-fourth of Colorado has coal deposits under it.

Young boys nine and ten years old worked in coal mines.

The town of Salida was started by the Denver & Rio Grande.

Women sometimes worked in coal mines.

In 1890 a cog railway was built to the summit of Pikes Peak.

CHAPTER TEN
Cowboys and Farmers

> I'm up in the morning before daylight,
> Before I sleep the moon shines bright

That is how a favorite cowboy song, "The Old Chisholm Trail," describes the workday of one of the West's most popular characters. The cowboy has ridden the range in Colorado since the 1850s, although today you will find him more often in a pickup truck than on a horse.

The cowboy and his horse, the ranch, the long cattle drives, and the cattle towns have become part of American history and folklore. Hardly a week goes by without an old movie or television program about the cowboy's West. Colorado was, and still is, cattle country.

Cattle were driven from Texas to the Pikes Peak country in 1859 because there was a good market for beef in the mining districts. Several of the major cattle trails, including the Dawson and Goodnight-Loving, came into Colorado. The longhorns — long-horned cattle — were driven over these hot, dusty, dangerous trails by the cowboys. The first cattle ranches were started because the miners wanted meat. The eastern plains of Colorado had once been called the "Great American Desert," but cattlemen found the grass there very nourishing for their cattle. For that reason they established their ranches on the plains and not in the mountains. The range was open and free for anyone who had the courage to risk the hard life of ranching.

The Open Range

The great days of ranching were called the open-range era. It lasted only about twenty years, from 1865 to the mid-1880s.

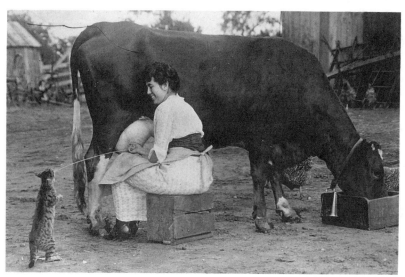

Cattle provided meat and milk for the thousands of people moving into Colorado every year. (Colorado State University.)

Coloradans had to wait until the Cheyenne and Arapaho Indians were removed from the eastern plains and the railroad arrived before they could fully enter into the cattle business. Once they started, the industry boomed here as it did in Texas, Wyoming, and Montana. By the mid-1870s, Denver was becoming the center of the livestock industry. Denver's railroad connections and stockyards made it a logical place to buy, sell, and ship cattle to meat markets and cattle buyers.

Operating a ranch looked easy and, in some ways, it was. All you needed at first were cattle, cowboys, and a branding iron. The grass and water were free. The cattle were turned loose to graze on the open range. Once or twice a year they were rounded up, branded, and driven to market or to the railroad's loading pen. Each ranch burned its own brand into its cattle and calf hides for easy identification.

The ranch itself had only a couple of quickly constructed buildings and a corral. Not much money was spent on them. Horses were not too expensive to buy. Wages for the cowhands, or "hands," as they were called, were another expense. Their pay averaged about $30 a month, plus room and board. A top hand might receive as much as $45. The number of cowboys that were needed changed with the seasons. More were required in the summer and during roundups and drives, but only a few were needed in winter.

The phrase "Grass is King" described the days of the open range. The cattle grazed on free grass and multiplied naturally. All the owner had to do was round them up, brand them, and sell them for a profit. Grass and cows were the road to fortune. No one in Colorado became more famous or wealthy by following this road than John Wesley Iliff.

John Wesley Iliff

John Wesley Iliff was no ordinary cattleman. He ran his cattle across a range that stretched more than 100 miles west from Colorado's eastern border and ran 60 miles north and south — over 650,000 total acres. His chief ranch headquarters was 40 miles from Julesburg. Northeastern Colorado was his range. Iliff did not own all of this land, but he controlled the water. That meant the land was his to use, because without water the land was useless for other ranchers or farmers.

John Wesley Iliff raised cattle to feed miners, railroad construction crews, and even Indians on reservations. (Colorado Historical Society.)

Twenty-eight-year-old Iliff had come to Colorado in the gold rush of 1859 and opened a store in Denver. He soon realized that there was a lot of money to be made in the cattle business, so he invested in a herd of cattle. Within ten years Iliff was purchasing 10,000 to 15,000 Texas longhorns each spring at $10 to $15 each. He fattened them on his range for a year or two and then sold them for $30 to $50 each. He hired about forty hands in the summer and about twelve in the winter to herd his cattle. Iliff became a rich and powerful man in Colorado.

By the 1870s, however, he realized that the days of the open range would not last forever. Farmers were moving onto the plains, and towns were being built where once there had been only open space and cattle. Iliff also understood that the ranching methods in use then were not the best. He began to make changes. For example, he brought in better breeds of cattle. Shorthorn and Hereford beef was much better than the tough and stringy longhorn meat. Ranchers had been losing a third or more of their herds during the storms and harsh weather of winter by letting the cattle graze on their own. Iliff decreased these losses by building shelters for his animals and by cutting hay for winter feed. He used sound business practices to run his ranch and refused to borrow money. Iliff was one of the first ranchers to understand that the range could be overgrazed by too many cattle. He worked hard to keep it free from overcrowding and disease.

John Iliff was one of the most advanced cattlemen of his time. After the open range ended, people realized that he had introduced scientific ranching, the basis of today's industry. Iliff died in February 1878, and his widow Elizabeth ably ran the ranch, becoming one of Colorado's best-known ranch women. Eventually she donated part of the family fortune to establish the Iliff Seminary at the University of Denver, Colorado's first college. Of Iliff, one of his friends said: "He was the squarest man that ever rode over these Plains."

The End of the Open Range

Iliff was right, the days of the open range would soon end. The coming of the farmer hurt; so did overgrazing the land and crowding too many cattle onto the range. By the mid-1880s, too much debt and poor management had put ranchers on shaky ground. Then came the harsh years of 1885–1887, which brought drought and terrible winters. Cattle died by the thousands. Panicked owners shipped all of the cattle they could and flooded the market. Because there were too many cattle for sale, the price collapsed. Finally, the poor management and borrowing to buy more cattle caught up with the ranchers. The days of open-range ranching ended.

In its place came ranching based on better breeds of cattle, fenced pastures, winter feeding, and more businesslike methods. Grass was no longer king, but the cattle industry now had a more solid foundation. By 1900 cattle were being raised throughout Colorado — from the eastern plains to the mountain valleys and in the far western parts of the state. Cattle raising had become one of the most important industries in Colorado's economy.

Although the open range disappeared, legends of cowboys and cattle drives lingered. Colorado even claimed to have one

Ranchers used windmills to pump up underground water for their cattle on the dry high plains. (Photo by Thomas J. Noel.)

real cattle town, like the more famous Dodge City, Kansas. Trail City, Colorado, six miles north of Holly on the Kansas border, was established in 1884. It lasted only about six years. Located on the National Cattle Trail, Trail City was a place where cowboys could "let off steam" after driving the herds up from Texas. When the days of the long drives and the open range came to an end, so did Trail City.

Cowboys

The hero of this time in history was the cowboy. His life has been made to look exciting in books and movies. Jack Keppel did not think so. He came to eastern Colorado in 1887 and worked on a ranch. Jack was a "greenhorn" who didn't even know how to ride a horse. His pay at first was $15 a month. In the summer of 1889, it was raised to $20. He learned to do all the ranch chores after a while, except milking cows; he said he was "not good at that." Jack had difficulties getting used to washing with and drinking alkali water. Its salty taste was terrible, and too much of it could cause illness. Like most cowboys, he drifted from place to place and worked for several ranchers before homesteading his own little ranch/farm. There was not much excitement or glamour in Jack's life. Mostly it was just plain hard work and a very lonesome existence.

Still, the cowboy's life was not all work and no play. When the cowboy went to town, he could have some fun. Sometimes he got too rowdy. For example, during the 1880s two cowboys were racing their horses in Denver. They crashed into a trolley car with this result:

> [The impact] smashed three of the roof supports, splintering the seats and breaking down the grip guard. One rider went hurtling through the car like a human cannon ball, and landed on all fours in the street on the other side. . . . His companion struck the side of the car and bounced back into the roadway. Marvelous to relate neither were hurt [nor were any horses or passengers].

In 1894 Perry Davis helped drive horses through eastern Colorado. He and his friends had to deal with dangerous river crossings, quicksand, unruly livestock, rapid weather changes, and many other problems before they reached the end of the trail. Davis wrote in his diary on September 17:

> Horses tore down wire fences; got badly cut and went through brush. Didn't pay for fences. Moved eight miles from Platte and camped for noon. Move about eight miles after dinner and water in Beaver [Creek] and pull into the hills a couple of miles and camp. Sheep here; feed short. See sand lizards; poison. Horses run into two bands of sheep, stampede.

It doesn't sound like much fun, does it? Being a cowboy was hard work.

Sheep

As a rule, cattlemen did not like sheep. Sometimes the sheep scared their horses, as Davis wrote in his diary. Both the cowboys and the sheepherders wanted the same range for their animals, and cattlemen believed the legend that cattle would not eat where sheep had grazed.

Although the sheep had come before the cattle — New Mexico settlers in the San Luis Valley had brought them north — sheep raising grew slowly. Not until the 1870s and 1880s did it spread very far. Troubles came quickly and lasted a long time. For almost forty years the cattlemen and sheep ranchers fought one another for the mountain valleys and river bottoms. Sometimes these fights became violent. In March 1877 a flock of 1,600 sheep was poisoned and clubbed to death near Pueblo as a warning to sheep ranchers to keep out of the area. These "cattle-sheep wars" also extended to Colorado's Western Slope. Smart sheepherders like Ann Bassett of Brown's Park had their sheep chew up grass at the head of any green valley that might attract cattlemen. The fighting did not end until the 1930s, when the federal government began to regulate use of public grazing lands.

Farming

A much greater threat to the cattleman was the farmer or home-steader. The name *homesteader* came from the Homestead Act, passed by Congress in 1862. This act let any American citizen, or anyone who wanted to be a citizen, choose 160 acres of public land for a farm, or homestead. After five years of living on the land and making improvements, the homesteader was given the land, or, after six months' residence, the land could be bought for $1.25 an acre. Homesteaders had to wait until the Indians were removed and the railroad came before they could settle very much of the eastern plains. They arrived after the cattle ranches were already established.

Farming in Colorado had begun with the fifty-niners. The miners needed more than meat to eat, so some of them turned to farming. They realized they could make more money by growing crops and selling them to other miners than they could by mining. They farmed along the rivers that came out of the mountains. Most of them did not have to learn any new skills, because they had been farmers back in the Midwest.

William Byers, in the very first issue of his newspaper, the *Rocky Mountain News,* told his readers that money could be made from farming. David Wall took that advice. He settled in the Golden area and established a farm. His site was perfect, because he could sell his produce to both the miners in the mountains and the residents of Denver and Golden. He irrigated, or watered, his crops by digging a ditch from Clear Creek. He made a nice profit until grasshoppers almost ruined him by eating his crops in 1862. Other farmers settled in the Huerfano, Arkansas, Platte, and Big Thompson river valleys.

Byers's dream of having homegrown products came true by the fall of 1859 in Denver. Yet Colorado farmers would not be able to provide all the produce and grain that were needed until after 1900. The farmers needed time to find out the length of the growing season, which crops could be grown successfully, and how much rainfall could be counted on during the growing season. Furthermore, equipment and some of the common farm animals had to be brought out to the West. Experienced hog

In Colorado's mountain valleys, ice farming was one way to make a living. (North Fork Historical Society.)

drivers drove 252 hogs on a march from the Missouri River in 1861, and the first colony of bees came by wagon train the next year. The first turkeys trotted all the way to Denver, making as many as twenty-five miles a day with help from a tailwind. The first cats arrived in 1859 and sold for as much as $25 apiece as pets. Cats were prized because they controlled rats and mice.

When the farmers moved away from the well-watered river valleys near the foothills to Colorado's eastern plains, they had to make some changes. The first thing they had to do was find water and get it to their crops. Without water, farming and settlement would fail. Building an irrigation system took more money and skill than most Coloradans had in the 1860s, so they had to work together.

Colony Settlements and Water Law

The first really successful plains farmers solved some of these problems with colony settlements. In a colony, a group of people joined together to plan a settlement and combine their skills and money. In this way they hoped to get all the needed finances, knowledge, skills, and labor to establish and maintain a town and an irrigation system. A group of farm families who moved

With hard work, enough water, and luck, farmers thrived. Such was the case for this family in Sterling. Their success is shown by a new clapboard house, new Eureka windmill, and fine clothes. (Colorado Historical Society.)

together also could overcome the loneliness of the eastern plains. Loneliness had always been a problem on the farming frontier, especially for the women and children.

The best known of Colorado's colonies was the Union Colony, which started the town of Greeley. It was named after Horace Greeley, who helped promote this well-planned town in his New York City newspaper. The Union colonists worked together to build an irrigation system so they could begin farming. Longmont was established using the same idea. These were the most successful of the many attempts during these years to plant agricultural colonies.

When the farmers began to take water out of the rivers, the question was asked, "Who has the right to use it?" There was not enough for everybody if settlements grew too fast. Because both mining and agriculture needed large amounts of water, Colorado was one of the first states to make water laws to decide how it should be used. From these laws came the doctrine of prior appropriation. It meant "first in time, first in right"; that is, the person who had the earliest water claim (say, April 1860) had the first right to use the water. The person with the second earliest date (for instance, May 1860) came next, and so on. The persons who held water rights could not waste the water; they had to make good use of it. In water law this is called "beneficial use." Water is still of major importance to Colorado's growth, just as it was over 100 years ago when these laws were being made.

Homesteading

Despite the success of colonies at Greeley and Longmont, most of the eastern plains were settled by individual farmers who hoped to make their fortune in this new land. They were encouraged by the railroads, which crossed the plains on their way to Denver and Pueblo. These railroads had land to sell to farmers, and they could make money by shipping the farmers' crops to market.

Imagine the plains being divided up like a giant checkerboard, with each section containing 640 acres (one mile square). The railroads were given much land along their tracks that they had to sell. They used some of it to start towns such as Wray, Yuma, Akron, and Ft. Morgan along the Burlington Railroad. Other railroad towns were Burlington, Flagler, and Limon on the Rock Island line. The railroads offered to sell their other sections of land to farmers and ranchers.

Settlers came with wonderful dreams of homesteading in eastern Colorado. What they found was quite different from the paradise they had imagined. Trees were in short supply, so there was no wood for fuel or building. They had to construct their homes with sod cut from the soil on their farms. These houses were cheap to build and fairly warm in the winter (when heated by a stove) and cool in the summer. Cornstalks, straw, corncobs, and even cow "chips" (dried manure) were used instead of wood in the stove. There were other problems, too, as Alvin Steinel noted in his *History of Agriculture in Colorado:*

> Mush and milk was the diet that sustained many a family through the pioneering period, although those properly equipped to farm soon had a garden under way and a supply of eggs and meat coming from a flock of hens,

For their 1880s homestead near Merino in Logan County, the Davis family used sod for the walls and buffalo hides for the roof. (Colorado Historical Society.)

with plenty of salt pork in prospect later. The obstacles to settlement which nature had set up in a semi-arid [dry] climate . . . were serious enough, but the problem was made doubly hard by the fact that free homesteads and cheap railroad land attracted a class of people who were generally without capital [money], and often without farming experience.

Most of the people stayed and tried to start a farm and home, despite all the problems.

Rainmaking

Settlers poured in and, for a while, so did the rains. The hopeful saying "Rain follows the plow" seemed to be true. The people didn't realize that they had settled during a wet cycle in the late 1870s and 1880s. When the dry years came, the farmers started to worry. They turned to anyone who promised to bring rain. As a result, so-called rainmakers appeared and practiced their "magic." Frank Melbourne, according to a *Denver Post* article on August 2, 1891, worked from a "mysterious little house from which the inventor controls the elements." He promised hope to eastern Colorado: "I have passed through Colorado three months ago and made it a point to take particular notice of the country through which I passed, the weight of the air and other points which the general traveler would not notice. . . . I can bring rain over an area of 250,000 square miles, and am positive I could bring it in Denver."

The "magic" of the rainmakers did not work, and in the late 1880s and 1890s much of eastern Colorado was abandoned. The farmers had been defeated by drought and low farm prices. Others would try their luck again after 1900 and would use what became known as "dryland" farming methods. These methods enabled families to grow wheat, broom corn, and some other crops without irrigation.

Through a slow trial-and-error process, Colorado farmers would find the right crops, seeds, machinery, and methods. Agriculture finally would take its place as an important part of Colorado's economy.

The Grange and Other Community Life

Hard work, drudgery, loneliness, and disappointment filled the lives of farmers. Working together in colonies made things better, but there was little help for the typical farmer. One organization for farmers did make life easier. The Patrons of Husbandry, popularly known as the Grange, had come to Colorado in the 1870s. It gave the farmers and their families social and educational opportunities by providing meetings, picnics, dances, and publications about farming methods. The Grange halls in the farming counties became social centers and places where farm families could learn about the latest farm machinery, stove, or cooking technique. Some of these Grange halls still exist. Is there one in your county?

County fairs were another opportunity for rural families to get together and a place to advertise local crops. Some towns had special days to promote themselves and their agriculture. For example:

LOAD 130 SACKS 16490 LBS OF POTATOES HAULED IN 4 MILES ON STUDEBAKER WAGON. TO NORTHERN COL. PRODUCE CO. GREELEY. BY H. FISHENGORD *Union Bank Corner 8th Ave & 8th St*

Sometimes, Colorado farmers made the "Great American Desert" yield a wealth of crops. This wagon
with 130 sacks of potatoes became part of the parade at Greeley's Potato Day festival.
(Denver Public Library.)

Rocky Ford	"Melon Day"
Greeley	"Potato Day"
Sterling	"Farmers' Picnic"
Longmont	"Pumpkin Pie Day"
Fort Collins	"Lamb Day"
Platteville	"Pickle Day"

On the Western Slope, Grand Junction sponsors "Peach Day" and Glenwood Springs celebrates "Strawberry Day." Since 1887, Pueblo has hosted the state's largest agricultural festival, the Colorado State Fair. It continues to attract fascinating farm exhibits and top country musicians.

Colorado's biggest rodeo and livestock show began in 1906. The National Western Stock Show is still held for ten days every January. Ranchers from all over North America meet in Denver to exhibit, inspect, buy, and sell all kinds of animals. Although the stock show traditionally happens during the coldest part of winter, hundreds of thousands come to the rodeo, the Beef Palace, and the Hall of Education, where you can see dozens of different kinds of animals, from rabbits to roosters to llamas.

QUESTIONS
1. What contributions did John Wesley Iliff make to the "science" of ranching?
2. What factors led to the end of the open range?
3. Compare and contrast the life of the cowboy with the life of the farmer.
4. What did the railroads have to do with farming settlements in Colorado?
5. Explain the concept of "first in time, first in right."
6. Why is water so important to Colorado?
7. Describe some of the problems faced by early homesteaders.

ACTIVITIES
1. Visit a ranch or farm in your county to see how ranching and farming are carried on today.
2. Ask your county agricultural agent to come talk to your class about farming and ranching.
3. Bring some records or tapes of cowboy songs and play them for the class. Show a video about the cowboy's life.
4. Study how water has influenced development in your county. Do you have any irrigation districts? Interview a district official.
5. Find out the history of an irrigation ditch in your area. Ask someone familiar with the ditch to walk with your class along a portion of it. You may hear some interesting stories!
6. Discuss how farmers and ranchers make your life better.

Books You and Your Teacher Might Enjoy

Sonora Babb. *An Owl on Every Post.* New York: McCall, 1970 (1994 University of New Mexico Press reprint). An awesome account of a girl growing up on a sodhouse farm in the southeast corner of Colorado.

Perry Eberhart. *Ghosts of the Colorado Plains.* Athens, OH: Swallow Press, 1986. The best guide to farming and ranching ghost towns.

Will James. *Smoky, the Cowhorse.* New York: Aladdin, 1993 (reprint). A great novel about a man and his horse.

Julie James-Eddy. *Homesteading Women.* New York: Twayne, 1992. Interviews of women who homesteaded in Colorado.

David Murdoch. *Cowboy.* New York: Knopf, 1993. The cowboys come to life in this historical overview.

Richard B. Townshend. *A Tenderfoot in Colorado.* London: John Lane and Bodley Head, 1923 (1968 University of Oklahoma Press reprint). Amusing account of an Englishman who took up ranching in Colorado during the 1870s.

Elliott West. *Growing Up with the Country.* Albuquerque: University of New Mexico, 1989. Find out what it was like for youngsters to live in a town or on a ranch or farm in the nineteenth century.

Laura Ingalls Wilder. *Little House on the Prairie* and other books. Though not specifically about Colorado, these books provide vivid descriptions of life on the farm.

Did You Know?

In the 1890s a well-broken saddle horse cost $50 or $60.

A pair of men's blue denim overalls sold for 50 cents.

CHAPTER ELEVEN
Western Slopers

On the Pacific side of the Continental Divide in Colorado lies the Western Slope. Its high mountains, river valleys, mesas (high, flat tablelands), and lonely stretches of semideserts and deserts are some of the state's most beautiful scenery and rugged land. This part of Colorado gives birth to the great Colorado River and two-thirds of the state's water reserves. Water always has been important to the state's growth and development, and it will continue to be in the future. Water is the lifeblood of the Western Slope.

Prospecting

These lands had been home to the Indians for many, many years — first the Basketmakers, then the cliff dwellers, and finally the Utes. At first, the high mountains kept the gold seekers of 1859 from invading this part of Colorado. They could not be kept out for long, however, and they found passes through those mountains. By midsummer the fifty-niners had arrived on the Western Slope in their search for gold. Most of them did not stay long. The loneliness, the threat of Indian attacks, transportation problems, and a hard winter drove out all but the most determined. This would be the pattern for the next decade, while other areas of the state gradually were settled. Breckenridge and Summit County had the only gold placers that proved rich enough to keep miners there for a couple of years. Then they, too, declined. The problem of moving goods through the Rocky Mountains killed interest in other mining areas, such as the San Juan Mountains and the Gunnison country.

Rumors of gold and silver still found their way east, however, and continued to lure prospectors to the Western Slope. All of them thought they could unlock its mineral secrets. Settlers tried to start homes, but their job was difficult until they could earn a living and transportation improved. Miner Daniel Conner wrote about the appearance of the first woman and her daughter in the mining district of Georgia Gulch, near Breckenridge:

> She [an old lady] brought her daughter with her, whom she addressed by the affectionate sobriquet [nickname] of "Sis." Sis was the first young lady to arrive in Georgia Gulch, and the fact that she waited upon customers gave the establishment a heavy run of business. . . . The common remark of the miners, when meeting friends, was first, "Boys, there is a *gal* in the gulch." "When did she come?" "Oh, I don't know, but she's there." "Hurrah! Hurrah for Georgia Gulch."

Until more women and families arrived, the Western Slope would not have permanent settlement. As late as the mid-1870s it was still being called an "unknown land." One author boldly forecast that in time it would become "thickly settled."

Mining finally provided the solution to most of the problems. The San Juan Mountains were prospected in the 1870s. Because of the activity there, the towns of Ouray, Silverton, and Lake City came into being and provided the base for more exploring. The neighboring Gunnison country began to be settled in the late 1870s and attracted a lot of attention in the early 1880s. The town of Gunnison was the transportation and business center. North and east of it were the silver mining districts and camps.

The Ute Land

Mining and the settlement that came with it also brought tragedy to the Western Slope, because most of it belonged to the Utes. This fact did not concern the miners and other newcomers. In 1863 and again in 1868, the United States government had promised this land to the Utes. It was to be their reservation, or land set aside for them. That agreement seemed fair, as it had been their home for hundreds of years. Then came the miners, who discovered and mined gold and silver. To them, it seemed unfair that the Utes should have all the land, especially since the Indians did not mine these treasures. It was the same clash of different cultures that had occurred when European settlers first came to the Americas centuries before.

The Colorado conflict reached the danger point in the San Juans in the early 1870s. This area was Ute hunting land. In 1873 the U.S. government officials and Ute leaders sat down once more to work out the terms of a treaty. In the resulting Brunot Agreement, the Utes gave up their claim to the San Juan Mountains. The miners could now start mining legally.

But that was not enough for these new settlers. Other lands held by the Utes seemed just as attractive to the miner, town builder, rancher, and farmer. Cries that the "Utes must go" were heard throughout Colorado. The Utes stood in the way of "progress," as Coloradans defined it in the 1870s. They must be conquered just as the mountains had been.

The Utes did not want to leave their homeland. Their most famous leader, Ouray, tried with all his skills to keep them there. Ouray was one Ute whom the white people respected. For instance, Ouray, the town named after him, held a "grand reception" for him in March 1879. Two hundred people turned out to honor him. The local band played for Ouray and his wife, Chipeta. The *Ouray Times* of March 15 praised this good man and hoped that he would be a "better friend than ever of the whites." Unfortunately, he could not control all of the Utes. Only six months later trouble came at the White River Agency near the present town of Meeker.

The United States Indian agent, Nathan Meeker, a good but stubborn man, wanted the Utes to farm, something they did not want to do. When Meeker ordered the racetrack plowed up to stop their horse racing and betting, tempers exploded. Meeker called for help, but it came too late. In September he and eleven men were killed by some Utes. The agency's white women and children were carried off into captivity. The newspapers screamed that a "Ute War" had broken out.

The column of troops that came to rescue Meeker and his co-workers was stopped by Ute warriors. The soldiers had to be

Ouray and Chipeta were Colorado's most famous Native American couple. They tried to keep peace between the Ute people and the whites moving into the tribe's Colorado homeland. (Museum of Western Colorado.)

rescued before they could march on to find a bloody scene at the agency. Ouray tried desperately to persuade his fellow Utes to release their prisoners to prevent a full-scale war. He succeeded, but the damage already had been done.

Not even Ouray could save the Ute homeland now. In 1880 he and other Ute people traveled to Washington and signed a new agreement. This one removed all the Utes involved in the Meeker incident from Colorado into eastern Utah. Only the Southern Utes, who had not participated, were allowed to stay on their reservation in what are now La Plata and Montezuma Counties. The next year the Northern Utes left Colorado. In 1882 the remaining land on the Western Slope was declared open for settlement. White settlers came on the heels of the retreating Utes.

The town of Ouray was named for the Ute leader. The Utes surrendered the San Juans to miners in 1873 after they struck gold and silver in these rugged mountains. (Denver Public Library.)

Ouray, the wise and dedicated Ute leader, did not live to see this final tragedy in his people's Colorado story. He died in August 1880, while working for approval of the agreement. No Indian leader stands taller in the history of Colorado than Ouray. And some of his people, the Southern Utes and the Ute Mountain Utes, live in Colorado to this day on their two reservations in the state's southwestern corner.

Transportation

At the time of the Ute troubles, transportation improvements began to come to the Western Slope. This was the other major development necessary to open this area of Colorado to white settlement.

The Freighters

First came the freighter to haul goods with his supply wagons and mule or burro pack trains. Later, stagecoaches carried in mail and passengers.

One of the most famous freighters was Dave Wood, who ran his freight teams in the San Juans and in other areas from the 1870s into the 1890s. Freighters hauled an amazing variety of things. You can imagine what some of them were: ore from the mines, oats, corn, mining equipment, dynamite, general supplies

Burros carried even this ore car and ore car railroad track out of Silverton to a mine high above that silver city. (Denver Public Library.)

for stores, furniture, and food. They charged by the pound and worked as long as weather permitted. In the snowy winter months they used horse or mule pack trains to bring supplies. Such travel could be very dangerous because of snow slides and extreme cold. Freighting was risky in all seasons, and the best efforts did not always satisfy customers. They complained to Dave Wood about the following matters:

> Poor oats are hard to sell — please send good ones neither musty or dirty.
>
> We don't put ourselves up as kickers but would like to know why it is you ship freight to others for less than you do us?
>
> 18 lbs. of cheese were destroyed in one of your wagons — got down between some barrels where it got mashed and gorged.
>
> You must have some goods of ours that has been in your possession a long time.
>
> Roads now getting in fair condition. You may load and ship our ore cabinet case, but I wish you or Mr. Marshall would personally look after the loading of same to see that no danger of either breaking the glass or rubbing the stand.

Dave Wood helped open the San Juans to white settlement as much as any other individual did, despite the complainers. Freighting — bringing in supplies — was absolutely necessary.

Railroads

The most dependable type of transportation was the railroad. Faster and bigger than supply wagons and stagecoaches, the iron horse could be depended on all year — usually. You already read about the Denver & Rio Grande and its effect on the settlement of Leadville, Colorado Springs, Denver, and Pueblo. The D&RG would be even more important in western Colorado. Without the railroad, settlement could not have come so easily or covered so much land.

The Denver & Rio Grande's narrow-gauge rails (only 3 feet wide) proved to be ideal for the mountains and canyons of the Western Slope. They were easier to build and take care of, and they could climb steeper grades up the mountains and make sharper turns. Narrow gauge also cost less than the 4-foot, 8½-inch broad gauge in general use throughout the United States. Palmer's railroad climbed through the Rockies and beyond to Utah and New Mexico.

One branch swung south and west from Alamosa to Durango, which the D&RG founded, and then up to Silverton. Another crossed Marshall Pass and went to Gunnison, then west to Montrose and Grand Junction, with other branches later going to Ouray and Lake City. Denver & Rio Grande tracks

In Telluride, these comfortable "palace cars" put an end to jokes about "To Hell You Ride." (Amon Carter Museum.)

reached the booming silver camp of Aspen in the 1880s. Both mining and farming regions were helped by rail connections. It took hard work, money, and courage to build into these new areas. The D&RG was not afraid to move into unexplored territory, and everyone benefited.

Other railroads were not about to let the Denver & Rio Grande have the Western Slope all to itself. The Denver, South Park, and Pacific Railroad raced the D&RG to Gunnison, only to come in second. The same thing happened to the Colorado Midland going into Aspen. Otto Mears was known for building wagon roads, but he also built a few railroads. He built short rail lines out of Silverton to tap nearby mining districts. A longer railroad, the Rio Grande Southern, stretched from Durango to Telluride and Ridgway. At one time Silverton had four narrow-gauge railroads and called itself the "Narrow Gauge Capital of the World."

The railroads brought growth to the mining regions because they lowered the cost of freight and made the mountain districts easy to reach. As on the Front Range, they also helped the farmer and rancher to ship their crops and cattle much more easily to markets. Without railroads, towns were considered "too dead to bury."

Railroads helped to start the tourist industry on the Western Slope. By the 1890s, travelers could buy tickets in Denver to take the "circle route." First, they rode the Denver & Rio Grande all the way to Silverton. Then they changed to Mears's Silverton railroad and traveled to Ironton. Here a thrilling stagecoach ride down a narrow canyon road brought them to Ouray, where they rejoined the D&RG for the trip back to Denver. It was as much fun as it sounds. The "Rainbow Route," as it was sometimes called, carried tourists through some of the most beautiful Colorado mountains and canyons. The ease and comfort of travel was amazing for a state only thirty years old. Today, tourists still travel by train over the Silverton-Durango and Chama-Antonito parts of the Rainbow Route.

The railroads brought some bad along with the good. In their rush to reach the Western Slope they often hurried too much. Poor construction of curves and bridges caused train wrecks. Someone said about the South Park Railroad that it was "poorly surveyed, poorly located, poorly engineered, poorly financed and in financial trouble during most of its history." The same could be said for other railroads, because they were slow in making a profit. Western Slopers grumbled about such problems, but they could also laugh about them. Old-timers said the D&RGW (as it was renamed when it reached Utah) meant "Dangerous & Rapidly Growing Worse." The little Crystal River & San Juan (CR&SJ) Railroad that ran to Marble was known as the "Can't Run & Seldom Jumps."

Hard-Rock Mining

The discovery of gold and silver, the removal of the Utes, and the coming of the railroads finally turned the Western Slope into a miners' delight. They scurried about the mountains looking for more minerals. Ranchers and farmers settled in the valleys, and town builders surveyed and built where the Utes had roamed only a few years earlier. In the 1880s and 1890s the Western Slope became a new frontier to settle.

Mining had called attention to the region in the first place. It had encouraged the railroads, settlers, and investors to come in and had advertised the Western Slope. Mining followed the same

Imagine dressing up as well as these men and women did for a fishing trip to Grand Lake. (Colorado Historical Society.)

pattern in western Colorado as it had in other parts of the state. First it boomed, then it busted. Gunnison mines had their moments of excitement, then faded away. Aspen replaced Leadville as Colorado's silver queen in the late 1880s. Within ten years it, too, fizzled. Then the San Juan Mountains in the southwestern corner of the state blossomed into a major mining region. With their wealth of gold, silver, and other minerals, the San Juans continued for over a hundred years as an important mining area.

Mining helped the farmer and rancher get started, because the miners were willing to pay high prices for farm and ranch products. When mining declined, farming and tourism became the main local industries.

Growth

The Western Slope, because settlement began later, found itself far behind the eastern part of the state in development, population, finances, and political power. During the 1800s, it never caught up, and it remained a poor "country cousin" to Denver and the rest of the state. It seemed as if the Western Slope was a colony of the older parts of Colorado. You may remember that the original thirteen colonies in America depended on England for money, trade, and manufactured products. In much the same way, the Western Slope depended on outside investors, bankers, and businessmen. This dependence created problems as the years went by, such as fights over water rights.

Water was one thing the Western Slope had in large amounts. The Eastern Slope and nearby states needed more and more of it for their farms and towns. The Western Slope wanted to use its own water for farming, cities, and mining. Both halves of the state looked to the same water sources to meet their needs. Who would be allowed to use them would be the important question of the twentieth century.

By 1900, after only one generation of white settlement, the Western Slope had developed its own way of life, based on its many resources. Some of the problems that had held back settlement for so long had been solved. Grand Junction had 3,503 people and was well on its way to being the largest Western

Slope city, although it was not anywhere near Denver's 133,859. Grand Junction's peaches and apples, grown in the heart of rich agricultural land with a long growing season, were already famous. The Grand Valley around Grand Junction had plenty of water and a mild climate. It became the Western Slope center of agriculture. The development of sugar beets, which became an important crop for all of Colorado, was pioneered here. Durango, Cortez, Montrose, and Delta were busy crop-growing areas, and Paonia rivaled Grand Junction in fruit growing.

Not all of the Western Slope grew at the same rate. The northwestern section continued to be a mostly empty land for many years. Some ranchers and farmers had moved into that area by 1900, but it still lacked railroads. No rich gold or silver strikes

Flumes like this watered the peach and apple orchards of Mesa and Delta Counties with the Colorado River's liquid magic. (Colorado Historical Society.)

*This is one of many orchards that made Palisade and Grand Junction famous for their
fruit harvest. (Colorado Historical Society.)*

attracted the miners, and what towns there were remained very
small. This was Colorado's last frontier.

The years after the early 1870s were exciting ones for Western Slopers. They saw their region grow and prosper. They
loved their land, even with the problems it presented. Most of
them probably would have agreed with newspaperman/poet
Cy Warman:

> I would stand amid these mountains, with their hue-
> less caps of snow,
>
> Looking down the distant valley, stretching far away
> below;
>
> And with reverential rapture, thank my Maker for
> this grand,
>
> Peerless, priceless panorama, that a child can under-
> stand.

QUESTIONS

1. Match the items that go together from the left and right columns.

Ouray	mining
Dave Wood	Ute Leader
San Juans	Denver & Rio Grande
narrow gauge	freighter

2. What problems would you have faced if you had built a railroad into the Western Slope 100 years ago?
3. You are a Ute in the 1870s; what would your reaction be to the settlement of your land?
4. How did mining contribute to the settlement of the Western Slope?

ACTIVITIES

1. Survey your class members to see whether they would rather live on the Eastern or the Western Slope. Discuss the differences between these two regions.
2. The only two Indian reservations in Colorado are in the southwestern corner of the state. How are the Utes doing there today?
3. Locate the two Western Slope counties that have only one town in them.
4. Draw a map showing the rivers and mountains that influenced the settlement of the Western Slope.
5. Read a book about Colorado railroading and report back to the class.

Books You and Your Teacher Might Enjoy

Harriet Backus. *Tomboy Bride*. Boulder: Pruett Pubishing, 1969. This is one of the best books you will read about turn-of-the-century life.

Edwin Bennett. *Boom Town Boy*. Chicago: Sage, 1966. A young boy grows up in Creede.

Daniel Ellis Conner. *A Confederate in the Colorado Gold Fields*. Norman: University of Oklahoma Press, 1970. Conner provides a firsthand look at 1860s Colorado.

Thomas Hornsby Ferril. *Westering*. Boise: Ahsahta Press, 1986. Have
    your teacher read you some of Ferril's poems about Colorado.
Marshall Sprague. *Massacre: The Tragedy at White River*. Lincoln: Bison
    Press, 1980. Well-written story of the bloody Ute War of 1880.
Duane Vandenbusche and Duane A. Smith. *A Land Alone: Colorado's
    Western Slope*. Boulder: Pruett Publishing, 1981. The history of
    Colorado's "Wild West."

Did You Know?

In Colorado in 1881 a person could buy:

thirteen loaves of fresh bread for $1

a "square meal" for 25–50 cents

one pound of sirloin steak for 10 cents

a ticket to a play for 25 cents

a daily newspaper for 5 cents

Denver shoe shine boys. (Colorado Historical Society.)

PART II

Colorado's Ups and Downs

United States		Colorado	
1901–1909	President Teddy Roosevelt preserves public lands	**1906**	Mesa Verde National Park established
1917–1918	World War I	**1913**	The Big Snow
1920	Population 105,710,620	**1920**	Population 939,629; Ku Klux Klan begins to haunt Colorado
1929	Great Depression begins	**1928**	Moffat Tunnel opens
1932	President Franklin Delano Roosevelt begins "New Deal"	**1929**	Stapleton Airport opens
1940	Population 131,669,275	**1940**	Population 1,123,296
1941–1945	World War II	**1941–1945**	Military bases boom
1956	Interstate Highway Act	**1950s**	Automobile suburbs boom
1960	Population reaches 178,464,236	**1960**	Population reaches 1,753,947
1969	First human on the moon	**1960s**	"Ski Country U.S.A."
1974	President Richard Nixon resigns	**1972**	Colorado votes no on Winter Olympics
1970s	Civil rights expanded for women	**1970s**	Oil, coal, and solar energy boom
1976	U.S. bicentennial	**1976**	Colorado Centennial
1980	Population 226,504,825	**1980**	Population 2,888,834
1990s	National hard times bring many to Colorado	**1993**	Colorado Rockies baseball team is born
1994	President Bill Clinton passes gun control law	**1995**	Denver International Airport opens
2000	Population estimated to be 260,000,000	**2000**	Population estimated to be 4,000,000

CHAPTER TWELVE
Hard Times

If you could ride a time machine back to 1900, what would you find? Many Coloradans your age would not be in school. They would be working on farms and in factories. You would also find many men and boys working in damp, dark mines or in hot, noisy smelters where gold and silver were taken out of ores. Miners and smelter workers often worked ten hours a day for $3 a day or less. Because of dangerous working conditions, these laborers were lucky to work an entire year without a serious accident or illness. Added to these problems were high unemployment and frequent strikes. Due to the low wages, dangerous working conditions, and other problems, miners and other workers sometimes refused to work. These group protests were called strikes. Hard times also meant that women and girls had to leave home and go to work.

The Depression of 1893

People blamed many of their troubles on the federal government. It had stopped buying silver and used only gold to back up paper money. That is, every note, such as a dollar bill, could be traded for a certain amount of gold. By the end of 1893, half of Colorado's silver mines had closed, throwing about 50,000 people out of work. Hundreds of businesses, including many banks, failed. Colorado, "the Silver State," sank into a depression along with the rest of the United States.

Boom days were over. One proof of this was slower growth. Between 1870 and 1890, Colorado's population jumped from 39,864 to 413,249. But between 1890 and 1900, the state grew to only 539,700. Not until 1930 would the number of Coloradans reach a million.

In the San Juan Mountains of southwestern Colorado, the depression crippled the silver industry. As silver mines closed and the supply of silver ore fell, silver smelters closed. Durango, the metropolis of southwestern Colorado, felt the pinch. Henry Strater, founder of Durango's famous Strater Hotel, lowered his room and meal rates. Even so, he could not attract enough business to cover his debts and had to sell his grand hotel. Another Durango resident, thirty-six-year-old Frank Burke, blew off the top of his head with a shotgun. He left behind a note: "Good bye all friends. Times too hard. The Boys can have a wake. . . . What I owe now I'll owe forever."

Millionaires lost their fortunes, went into debt, and were forced to sell everything. Horace Tabor, best known of the silver kings, was forced to sell his mines, opera houses, and office buildings. He even had to sell his mansion on Capitol Hill in Denver. The Tabors and their two little girls moved into the Windsor Hotel on Larimer Street. The second Mrs. Tabor, a beauty known as "Baby Doe," once wore a $7,000 wedding dress and a $75,000 diamond necklace. She spent her last years wearing rags. She lived until 1935, when her frozen body was found in a shack at the Matchless Mine in Leadville.

The nationwide depression of 1893 hurt farmers and ranchers as well as miners. Agriculture was also in trouble because of drought, overgrazing, and soil erosion. Because of the depression, farmers and ranchers had trouble paying their debts and could not get new loans from banks. Many people lost their land because they could not make payments on it, and the banks took over their property.

In 1894, hundreds of these homeless, jobless people drifted into Denver. The city let them camp along the South Platte River and tried to feed them. As the army of unemployed grew to over 1,000, Denver officials worried about disease, crime, and riots. City leaders told the jobless to take their problems to the federal government. Coloradans and other unemployed Americans planned a protest march to Washington, D.C. When some of them finally reached the national capitol, their leaders were arrested for walking on the Capitol lawn. The defeated

protesters went back to their homes — if they had homes to go
to — as hungry and poor as ever.

The Populist Party

The depression of 1893 led to political unrest. Many people felt
that neither the Democrats nor the Republicans could deal with
the country's problems. They turned to a new political party
called the People's Party, or the Populists. The Populists, who
had organized on a national level in 1891, talked about reform-
ing, or improving, the political system and doing more for farmers, miners, and factory workers. This new political party
proposed the following reforms:

1. Have the federal government buy up all the silver that
   could be produced at $1.28 an ounce and use it to make
   more money.
2. Nationalize (have the government own and operate) the
   railroads and lower their rates.
3. Set up a maximum workday of eight hours.
4. Start taxing people's income instead of their land, and
   have richer people pay a larger share of the taxes.

*Out-of-work
Coloradans gathered
in Denver along the
South Platte River
and looked for help.
(Denver Public
Library.)*

5. Let voters draw up and circulate petitions to change laws or make new ones.

6. Use the secret ballot in elections.

Many Americans liked these ideas. In 1892 Coloradans elected the Populist candidate for governor, Davis H. Waite. Waite, a newspaper editor from Aspen, was an old man with a long beard and a loud voice. He promised to reform Colorado even if "blood should flow to the horses' bridles." After he said this, the governor's enemies called him "Bloody Bridles" Waite.

The City Hall War

Governor Davis H. Waite, the most radical reformer to ever govern Colorado, tried to help miners, farmers, and poor working people get better pay and better working conditions. (Thomas J. Noel Collection.)

One of Waite's reforms came close to causing bloodshed. Like many Coloradans today, Governor Waite thought that Denver was a wicked place run by corrupt, dishonest officials. Proof of the city's corruption had come in 1891, when Denver Mayor Wolfe Londoner was forced to resign. A court trial showed that he had been elected with hundreds of illegal votes. People had been given free drinks and a dollar each time they voted for Mayor Londoner.

When he was elected, Governor Waite complained that some of the saloons and gambling halls in Denver stayed open illegally all night long and on Sundays. He fired two police commissioners for letting these places stay open despite the law. The two fired Denver officials said they would rather fight than leave their jobs. Governor Waite called out the state militia, which surrounded City Hall with guns and cannons. Policemen and firemen who worked for the commissioners went to City Hall to stop the governor and his troops from kicking out their bosses. Soon the windows of Denver's City Hall bristled with rifles and pistols.

According to one story, the gambler "Soapy" Smith climbed to the top of the City Hall bell tower and began waving a stick of dynamite. "I'm closer to heaven than you gentlemen," Soapy yelled down at the governor's soldiers. "But if you come any closer, you may get there first!" A huge crowd gathered to see the battle. Governor Waite, however, avoided bloodshed by withdrawing his troops, and Denver remained unreformed. The site of the City Hall War is marked today by the old City Hall bell at Fourteenth and Larimer Streets near Larimer Square.

Women's Rights

Governor Waite and the Populists were more successful in their plan to let women vote. Colorado women were first allowed to register and vote in 1894. Colorado became the second place in the world, after New Zealand, where men voted to give women full voting rights.

Many women entered politics and other careers because new goods and machines helped free them from housework. New inventions such as electric iceboxes, sewing machines, and vacuum cleaners made it easier to manage a household.

Colorado men voted to give women voting rights in 1893. This made Colorado the second state (after Wyoming) to grant women's suffrage. (Colorado Historical Society.)

Factory-made clothing and packaged food enabled women to spend less time sewing and cooking than they had in earlier times.

Even before these advances, women had worked in fields, factories, and businesses as well as in the home. One of the hundreds of women running ranches in Colorado was Elizabeth Iliff. After the death of her husband, John W. Iliff, Elizabeth took over their vast cattle kingdom and ran it. Other nineteenth-century women added to their family's income by taking in boarders, baby-sitting, and running shops, restaurants, hotels, and other businesses. Farm women often sold butter, eggs, chickens, and produce. With advanced technology, women could manage home-based businesses and work outside of the home.

Many women participated in athletics. High school girls' basketball teams gained popularity after 1900. In the early days, however, some people said girls should not play sports. For example, Durango girls had to receive permission from the principal, superintendent, and school board before they took to the floor! Proving that women could be winners, in July 1906 the Holly Bloomer Girls defeated the Lamar Cardinals, a men's team, 7–2.

Once women could vote, they began to make even bigger contributions to the community. They worked for better schools, churches, and health care. Women's clubs fought everything from political corruption to saloons. Individual women ran newspapers such as the *Queen Bee,* a Denver weekly published by Caroline Churchill. Women also wrote many best-selling books, such as Helen Hunt Jackson's *A Century of Dishonor,* which drew national attention to the mistreatment of American Indians. Mary Lathrop, a Denver resident, became one of the state's first female attorneys. Her services were sought by some of the most famous badmen in Colorado, including Denver's leading gambler, "Big Ed" Chase. In the 1894 election, three women were elected to the state legislature. Many people dreamed of the day when Colorado would have a female governor or U.S. senator.

When bicycles
became popular
around 1900,
women made
"wheeling" popular
recreation for both
sexes. (Photo by
Charles Lillybridge.
Colorado Historical
Society.)

Colorado women entered rodeo competitions all over the West. They were treated no better
than men by bucking broncos. (Denver Public Library.)

Boosterism

Some people thought that a cheerful attitude and willingness to work harder would end the hard times in Colorado. These "boosters" tried to cheer everyone up with public carnivals such as the Festival of Mountain and Plains, which showcased Colorado-made products during the 1890s and early 1900s. Another Denver festival that tried to improve business was the National Western Stock Show. Held every January since 1905, this is still Denver's biggest festival. Some 300,000 people attend the Stock Show to see cattle, hogs, horses, llamas, rabbits, sheep, and other livestock. At the auctions, prize-winning animals sell for hundreds of thousands of dollars each. Families from all over the western U.S. and Canada come to look at new products, new animal breeds, and new ways to improve livestock to feed the rest of the country. The rodeo features bronco riding, bull riding, calf roping, precision horse riding, and many other competitions. The National Western Stock Show is a reminder that Colorado is an agricultural state, long dependent on its farmers and ranchers.

Foremost among Colorado's boosters were the newspapers. The *Rocky Mountain News* has been promoting Colorado as the promised land since William N. Byers founded it in 1859. During the 1890s the *News* faced new competition that made even more sensational claims that Colorado was heaven on earth—the *Denver Post*. A gambler named Frederick G. Bonfils and a bartender named Harry Tammen purchased the *Post* in 1895. These two characters made the *Post* the most popular and profitable newspaper in the Rockies. One example of their colorful headlines was "Does It Hurt to Be Born?"

Trouble in the Mines

Even booster newspapers could not hide the trouble brewing between Colorado workers and their bosses. The multimillion-dollar Cripple Creek gold boom of the 1890s was one of the few bright spots in Colorado after the 1893 depression. Miners and mine owners of Cripple Creek had agreed in 1894 that miners would work no more than eight hours a day for no less than $3 a day.

Along with other workers, miners had found that they had more power as a group. They formed labor unions to help them work for better working conditions. The miners' biggest union was the Western Federation of Miners (WFM). This union, headquartered in Denver, tried to organize hard-rock miners throughout the West. By 1903, the WFM had formed forty-two local chapters in Colorado. The union's star promoter was William D. Haywood, nicknamed "Big Bill." He stood nearly six feet tall, weighed over 225 pounds, and had lost one eye in a childhood fight.

Haywood had started working in the mines as a teenager. He saw how dangerous the work was when a rock fell from the roof of the mine and crushed a friend's head. Shortly afterward, Big Bill smashed his own hand in an accident. While he was unable to work, his family had no worker's insurance or sick pay. These accidents and the working conditions in most mines convinced Haywood that working people should join unions to work for safer, more rewarding work.

Despite the 1894 Cripple Creek agreement, many Coloradans still labored ten or twelve hours a day for low wages. In 1903, Haywood and the WFM began a statewide crusade for the

Many Colorado strikes were settled by the Colorado National Guard. Here a guardsman patrols the Emmett Mine in Leadville during the 1896 strike. The guard protected mine owners, their mines, and "scab" labor from strikers, who were sometimes jailed or deported. (Amon Carter Museum.)

"Big Bill" Haywood organized Colorado miners to fight for a minimum wage of $3 a day and a maximum work-day of eight hours. (Denver Public Library.)

$3, eight-hour day. From Idaho Springs to Cripple Creek, and from Leadville to Telluride, miners walked off the job. Numerous brawls and injuries and several murders (committed by people on both sides) created extreme bitterness between labor and management. Violence peaked on June 6, 1904, when someone dynamited the Independence Mine railroad depot in the Cripple Creek District, killing thirteen men and injuring many more.

Governor Waite had sided with the miners in 1894, but Governor James H. Peabody, elected in 1902, sided with the mine owners. Governor Peabody sent the Colorado National Guard to protect the mines and strikebreakers who continued to work despite the strike. Striking miners were illegally arrested and locked in jails. Some were loaded on railroad cars and shipped to Kansas. The *New York Times* of August 11, 1904, called Colorado's 1903–1904 labor wars "a reign of terror." The strikers were crushed and so was their union, the WFM.

Three Governors in One Day

Although Governor Peabody defeated the Western Federation of Miners, he made enemies in doing so. In the 1904 election, Coloradans voted him out of office. However, the Republican-controlled supreme court and state legislature charged that the Democratic winner, Alva B. Adams, had been elected with illegal votes. They reinstated Peabody. Angry Democrats then persuaded the Republicans to replace Peabody with his lieutenant governor, Jesse F. McDonald of Leadville. In one day, Colorado had three governors! This confusion showed that the state was in trouble.

Some Coloradans were shocked by the rotten politics, miserable working conditions, and poverty of the working class at the turn of the century. A few determined men and women decided that the time had come to begin social, political, and economic reform.

QUESTIONS

1. What would a weekday be like for a person your age in 1900?
2. What kind of work were Coloradans doing in 1900?
3. What federal action ended Colorado's silver boom? Why?
4. Do you agree with the Populist party ideas? How many of their plans have become law today?
5. List several reasons why Davis H. Waite was unpopular with some Coloradans.
6. What developments during the 1890s and early 1900s allowed women more freedom?
7. What were Colorado miners striking for in 1903–1904?

ACTIVITIES

1. Visit a nursing home and ask some of the people there what life was like when they were your age. What do your grandparents and the elderly people in your neighborhood say? Do they remember "the good old days" or "the bad old days"?
2. To find out what school was like around 1900, visit the old Broadway School classroom at the Colorado Heritage Center in Denver or schoolhouse museums throughout the state.
3. To find out what mining was like, tour mines in Breckenridge, Cripple Creek, Georgetown, Leadville, Silverton, and other mining towns. Write a report about the life of a miner in one of these mines.
4. In your school library (or the public library), look up your town's newspaper for March 17, 1905 (and the day afterward). What does it say about the day Colorado had three governors? In your class, hold a three-way debate among students acting as the governors. Prepare questions in advance about their plans to "clean up" Colorado politics.
5. Imagine you are a reporter in 1893 and 1894. Write a newspaper account of the day women won the vote in Colorado. Write another account of the first day women voted in Colorado.

6. Study the Western Federation of Miners. Make an illustrated time line showing its history.

Books You and Your Teacher Might Enjoy

Colorado Suffrage Centennial, 1893–1993. Denver: Colorado Committee for Women's History, 1993. This booklet provides an excellent overview of the national and Colorado women's suffrage movements.

Anne Ellis. *The Life of an Ordinary Woman*. Boston: Houghton Mifflin, 1929 (1989 University of Nebraska Press reprint). In a fascinating autobiography, Ellis describes life in Colorado mining camps.

Gene Fowler. *Timber Line*. New York: Covici-Friede, 1933 (1974 Comstock Editions reprint). Colorado's best-known newspaperman wrote this funny, best-selling tale of Denver and the *Denver Post*.

William D. Haywood. *Big Bill's Book*. New York: International Publishers, 1929 (various reprints). This rip-roaring autobiography of Colorado's most powerful and feared labor leader provides an unusual view of Colorado's labor wars.

Representative Women of Colorado. Denver: Williamson-Haffner, 1911. If you can find this rare book, take a peek at the hairstyles and costumes to see how women looked way back then.

Janet C. Robertson. *The Magnificent Mountain Women: Adventures in the Colorado Rockies*. Lincoln: University of Nebraska Press, 1990. This book gives a lively account of some adventurous women of earlier times.

Duane A. Smith. *Horace Tabor: His Life and the Legend*. Niwot: University Press of Colorado, 1973, 1991. The most accurate and readable account of Colorado's colorful and celebrated silver king.

George C. Suggs. *Colorado's War on Militant Unionism*. Detroit, MI: Wayne State University Press, 1972 (1991 University of Oklahoma reprint). This account of the 1903–1904 labor war is the best you will find.

Did You Know?

There were twenty males for each female in Colorado in 1860; by 1900, there were five women for every six men.

Colorado has had 100 different railroad companies over the years. Many of them went out of business after the depression of 1893.

Denver had almost 500 different grocery stores in 1900.

German-born people were the largest ethnic group in Colorado in 1900.

People born in Illinois were the most numerous American-born immigrants to Colorado in 1900.

In the early 1990s, reformers began to reach out to Colorado's needy, such as this poor girl looking for help at a Denver shelter. (Denver Public Library.)

CHAPTER THIRTEEN
Colorado's Reformers

The two decades between the Spanish-American War of 1898 and America's involvement in World War I in 1917 are known as the Progressive Era. During these years the idea of reform — changing things for the good of the people — was sweeping the nation. Colorado had its own group of dedicated reformers, people who worked to improve the lives of young people, better the conditions in mines and in prisons, provide educational opportunities, and make the state more beautiful with parks and wilderness areas.

The "Kids' Judge"

Benjamin Barr Lindsey was a tiny man. He weighed only ninety-eight pounds and stood barely five feet, five inches tall. Nevertheless, he stands tallest among Colorado's reformers. Lindsey spent his life working for the poor and the powerless and especially for their children.

Perhaps Lindsey loved underdogs because he grew up as one. His family came to Denver in 1880, from a farm in Tennessee. The Lindseys moved into a shack on West Colfax Avenue. After Ben's father committed suicide, the boy began delivering the *Rocky Mountain News* in the morning and working as a janitor at night. He also kept going to school and did not stop until he became a lawyer.

Constant hard work and poverty depressed Ben, as he recalled later in his book, *The Beast:*

> It seemed to me that my life was not worth living—that every one had lost faith in me— that I should never succeed in the law or any- thing else—that I had no brains—that I should

> never do anything but scrub floors and run
> messages. . . . I got a revolver and some car-
> tridges, locked myself in my room, confronted
> myself desperately, in the mirror, put the muz-
> zle of the loaded pistol to my temple, and
> pulled the trigger.

The gun misfired, and Lindsey took a second look at his life. He decided "to crush the circumstances that had almost crushed me." Thus began Ben Lindsey's lifelong crusade to help humanity.

His biggest concern was the treatment of juvenile delin-quents. Lindsey found that putting these young offenders in jail with older criminals was like sending them to a school for crime. Adults in prison would tell youngsters how to steal, use weap-ons, and commit other crimes. After Lindsey became a judge, he created separate courts and separate prisons for people aged six-teen or younger. The "Kids' Judge" made the Denver Juvenile Court a model not only for America, but for the world. In a 1914 national poll for *American Magazine,* the Denver judge was listed among the ten "greatest living Americans."

The little judge had many big ideas for reform. He attacked child labor, divorce laws, and corrupt politics. He thought that many corporations had too much political influence, and he worked to take away their power. Lindsey soon found that nei-ther the Democrats nor the Republicans supported his ideas, so he ran as an independent candidate for governor of Colorado in 1906. He lost.

In 1912, Lindsey and other Coloradans joined former presi-dent Theodore Roosevelt in forming the new Progressive Party. The Progressives pushed social, political, and economic reforms. Lindsey made many enemies, including the Ku Klux Klan, a group that persecuted nonwhites, Catholics, Jews, and recent immigrants. During the 1920s he left Colorado for California, where he continued to crusade for reform until his death in 1943.

"Honest John" Shafroth

Another man who worked hard for change in Colorado was John F. Shafroth. He became a favorite of reformers in 1904, when he resigned from the U.S. House of Representatives after learning that some people had voted for him illegally. In 1908, voters remembered "Honest John's" action and elected him governor. In 1913 they elected him to the U.S. Senate.

As governor, Shafroth helped turn some of the ideas of Governor Waite and the Populists into law. For example, Colorado adopted the voter initiative process in 1910, after voters approved this tool of democratic government. The initiative means that if you think a law should be passed, you can draw up a petition. If enough people sign your petition, the issue goes on the ballot at election time so that everyone can vote on your idea. With the initiative, ordinary people, as well as the governor and the legislature, can make laws.

Judge Ben Lindsey (far left, with moustache) was shorter than some of the troubled youngsters and gang members he helped by setting up the Denver Juvenile Court. (Colorado Historical Society.)

Many other reforms took place during the Shafroth administration. Campaign contributions from corporations were regulated. Voters were given a chance to help pick their party's candidates in primary elections. A Public Utilities Commission was set up to serve as a watchdog over agencies providing electricity, gas, water, transportation, and other utilities. Earlier, in 1907, a state civil service law had been passed to stop the "spoils system" under which a governor could hire and fire state employees at will.

Governor Shafroth was interested in improving prisons, as well. He put Thomas J. Tynan in charge of the state prison at Canon City. Tynan found that the 700 or so inmates were sitting around doing nothing. Their idleness "sort of got on my nerves," he said, and he put the convicts to work building roads, running a ranch, growing their own food, and building a new prison hospital. Because of Tynan's programs, the penitentiary in Canon City became a busier, less troubled place. Taxpayers were happy because these work projects cut the cost of running the prison.

Colorado passed an eight-hour workday law for people working in mining and other dangerous occupations. State inspectors went into mines and factories to look for work hazards and to report abuses of the new child labor laws. Passing laws and reporting violations of them did not always solve the problems, however. Sometimes laws were not or could not be enforced.

Josephine Roche, Mine Owner

One of the deadliest labor wars in American history occurred in spite of new labor laws. In 1913, coal miners in southern Colorado went on strike. Their union, the United Mine Workers (UMW), wanted a wage increase, stricter enforcement of the eight-hour workday law, and safer working conditions. In addition, miners wanted the right to live outside company towns.

The Colorado Fuel and Iron Company, which controlled many Colorado coal mines, refused to recognize the UMW or listen to its complaints. Thus began a bitter, bloody strike

that led to the Ludlow Massacre of April 1914. Almost 100 people lost their lives as mine owners and the Colorado National Guard forced strikers to leave Ludlow and other nearby southern Colorado coal camps. Strikers and their families, after being thrown out of the company towns, moved into tents at Ludlow, a camp between Walsenburg and Trinidad. They found themselves surrounded by the Colorado National Guard armed with machine guns. To escape the gunfire, strikers and their families dug holes under their tents.

Prisoners at the state penitentiary in Canon City built many of the first paved roads in Colorado, including Canon City's Skyline Drive. (Photo by Glenn Cuerden.)

After this tent town caught fire on April 20, 1914, three mothers and eight of their children were found suffocated to death under the tent in which they had been hiding. To add to this tragedy, the miners lost the strike and had to go back to work under the same dreadful conditions as before. To honor the dead and remind people of the struggle, the United Mine Workers erected a large monument at Ludlow. The horror of Ludlow inspired Josephine Roche, the daughter of a mine owner, to push for reform. She became one of Denver's first policewomen in 1913. She worked with Judge Ben Lindsey to make Colorado a better place to bring up children. Officer Roche, according to Judge Lindsey, "could break up a dance hall row [fight] or a riot in front of a saloon better than an experienced policeman." Known as Denver's "lady cop," she visited dance halls at night to enforce a city law that required anyone under age twenty-one to write down his or her name and address. If you did not sign in, you were not allowed into the dance.

When Josephine's father died in 1927, she became the biggest stockholder of the Rocky Mountain Fuel Company. That is, she owned more of the company than any other person. Now she was able to tackle an issue that had troubled her for years. At the age of twelve, she had asked her father if he would show her one of his coal mines. "It would be too dangerous," he told her. "Then how is it safe for the miners?" the girl had asked. Her father did not have an answer.

After Roche grew up and became an owner of the coal company, she visited its mines around the state. She saw for herself how unsafe the mines were and took steps to improve them. In 1928, she raised the base wage to $7 per day, the highest salary paid in the Colorado mining industry. Other mine owners criticized her and predicted that the Rocky Mountain Fuel Company would lose money and soon fail.

When the depression of 1929 brought hard times, Roche donated her salary as vice president to help keep the Rocky Mountain Fuel Company open. The United Mine Workers union loaned money to the company so it could stay in business while many other mines were closing. Because Josephine Roche had worked with the union instead of against it, the miners also volunteered to accept wage cuts and work fewer days so that no one would have to be laid off. With these measures, Roche was able to keep her mines open throughout the Great Depression of the 1930s.

Roche's solution to the problems of the depression attracted the interest of President Franklin D. Roosevelt and his wife, Eleanor. They asked her to come to Washington as assistant secretary of the treasury. She accepted and became the second-most prominent woman in the federal government (the first was Frances Perkins, the secretary of labor, who had been Roche's classmate at Columbia University). Josephine Roche later served as director of the National Youth Administration and the Public Health Service.

In 1934, Roche became the first woman to run for governor of Colorado. She narrowly lost the Democratic party nomination to Edwin C. Johnson, a farmer from Craig.

Emily Griffith and the Opportunity School

Emily Griffith, a Denver schoolteacher, noticed that many Coloradans lacked education and the ability to speak, read, and write English well. In 1916, she opened her Opportunity School and offered free courses "for all who wished to learn." Evening and weekend courses were held for working people to teach them English and job skills. Today, the Emily Griffith Opportunity School still teaches students of all ages how to fix everything from automobiles to airplanes, how to run computers and word processors, and hundreds of other skills that help them find work.

Hal Borland

While Emily Griffith and Josephine Roche were working to improve Colorado, Hal Borland was growing up near Brush and later in Flagler, both in eastern Colorado. His father published the *Flagler News* from 1915 to 1931. Young Hal graduated from high school in 1918, worked at the *Denver Post*, went to the

Schoolteacher Emily Griffith founded Denver's Opportunity School in 1916 so people of all ages could learn English and job skills. (Denver Public Library.)

University of Colorado, and then returned to Flagler to be editor of the *News* in 1920–1921. All the while, he watched and remembered the world about him on the prairies.

In 1921, he moved to the East Coast and became a long-time columnist for the *New York Times*. Over the years, he won many awards for his writing. Hal Borland wrote excellent books about his earlier days in Colorado. This youngster's vivid memories make *Country Editor's Boy* and *High, Wide and Lonesome* good reading.

"Boss" Speer's City Beautiful

While some men and women tried to improve jobs, jails, and schools, others began to look closely at Colorado's cities, which had become crowded, ugly, and unhealthy. The best known of Colorado's city beautifiers was Mayor Robert W. Speer of Denver. He had come to Colorado in 1878 from Pennsylvania with raw and bleeding lungs. Like thousands of other tuberculosis (T.B.) victims, Speer had been told by his doctor to try the high, dry Colorado climate. These "lungers," as they were called, flooded into the state, creating a "health rush" as big as the mining rushes. Tuberculosis hospitals were built all over the state. On the streets you would see people coughing into sputum cups. Nowadays, new drugs and better health care have almost wiped out T.B., but at one time it was the nation's major killer.

Speer, like many other lung disease victims, improved in Colorado's sunshine and dry air. Once he regained his health, he jumped into politics. Speer and others persuaded the state legislature to create the City and County of Denver. Denver, which had 133,859 citizens in 1900, had been part of Arapahoe County. It needed a stronger government to cope with its special problems, so Denver County was carved out of Arapahoe County.

With the help of many illegal votes, Speer was elected mayor of the new City and County of Denver in 1904. He was called a "boss" because of his powerful and corrupt political machine. "I am a boss," Speer admitted, but added, "I want to be a good one." Was he? Many people thought so. His dream of a "City Beautiful" continues to inspire Coloradans.

One of "Boss" Speer's first orders was to remove the "Keep Off the Grass" signs from city parks. Then he converted the banks of Cherry Creek, which had been used as a dump, to Speer Boulevard. The new mayor also began buying land to create more parks. Parkways were built between the parks so that city residents could walk, run, or bicycle all over town on paths edged with trees, shrubs, and flowers. Coloradans found plenty to do when they visited Denver parks. Mayor Speer put in playgrounds, tennis courts, and golf courses and built lakes for fishing, swimming, boating, and ice-skating.

Speer also installed miles of sewers, paved streets, and sandstone sidewalks. Fancy streetlights and trash cans were put on downtown streets. In addition, he worked to outlaw billboards, bury power lines, and limit building heights to save Denver's view of the mountains. By the time Speer died in office in 1918, he had given away 116,000 shade trees to citizens who promised to plant and take care of them. He had doubled the park space and improved public health, education, and welfare. Denver had become one of the handsomest big cities in the United States.

Denver was not the only place to profit from Mayor Speer's vision. He helped create mountain parks in Jefferson, Clear Creek, and Douglas Counties. The City of Denver purchased 21,000 acres for twenty-seven Denver mountain parks in those counties. Later mayors developed these parks into various attractions such as the Red Rocks Park Outdoor Amphitheater and the Winter Park Ski Area. Thanks to Mayor Speer, some of Colorado's beautiful mountains are open to the public for recreation.

Mayor Speer's City Beautiful dream included four steps: (1) converting the run-down heart of Denver into Civic Center Park; (2) connecting Civic Center by tree-lined boulevards and parkways with neighborhood parks; (3) making large neighborhood parks, such as City Park and Washington Park, into neighborhood civic centers surrounded by schools, libraries, churches, and other public buildings; and (4) preserving some mountain areas for the public by creating a mountain parks system.

The idea of mountain parks also caught on in other communities. Boulder, Fort Collins, Colorado Springs, Pueblo, Trinidad, and Canon City all created city parks outside their city limits. Many cities and towns all over Colorado, inspired by Mayor Speer's City Beautiful vision, established city parks.

John Otto: Creation of a Monument

One of Colorado's most spectacular parks is just outside Grand Junction. In the early years of the twentieth century, John Otto

Mayor Robert W. Speer transformed a drab and dusty Denver into a City Beautiful by planting more than 100,000 trees and doubling the number of public parks. (Denver Public Library.)

settled near Grand Junction among some fabulous redstone canyons carved by the Colorado River. In May 1907 he wrote, "I came here last year and found these canyons, and they feel like the heart of the world to me. I'm going to stay and build trails and promote this place, because it should be a national park. Some folks think I'm crazy, but I want to see this scenery opened up to all people."

Otto worked to realize his dream, and the Colorado National Monument was created on the outskirts of Grand Junction in 1911. Otto became the area's caretaker at a salary of $1 a month. Although Otto got his monument, he lost his wife. She left him in 1911, explaining in a letter to her parents that she "could not live with a man to whom even a cabin was an encumbrance [a burden]. He wanted to live in tents or without tents, outdoors."

She left for good, but he stayed with the Colorado National Monument, always working to improve and promote it. Today thousands of tourists admire the spectacular canyons and enjoy the views of nearby Grand Mesa and the Book Cliffs, which look like partly opened books.

Naturalist Enos Mills

Colorado's best-known naturalist was Enos Mills. At the age of fourteen, Mills left the Kansas flatland for the mountains of Colorado. Arriving in Estes Park, he found a job at the Elkhorn Lodge washing dishes, chopping wood, and serving afternoon tea to the tourists.

During his spare time, Enos explored the mountains. He learned to love the alpine meadows, the spruce and aspen forests, and the flower-lined mountain brooks. He wanted to share them with others and began guiding tourists into the backcountry. To be nearer to his beloved mountains, Mills built a log cabin (now a museum) at the base of Longs Peak.

Mills spent winters as well as summers in the mountains in order to enjoy the "frozen music" of the snowbound Rockies. He camped out alone under the stars or in snow caves, skied the

John Otto, a hermit fascinated with the strange rock formations near Grand Junction, helped convert the area into the Colorado National Monument. (Museum of Western Colorado.)

Continental Divide, and raced avalanches. He tracked grizzly bears, watched beavers build their homes, and studied the rocks that showed how glaciers had carved out mountain valleys.

Mills began writing magazine articles and books that were read all over America. Soon people asked him to give talks about

Enos Mills, Colorado's foremost naturalist, fought for the creation of Rocky Mountain National Park. (Denver Public Library.)

the Rockies. In his writings and his speeches, this self-educated naturalist crusaded for preservation of at least one small section of the Rockies. He wanted a national park because national parks were protected from development, logging, and other uses. They existed solely for the enjoyment of nature. In this desire he was joined by the Colorado Mountain Club. Club members claimed that a mountain park would be a place where everyone could enjoy hiking, fishing, picnicking, camping, skiing, and snowshoeing — or just watching the marmots and mule deer, the elk and the water ouzels.

In 1915, the dream of Enos Mills and others came true when President Woodrow Wilson signed a bill in Washington that created Rocky Mountain National Park.

Enos Mills spoke out strongly in favor of wilderness protection. Because he had little tolerance for anyone who opposed him, he made many enemies. Cattle and sheep raisers, miners, and loggers who had used the land resented him and his ideas about saving wildlands. Other critics thought that state and local governments, not federal agencies, should control Colorado land use.

Some people must have been relieved when Enos Mills died in 1922, but his friend Judge Ben Lindsey declared:

> Like all great men, Enos Mills was perhaps least appreciated while he lived. . . . I think all will agree that Mills, his work and what he stood for, cannot be too much known and understood. It means far more to our children than the work of men after whom many of our mountain peaks have been named. Some of these men, like Zebulon Pike, discovered the bodies of our mountains. Mills discovered their souls.

As twentieth-century life becomes more crowded and urban, Coloradans have grown to appreciate people like Enos Mills and

Year-round snow helps make the Rockies both a winter and a summer playground. (Colorado Historical Society.)

John Otto — people who fought for national monuments, parks, forests, and grasslands. Can you imagine what our state would be like without public parks?

QUESTIONS

1. Teenage crime is one of the growing problems in America. What did Judge Ben Lindsey think should be done about it?
2. List some of the accomplishments of Josephine Roche.
3. Why was Josephine Roche able to keep her mines open when others were closing?
4. Why do adults often go to schools like the Emily Griffith Opportunity School for continuing education classes?
5. When were the parks nearest your home created?
6. List the four steps of Mayor Speer's plan to improve Denver.
7. How did creation of Rocky Mountain National Park further Enos Mills's cause?

ACTIVITIES

1. Sit in on a juvenile court case in your town. How are young lawbreakers treated?

2. Do the parks, playgrounds, and waterways in your community need beautification? Organize a cleanup and keep a list of all the different litter you find. One person's trash may be another person's treasure! Look for old coins as well as bottles, cans, and newspapers that you can recycle.

3. How many of Colorado's national parks, monuments, forests, and grasslands have you visited? Ask other members of the class to tell you about the ones they have visited.

4. What recreational and educational programs do your local, state, and national parks offer for your class? (Look up the parks in the phone book and call to ask.)

5. As a class, study one of Colorado's national parks, monuments, forests, or grasslands. Prepare a presentation with details about the site's wildlife, landforms, major attractions, and other features. Use maps, illustrations, models, and any other display methods you can think of.

Books You and Your Teacher Might Enjoy

Elinor Bluemel. *The Opportunity School and Emily Griffith, Its Founder.* Denver: Green Mountain Press, 1970. This biography tells how one Denver schoolteacher made thousands of lives better.

Hal Borland. *High, Wide and Lonesome* and *Country Editor's Boy.* Philadelphia: J. B. Lippincott (1970). Boyhood memories of growing up on the high plains of eastern Colorado by one of Colorado's most celebrated writers.

Curt W. Buckholtz. *Rocky Mountain National Park: A History.* Niwot: University Press of Colorado, 1983. This well-illustrated book tells the story of Colorado's most popular tourist attraction.

Alan J. Kania. *John Otto of Colorado National Monument.* Boulder, CO: Roberts Rinehart Publishers, 1984. The strange story of the hermit of the spectacular canyons of the Colorado National Monument.

Ben B. Lindsey and Harvey J. O'Higgins. *The Beast.* New York: Doubleday, Page & Co., 1910. Judge Lindsey and a co-author wrote the classic account of political corruption in turn-of-the-century Colorado.

Enos A. Mills. *The Spell of the Rockies.* Boston: Houghton Mifflin, 1911. One of a dozen books on the wonders of the Colorado Rockies by the noted naturalist who led the crusade to establish Rocky Mountain National Park.

Thomas J. Noel and Barbara S. Norgren. *Denver: The City Beautiful and Its Architects.* Denver: Historic Denver, Inc., 1987 (1993 reprint). A richly illustrated overview of how Mayor Speer transformed a dusty, drab Denver into a City Beautiful.

Did You Know?

Arapaho Indians named the Never Summer Mountains in Rocky Mountain National Park. Their word, Ni-chebe-chii, *translates as "Never-No-Summer."*

Ripples from ancient inland oceans can be seen in the sandstone of the Colorado National Monument.

Denver's mountain parks include a ski area, Winter Park.

Judge Ben Lindsey established the world's first juvenile court in Denver in 1901.

CHAPTER FOURTEEN
The Automobile Age

For many Americans, life seemed to speed up after the arrival of the automobile. During the 1920s, the horseless carriage changed where people lived, worked, and played. Autos enabled Americans to move to new suburban homes and still work, go to school, and play in the city.

Cars cost a lot of money, but during the 1920s many people had money. World War I (1914–1918) had strengthened the Colorado economy. When the war began in Europe in 1914, Colorado farmers and ranchers found European markets for their crops and livestock. Colorado's mining industry also enjoyed new booms in copper, lead, zinc, tungsten, molybdenum, and coal.

When early automobiles broke down, motorists often had to push them into town for repairs. (Colorado Historical Society.)

World War I was also a tragic time. About 43,000 Coloradans joined the armed services, and 1,000 of them died. After the war ended on November 11, 1918, an even deadlier menace swept the globe — the 1918 worldwide influenza ("flu") epidemic. In ten months, it killed more than 500,000 Americans — 7,783 in Colorado. Every community in Colorado mourned its losses. One issue of the *Silverton Standard* (October 26) listed over 125 deaths. Rocky Ford, La Junta, and other towns banned public meetings. Throughout the state schools closed, and people stayed home. If they went out in public where they might catch the disease, they wore masks over their mouth and nose. Following the double tragedy of war and flu, the 1920s proved to be a safer, happier decade. Colorado developed a broad-based economy that included mining, agriculture, industry, and tourism. Most Coloradans received decent wages for a forty-hour work week, and many families saved money to buy their own cars and new homes.

Growth of Water Use

New housing subdivisions were made possible by new massive water projects. In the old days, people usually settled along creeks or rivers where water could be found. In the early 1900s, a new trend developed: Federal, state, and local governments began building dams and tunnels to deliver water to places people wanted to live.

People on the Western Slope benefited from the first major rearrangement of Colorado's waterways. This U.S. Reclamation Service project of 1909 funneled Gunnison River water through a tunnel under Vernal Mesa to the farms and ranches around Delta and Montrose. A few years later, water from the Roaring Fork River was diverted under Independence Pass to Twin Lakes and the Arkansas River to benefit sugar beet and melon growers in southeastern Colorado. Later, the Fryingpan-Arkansas project took even more water from the Aspen area to further increase the streamflow of the Arkansas River, which waters Leadville, Salida, Canon City, Pueblo, La Junta, Las Animas, Lamar, and many smaller towns.

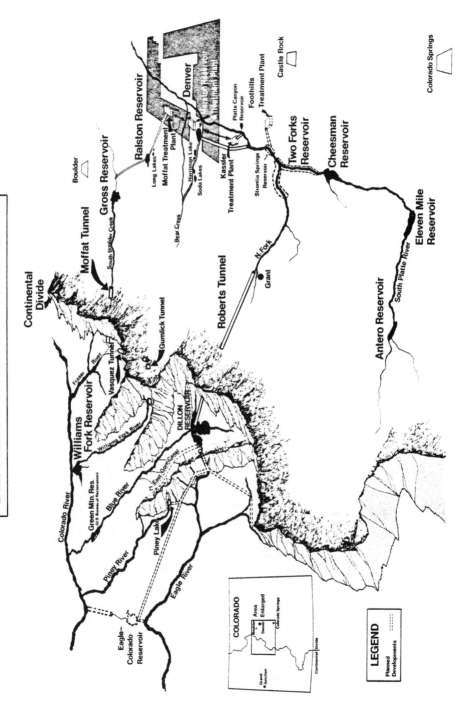

Water Supply System
DENVER WATER DEPARTMENT

Continental Divide

Moffat Tunnel

Gross Reservoir

Boulder

Ralston Reservoir

Long Lakes

Moffat Treatment Plant

Harriman Lake

Soda Lakes

Denver

Platte Canyon Reservoir

Foothills Treatment Plant

Castle Rock

Colorado Springs

Kassler Treatment Plant

Strontia Springs Reservoir

Two Forks Reservoir

Cheesman Reservoir

South Boulder Creek

Bear Creek

Gumlick Tunnel

Vasquez Tunnel

Fraser River

Williams Fork Reservoir

Roberts Tunnel

N. Fork

Grant

Eleven Mile Reservoir

Antero Reservoir

South Platte River

Colorado River

Green Mtn. Res.
(U.S. Bureau of Reclamation)

Williams Fork River

Blue River

DILLON RESERVOIR

Eagle-Colc Canal

Piney Lakes

Piney River

Eagle—Colorado Reservoir

Eagle River

COLORADO

Area Denver Enlarged

Grand Junction

Colorado Springs

Continental Divide

LEGEND

Planned Developments

The Colorado River, with headwaters in Rocky Mountain National Park, was dammed by the Big Thompson–Colorado project. This dam created Lake Granby and Shadow Mountain Reservoir for water storage. Water from these man-made lakes was channeled under the Continental Divide through a thirteen-mile tunnel that empties at Estes Park into the Big Thompson River. Since hydroelectric plants were a part of this $169 million project, electricity as well as water was provided for northeastern Colorado.

These water projects gave agriculture a big boost during the first twenty years of the twentieth century. Sugar beets and wheat became more important than mining to Colorado's economy.

Agriculture, like mining, had its ups and downs. Following the good years between 1900 and 1920, lower farm prices, the Great Depression, and the terrible drought of the 1930s left the eastern plains littered with ghost towns. Dry ditches, broken windmills, and the sun-baked skeletons of abandoned ranch houses are reminders that agriculture can be as risky as mining.

In a state where only a few inches of rain may fall in a year, water projects continue to be a key to Colorado's growth. These projects often have taken water from the sparsely populated

Irrigation allowed farmers in eastern Colorado to grow sugar beets by the trainload. Sugar became the state's number one crop during the early 1900s. (Photo by Roger Whitacre.)

Western Slope, where most of the precipitation falls, to the much more heavily populated Eastern Slope. Western Slope residents have resented losing water that is so important to their towns, mines, ranches, and fruit orchards. Over the years, major water projects grew more costly, and people began to criticize them. Many people began to question the wisdom of building bigger dams to rearrange natural waterways.

Prohibition

Water was not the only drink to interest Coloradans during the 1920s. In a statewide vote, a majority decided to outlaw, or prohibit, the sale of alcoholic beverages beginning January 1, 1916. A large minority voted against prohibition, and some of them continued to drink liquor regardless of the law. Leadville and other depressed mining towns discovered a new industry — making "moonshine" (illegal) whiskey. Old mines proved to be perfect hideouts for the stills used to make the liquor from sugar. Entire trainloads of beet sugar traveled to Leadville, and "Leadville Moon" became a famous Colorado brand. To deliver the moonshine, automobiles were fitted with big engines up front and secret trunks in the rear to carry heavy loads.

Growth of Technology

Another liquid that became precious during the early years of the twentieth century was oil. Colorado's first oil well had been dug near Florence in 1862, but the industry did not begin to boom until the 1920s, when the automobile age began to accelerate.

Electric radio sets and record players became popular during the 1920s. New dance crazes like the Charleston swept the country. To the distress of parents, young "swingers" danced late into the night to electronic music. The switch from silent movies to "talkies" added to the noise level.

The telephone, which had been around since the 1880s, became a common sight in homes. "Ma Bell," as Mountain States Telephone Company has been nicknamed, was formed in 1911 as a combination of various smaller, competing phone

Between 1900 and 1920, hundreds of little towns flourished on the Colorado high plains. Many of them built one-room schoolhouses, as did Lone Valley in Weld County, where this student escaped class on stilts. (Photo by Thomas J. Noel.)

KOA radio began broadcasting from Denver in 1924. After moving into this building at 1625 California Street and becoming part of the National Broadcasting Corporation, KOA's booming voice could be heard all over Colorado. (Denver Public Library.)

Florence, a small town on the Arkansas River, produced Colorado's first oil. When automobiles began consuming an endless amount of fuel, this oil town boomed. (Colorado Historical Society.)

companies. Today US West, the successor to Mountain Bell, is one of Colorado's biggest employers. Nearly every household — and many cars — has at least one telephone.

The radio, or "wireless," was introduced to Colorado in 1920 by Dr. W. D. Reynolds, a Colorado Springs physician. He started the first radio station in Colorado — KLZ. In 1924 the powerful KOA station began broadcasting from Denver, and by 1950 Colorado had thirty-four radio broadcasting stations. In 1952, the first television station, Channel 2, began operations in Denver. Channel 6, the pioneer public broadcasting and educational station, first went on the air in 1956. By the 1980s, cable television would become Colorado's most famous growth industry.

Bicycles

Bicycles had invaded Colorado long before automobiles did. The craze had begun back in 1879 when a Denver shopkeeper began selling bicycles. Few people bought these early "bone shakers." To attract customers, one bicycle salesman rented out a dance hall and offered riding lessons. He also tried to promote two-wheelers by bicycling around the city, but the police arrested him for scaring horses. These bikes had a front wheel six feet high and a tiny back wheel.

Only after the arrival of the "safety" bike (much like today's mountain bike, but without gears) with air-filled tires, good brakes, and ball-bearing wheels did bicycling become comfortable and popular. By 1900, the Denver Wheel Club boasted 25,000 members. Bicycle clubs across the state competed in century rides — pedaling 100 miles in a day.

A magazine claimed that "for the cyclist, exhalation and exhilaration take the place of depression and weakness." It added that the exercise would bring a sparkle to your eye and pink to your cheeks and would brush away "the cobwebs in the brain."

Bicyclists, after fighting potholes, mud, and dust, organized to pressure city councils, county commissioners, and the state legislature to build better roads. These improved highways paved the way for automobiles, which drove many two-wheelers off the road. In the 1920s, the car craze replaced the bicycle craze. Bicycles did not make a major comeback until the 1970s. Fat-tired mountain bikes became popular in the 1980s and 1990s and extended the love affair many Coloradans have with their bicycles.

Early Autos

The fast-growing popularity of automobiles in the early 1900s eventually doomed the old streetcar systems. Once Aspen, Boulder, Colorado Springs, Cripple Creek, Denver, Durango, Fort Collins, Grand Junction, Greeley, Pueblo, and Trinidad all had hometown streetcar companies. Horses pulled the first streetcars until they were replaced by electric trolleys. Streetcars enabled cities to grow outward into streetcar suburbs — neighborhoods along or near streetcar lines. Many of these early suburbs later were annexed to the mother city. Other suburbs, such as Aurora, Englewood, Littleton, and Lakewood in the Denver area, have remained independent towns. Although the growth of suburbs began with streetcars, automobiles greatly speeded up the process.

One of the first automobiles in Colorado was ordered by David W. Brunton, a Denver mining engineer. He had his electric car shipped to Denver from Boston. Brunton spent a whole day putting his car together, and on May 10, 1899, took it for a spin on the streets of Denver. Crowds followed the "horseless carriage" around to see how it would behave. How fast would it go? How did it stop? What droppings would it leave behind?

Automobile ads began appearing in the newspapers, such as this one in the *Denver Post* on May 1, 1900:

$750 LOCOMOBILE $750

The famous Steam Wagon. Cheap to buy.
Cheap to run. No noise, odor, or vibration.
Any person can run it from one to
40 miles per hour.

Dr. F. L. Bartlett of Canon City ordered an Oldsmobile in 1901. After finally putting together all the pieces shipped by railroad from Detroit, the doctor went to a nearby pasture to

Where automobile roads were poor or absent, cars were shipped by rail. These shiny new cars are about to get dusty on the dirt roads of Rifle. (Colorado Historical Society.)

practice starting, stopping, and steering. Then Canon City's main street was cleared of all horses so he could try out the first internal-combustion car in Colorado. Dr. Bartlett gave free rides to anyone brave enough to climb into his machine.

Improved Highways

With the increasing demand for better roads, the Colorado State Highway Commission was created in 1909. After the Federal Highway Act passed in 1916, Colorado received federal matching funds for road construction. By 1921 our state was spending over $10 million a year to build auto routes.

Towns began to measure their progress by how many miles of their roads were paved. Some farsighted people realized that automobiles would turn Colorado into a tourist haven. One of them was Spencer Penrose, who had made a fortune in Cripple Creek gold and retired to Colorado Springs. Penrose tried out a new car every year, spending as much as $5,000 per vehicle. With a stable full of horseless carriages, Penrose had a special interest in the good roads campaign. To prove that automobiles could master the mountains, Penrose built an auto road to the top of Pikes Peak.

As America's most famous mountain, Pikes Peak had long attracted tourists to Colorado Springs. Penrose's new road brought car caravans — groups of drivers eager to make the climb. To entertain his fellow automobile lovers, Penrose started the Pikes Peak Hill Climb on July 4, 1916. This demanding race still attracts daredevil drivers who roar up the 14,110-foot mountain faster than a mile a minute.

Auto Tourists

Automobiles allowed both residents and out–of–state visitors to tour Colorado in growing numbers. Soon tourism became a major part of Colorado's economy. Exploring ghost towns became a popular pastime after a woman from Boulder began prowling old mining towns in the 1920s. She was Muriel Sibell Wolle, an art professor at the University of Colorado at Boulder. Although rough auto trips into remote and rugged mountain

Millionaire Spencer Penrose introduced elephants, as well as automobiles, to Colorado Springs. He used this giant, "The Empress of India," to carry players around the golf course of his Broadmoor Hotel. (Colorado College Library.)

ghost towns terrified her, Wolle managed to visit every ghost town in Colorado. Once she reached a town, she read the town's old newspapers, asked old-timers to tell her about the town, and drew sketches of the decaying buildings and mines. She put all this together in *Stampede to Timberline*, a best-selling ghost town guidebook since its first publication in 1949.

Automobile tourists also headed for Colorado's many natural springs and their resorts. Eldorado Springs, Glenwood Springs, Idaho Springs, Ouray, Manitou Springs, and Steamboat Springs were among the most famous Colorado spas. To make touring inexpensive, many towns set up auto camps where motorists could camp out. These auto campers of the 1920s were the fore-runners of today's camper and mobile home travelers.

Boulder's Chautauqua Park, Canon City's Royal Gorge, Denver's Elitch's Gardens, Pueblo's Mineral Palace, and Wray's Flirtation Point lured vacationers. Yet the Rocky Mountains themselves remained the greatest attraction, a place to cool off with a snowball fight even in August.

The Air Age in Colorado

Soon after automobiles appeared, people began experimenting with wings and car engines. The auto age soon became the air age. Various Coloradans had been tinkering with airplanes for a decade before Denver built a municipal airport. What began as two dusty runways, a tiny terminal, and a windsock in 1929 became Stapleton International Airport. It was named for Denver Mayor Benjamin F. Stapleton, who built the airport.

Originally, pilots avoided Colorado for the same reason that the first railroad companies did — the mountains were too high and too dangerous to cross. Once again, Coloradans worked to attract a new transportation system. On May 31, 1925, 10,000 people gathered in a vacant field in east Denver. They cheered as a World War I biplane slowly lifted off the ground carrying 325 pounds of mail (13,000 letters). It was the first airmail flight out of Denver. Three years later, Western Air Express began carrying passengers as well as the mail.

Boulder's Chautauqua delighted early tourists. Now restored, it also captures modern visitors with its musical shows. (Boulder Historical Society.)

Frontier Airlines, once Colorado's largest home-state airline, began as Monarch Airlines. Monarch opened in 1946 with passenger flights from Denver to Durango. In 1950, it merged with Challenger Airlines of Denver and Arizona Airways to become Frontier Airlines. By 1980, Frontier was flying to a half-dozen Colorado towns and almost 100 cities in the United States, Canada, and Mexico.

Aspen Airways, Pioneer Airways, Rocky Mountain Airways, and Trans Colorado Airlines also connected Colorado cities before they were bought out by Continental or United, the two major Colorado carriers. A dozen national and international airlines now serve Colorado. The story of Robert F. Six is probably the best-known Colorado legend of the skyways. In 1936, Six took over Continental Airlines. When he retired forty-four years later as president of Continental, it had become one of America's biggest airlines and had moved its headquarters from Denver to Los Angeles.

Colorado's isolation from major cities and the East and West Coasts ended with the arrival of the airlines. Colorado is now only a few hours away from San Francisco and New York and twelve hours from any airport in the world. Stapleton Interna-

This daredevil pilot flying over Denver's Park Hill neighborhood in about 1919 had a bird's-eye view of then-undeveloped Aurora in the background. (Thomas J. Noel Collection.)

tional Airport had become one of the seven busiest airports in America by 1995, when it was replaced with Denver International Airport.

Airplanes and automobiles have largely solved Colorado's old problem of geographic isolation. Colorado is a large state whose long distances as well as high mountains have challenged travelers. Thanks in part to the automobile and the airplane, Colorado has become a popular place both to visit and to live, connected by quick airline flights to the rest of the world.

QUESTIONS

1. Why are water projects such as damming and tunneling so important in Colorado?
2. List some of the projects that have shifted Western Slope water to other areas of Colorado. Do any of these projects affect your water supply?
3. List three changes in communication and three changes in transportation that affected Colorado in the 1920s.
4. What are the leading tourist attractions in your county?
5. Why were both railroads and airlines slow to put routes through Colorado?
6. What did streetcars and automobiles have to do with the growth of suburbs?

ACTIVITIES

1. As a class project, research your town's water resources. Where does your water come from? How is it stored? Organize a class trip to check out your water supply.
2. The automobile greatly affected the state of Colorado. Look at advertisements for automobiles in old newspapers. They show the models, prices, and dealerships for automobiles in your community.
3. Research early automobiles. How did they run? Draw diagrams to compare the electric auto with the internal-combustion car.
4. Find out if there is a monument in your community dedicated to World War I soldiers. If so, visit it and draw it or

write a description of it. Do research in old newspapers to find out how many local soldiers fought in that war.

5. Visit your local museum or library to find old advertisements of Colorado tourist attractions in the 1920s. How do these advertisements compare with today's ads?

Books You and Your Teacher Might Enjoy

Colorado Department of Transportation. *The High Road.* Denver: Colorado Department of Transportation, 1976. A brief illustrated overview of Colorado highway construction.

Jeff Miller. *Stapleton International Airport.* Boulder, Pruett Publishing, 1983. Between 1929 and 1995, this airport welcomed millions of travelers to Colorado.

Marshall Sprague. *Greetings from Colorado: A Glimpse at the Past Through Post Cards.* Portland, OR: Graphic Arts Center, 1987. This book shows the lovely postcards that attracted visitors to Colorado.

Did You Know?

Sixty-nine percent of Colorado's rain falls on the Western Slope.

Colorado has the highest paved auto route in the country — the road to the top of Mount Evans.

Work began on Interstate 25 in 1948 and on Interstate 70 in 1957.

The Eisenhower Tunnel on Interstate 70 is 1.693 miles long and is 9.1 miles shorter than the old Loveland Pass route.

CHAPTER FIFTEEN
The Depression, Recovery, and Growth

For every economic boom there has been a bust. Colorado's silver boom ended with the Panic of 1893 and the depression that followed. The good times of the 1920s ended with the Great Depression of the 1930s, which began with the 1929 New York Stock Market crash. The crash itself had been caused by reckless spending and borrowing. Hoping to make big profits, people borrowed money to buy stock, or part ownership, in companies. When many of the companies failed, the stockholders lost everything. Stock values fell, companies went out of business, and banks failed. In the depression that followed, millions of people in America lost their jobs. Recovery came very slowly and only after the federal government spent billions of dollars to put people back to work.

Uncle Sam, as Americans called the U.S. government, became more important to Coloradans than state or local governments, which did little to relieve the problems of the Great Depression. Local politicians let Uncle Sam rescue the unemployed, hungry, and homeless.

Even people who had saved their money in banks were hurt by the Great Depression. In Colorado, 66 of the state's 237 banks failed during the 1930s. For a time, all banks were closed so that the federal government could determine which ones had enough money to reopen. After the stronger banks reopened, the federal government promised to insure deposits. This program, the Federal Deposit Insurance Corporation, is still in effect. It means that if a bank fails, the government will pay people whatever they had put in that bank, up to $100,000.

"Hey, brother, can you spare a dime?" This was the 1930s plea of busted Coloradans, such as this old cowpoke. (Photo by Glen Cuerden.)

Even worse than losing stocks and bank savings, many people lost their jobs. By 1933, about a quarter of all Americans were out of work, including some 65,000 Coloradans. No longer did people talk about buying cars and new houses; they just hoped for enough to eat. They hunted jackrabbits for stews, captured coyotes for the $5 bounty, and panned for gold.

Young people who could once afford to rent their own apartments moved back into their parents' homes. Grandparents, aunts, and uncles also moved in with relatives, and everyone worked to make ends meet. Many families planted vegetable gardens and raised rabbits, chickens, pigs, and goats to help put food on the table.

In depression-hit neighborhoods such as The Grove in Pueblo and Globeville in Denver, children crawled under parked railroad grain cars to drill holes in the car bottoms. They let the wheat run into bags and took it home to their mothers for bread making.

The depression was especially hard on retired older people without families to help them. The poorest of them could be seen poking around in garbage cans for food and clothing. If they had a little money, these senior citizens shopped at the many pawn shops, flea markets, and secondhand stores that opened during the 1930s. To help the elderly poor, the state of Colorado set up an old-age pension (savings) plan. It paid needy persons aged sixty or over $45 a month, using money from taxes on liquor (which became legal again in 1934) and other items. A few years later, President Franklin D. Roosevelt and Congress set up the federal Social Security system to aid the old and the disabled.

African Americans and Mexican Americans also suffered. For example, in Five Points, Denver's black neighborhood, Benny Hooper turned his nightclub into a soup line. People who had dined and danced at Hooper's Casino in the 1920s lined up there in the 1930s for jackrabbit stew. Benny ran the stew line with the same hospitality that had made his Welton Street nightclub one of the hottest jazz joints of the 1920s.

Agriculture

Farmers were hit hardest by the depression. They found that raising their crops and animals cost more than these products earned on the market. Apples that once had sold for $1.45 per bushel now brought only 42 cents per bushel. Pigs that had sold for $12 in 1929 sold for $3 at the bottom of the depression in

Junk collectors haunted Colorado's cities during the Great Depression. They collected old bottles, metal cans, cardboard, newspapers, and other trash for recycling. (The Denver Post.)

1933. Wheat prices fell from 96 cents a bushel to 37 cents. Many people lost their farms and moved into cities.

To survive, farmers began to work together. During the 1920s, groups such as the Monte Vista Potato Growers' Cooperative and the United Fruit Growers Association of Palisade had shown the advantages of cooperation. Soon farmers all over the state began to form co-ops (short for "cooperatives"). These organizations enabled farmers to pool their money to buy farm machinery and build grain elevators that could be shared. Today, as you travel around Colorado, look for the co-op grain elevators. They are the tallest landmarks in many farm towns.

Farmers also continued to use dryland farming methods. They grew crops that did not need much water such as winter wheat. To help save what little water there was, they plowed deeply and weeded carefully. Using these methods, and taking advantage of winter snows, dryland farmers could prosper without irrigation. Colorado State University at Fort Collins helped farmers by developing drought-resistant varieties of wheat, corn, and other crops.

Even the best dryland farming techniques, however, were of little use in the drought and dust storms that swept the Great

Even this tiny girl on a South Platte Valley farm went to work during the Great Depression to help feed her family. (Colorado Historical Society.)

Some Hispanic families got through hard times by making their own homes out of adobe. Hispanics also gathered their own firewood and piñon nuts, hunted deer, elk, and rabbits, and made their own bread. Note the homemade oven beside this adobe house near Trinidad. (Colorado Historical Society.)

Fruit growers on the Western Slope weathered the lean years by forming co-ops to share expenses and promote their apples and peaches. (Photo by Thomas J. Noel.)

Plains during the 1930s. LeRoy Hafen, a leading Colorado historian, wrote in his journal on April 10, 1935: "We had our second dust storm over Denver. It was almost suffocating. Part of the night I slept with a wet towel over my face to strain the dust." Southeastern Colorado saw some of the worst storms. One person who witnessed one wrote, "Great dust storms are at once magnificent and terrifying. They move forward in sky-high walls, black and ominous, and plunge the land into darkness." If anything green survived the drought and the "black blizzards," it often was eaten by the grasshopper plagues that added to farmers' woes during the 1930s.

In spite of these hardships, men and women of the region kept their humor. One farmer commented, "Part of my farm blew off into Kansas yesterday, so I guess I'll have to pay taxes there, too." Another said to a stranger who commented that a cloud in the sky might mean rain: "Hope so, not so much for my sake as the children's. I've seen rain."

Colorado, along with the rest of America, sank into poverty. In such troubled times, it is comforting to at least have someone to pin the blame on: Angry voters threw the Republicans out of office and elected mostly Democrats during the 1930s.

The New Deal

In 1932, Franklin D. Roosevelt, a Democrat, was elected President of the United States. Roosevelt promised a "new deal" for the poor, the elderly, farmers, and owners of small businesses. He believed recovery from the depression was possible only if the federal government helped people.

Democrat Edward P. Costigan was chosen for one of Colorado's U.S. Senate seats. He was a small, dark man whose mother was Spanish. This made him popular with Colorado's Mexican American voters. Costigan, a lawyer educated at Harvard University, entered politics after being beaten up for complaining about illegal voting. As a result, Costigan became a champion of reform. He worked with Judge Ben Lindsey, ran for governor of Colorado on the Progressive Party ticket in 1912, and helped Josephine Roche run for governor in 1934. In 1932, Senator

Costigan worked for Roosevelt's election. The New Deal helped Americans, including Coloradans, in many ways. For example, miners were aided by the Silver Purchase Act of 1934. Under this law, the federal government began buying up all the silver that could be mined for $1.29 an ounce. In addition, the government began buying gold at $35.00 an ounce. Old mines reopened and miners went back to work. Two New Deal programs that had a huge impact on Colorado's recovery were the Works Progress Administration and the Civilian Conservation Corps.

Dust storms nearly buried small towns in southeastern Colorado. Imagine what this 1934 black blizzard did to Burlington! (Denver Public Library.)

The WPA

The largest New Deal program, the Works Progress Administration (WPA), spent over $110 million in Colorado and provided work for about 150,000 people. The unemployed were hired to build roads and bridges, schools and libraries, ball fields and swimming pools, sewers and airports. A new high school in Clifton, a giant water tower in Walsh, and a golf course in Greeley were among the thousands of WPA projects in Colorado. The WPA also set up a drama program for out-of-work actors,

Civilian Conservation Corps (CCC) teenagers constructed the outdoor amphitheater at Red Rocks. It is Colorado's most unusual and beautiful theater. (Thomas J. Noel Collection.)

actresses, and playwrights and created a Federal Writers Project that employed out-of-work writers to produce a WPA guidebook to Colorado.

The CCC

Young men aged eighteen to twenty-five found jobs with the Civilian Conservation Corps (CCC). The CCC paid unemployed youths $30 per month (with $25 of that sent home to their families) to work on outdoor projects. The CCC "boys" built hiking trails and campgrounds, fought forest fires, built dams, and did many other jobs on public lands. Red Rocks outdoor theater near Denver, the Flagstaff Mountain road near Boulder, a dormitory for Ute Indians at Ignacio, a gym at Hugo, and the Winter Park Ski Area were among the many CCC projects in Colorado. Whenever you enjoy the outdoors in Colorado, you may be fishing in a lake that CCC workers dammed, camping at a shelter they erected, or driving over backroads they built.

Colorado ranchers were enthusiastic about another New Deal idea that used CCC labor. The Taylor Grazing Act was named for U.S. Representative Edward Taylor of Glenwood Springs. Under this act, livestock owners were charged a small fee for grazing their animals on federal lands. The fee was used to build watering places and to fence and maintain the land, often with the help of CCC workers. Colorado rancher Farrington R. Carpenter of Hayden went to Washington to get the grazing plan started. Thanks in part to Taylor and Carpenter, this federal program still works today.

World War II and Recovery

Although the federal government spent billions to end the Great Depression, not everybody found work. The economy did not really recover until the United States entered World War II in 1941. American workers made weapons and supplies, not only for our own armed forces but also for those of Great Britain, France, Russia, and our other allies. Colorado beef, lamb, and

With fathers off to war, many young-sters helped raise cattle and sheep to feed World War II troops fighting in Europe and in the Pacific. (Amon Carter Museum.)

pork, as well as wheat and sugar, fed people all over the world during wartime. Farmers and ranchers began to thrive for the first time since World War I.

With 138,832 Coloradans fighting in World War II, manpower became short at home. Companies began to use one of America's most overlooked resources — womanpower. Women worked in factories, ran farms and ranches, drove buses, and managed businesses. Even the old superstition that women in mines would bring bad luck proved false. The war gave women a chance to prove that they could do "man's work."

Wartime shortages also taught Coloradans to recycle everything from car tires to newspapers. Four-H clubs, scout troops, church groups, and civic clubs supported the war effort by collecting millions of tons of old newspapers, scrap iron and steel, rubber, tin cans, bottles, kitchen grease, and other recyclable items that had been thrown away before. Families learned to grow their own vegetables in "Victory Gardens."

World War II changed Colorado's economy. The minerals vanadium, molybdenum, and tungsten were mined to help make steel stronger and lighter. The Climax Molybdenum Mine near Leadville became the biggest and richest mine in all of Colorado's history. After the United States introduced the nuclear age by bombing Hiroshima and Nagasaki in Japan, the Western Slope became a prime region for mining and processing radium and uranium, minerals used for nuclear weapons and power plants. Unfortunately, the mining, milling, and processing of these radioactive materials have left hazardous wastes that can cause health problems.

Military bases and hospitals built during the two world wars are still very important to Colorado's economy. Lowry Air Force Base in Denver did not close until 1994, and Fitzsimons Army Medical Center in Aurora is still open. These and other military installations pumped millions of dollars into Colorado by hiring local people and buying local supplies.

Spin-offs from other military projects have changed Colorado in many ways. Camp Hale near Leadville is a good example. During World War II, the U.S. Army trained soldiers in

Some Colorado mines reopened in the 1930s and 1940s when Uncle Sam began paying a good price for gold, silver, and certain other minerals. Dredge mining around Breckenridge left miles of rock piles and this mining monster, which you can still see in French Gulch. (Photo by Thomas J. Noel.)

winter warfare there. For fun on weekends, the soldiers skied around the old silver city of Aspen. After the war, some of these ski troopers remembered the sparkling powder snow and the scenic slopes surrounding the quaint old mining town. They came back and helped convert a near ghost town into the world-famous Aspen ski resort. Later, some of the Camp Hale veterans helped lay out some of the thirty other ski areas that now make Colorado America's most popular spot for winter sports.

Colorado Springs

Colorado Springs is a good example of the growth created by World War II. Thanks to military installations, the Springs replaced Pueblo as Colorado's second-largest city. Colorado Springs had been founded by General William J. Palmer and the Denver & Rio Grande Railroad. Located at the base of Pikes Peak, the town for years had attracted many English tourists and settlers. It also had become a haven for many health seekers with tuberculosis, asthma, and other lung diseases. Their doctors had recommended Colorado for its high, dry, sunny climate.

Over the years, Colorado Springs became known for Colorado College and the Broadmoor Hotel, Colorado's finest resort to this day. Spencer Penrose spent millions to transform the old Broadmoor Dairy and Casino into a vacationer's dream, complete with a golf course, ski area, ice-skating rink, and zoo. After a monkey bit one of the hotel guests, the zoo was moved to nearby Cheyenne Mountain, where it thrives to this day.

During World War II, Fort Carson Army Post and Peterson Air Force Base became huge military bases and brought thousands of newcomers to Colorado Springs. After the war the Springs also became the home of the U.S. Air Force Academy and of the North American Air Defense Command, where Canada and the United States share a space-age military operations center.

The Postwar Boom

The federal government's large projects and paychecks brought Colorado out of the depression during the 1940s. After World War II ended in 1945, many army and air force veterans who had been stationed in Colorado during the war decided to move here. Some settled in Aurora, a small farm town whose population in 1940 was 3,437. By the 1980s, Aurora had become Colorado's third-largest city.

World War II trans-formed the sleepy farm village of Aurora. Thousands of jobs at Buckley Air Base, Lowry Air Force Base, and Fitzsimons Army Hospital inspired new housing subdivisions in the 1940s and 1950s. Hoffman Heights, the first big subdivision in what is now Colorado's third-largest city, is below this B-36 bomber. (Thomas J. Noel Collection.)

Lakewood in Jefferson County is another modern-day boom town. During World War II, a giant weapons factory was established there. After the war ended, this complex became the Federal Center, housing many of the government offices that have given the Denver metropolitan area the nickname of "Little Washington, D.C." Thanks in part to thousands of government jobs at the Federal Center, Lakewood has grown into the fourth-largest city in Colorado.

Since 1945, Colorado has become one of America's fastest-growing states. After relatively slow growth between the Crash of 1893 and World War II, our state has boomed in recent decades, as the following table shows:

Colorado Population

1900	539,700	1950	1,325,089
1910	799,024	1960	1,753,947
1920	939,629	1970	2,207,259
1930	1,035,791	1980	2,888,964
1940	1,123,296	1990	3,294,394

By the 1960s, newcomers outnumbered natives in many areas of the state. After two world wars and the Great Depression, our state has enjoyed a boom similar to the gold and silver booms of the 1870s and 1880s. As we shall see, however, not everyone has shared in the postwar prosperity.

QUESTIONS

1. List three ways that Coloradans of the 1930s helped themselves and their families cope with the depression.
2. What was the CCC? How did it open up Colorado's backcountry for recreation?
3. What New Deal program continues to help elderly and disabled Americans today?
4. Discuss two important ways that Colorado farmers survived the depression years.
5. How did World War II speed up Colorado's growth?
6. Why is Denver sometimes called "Little Washington, D.C."?
7. Calculate the percentage growth of Colorado's population for each decade between 1900 and 1990. In which decade did the greatest growth occur?

ACTIVITIES

1. Ask some of the older people in your town or your grandparents about their lives during the Great Depression.
2. Look around your town for bridges, schools, parks, and other public works. See how many have a WPA (Works Progress Administration) sign on them.
3. Call the oldest bank in your community and ask if your class can take a field trip there. You might ask the bank president how his or her bank would deal with another depression.
4. Make a chart showing your town's growth since 1900.
5. List some of the federal offices in your county. You can find them in the phone book under "United States Government."

6. Check into your local recycling programs. How many things that people usually throw away can be collected and sold for cash?

Books You and Your Teacher Might Enjoy

Stephen H. Leonard. *Trials and Triumphs: A Colorado Portrait of the Great Depression, With FSA Photographs.* Niwot: University Press of Colorado, 1993. Lively text and 150 photos capture the impact of the Great Depression on Coloradans.

Marshall Sprague. *Newport in the Rockies: The Life and Good Times of Colorado Springs.* Athens, OH: Swallow Press, 1971.

The WPA Guide to 1930s Colorado. Lawrence: University Press of Kansas, 1987 (reprint of *Colorado: A Guide to the Highest State*, 1941). This guidebook was compiled by workers in the Writers' Program of the Works Progress Administration.

Did You Know?

The 1930s Dust Bowl blew farmers off of what are now the Pawnee and Comanche National Grasslands.

"Brother, Can You Spare a Dime?" became a theme song for the Great Depression.

For farmers, the Great Depression began early — in the 1920s.

During World War II, women found work in factories, mines, and other traditionally male workplaces.

Lincoln School in Sterling, 1942. Fifth-grade boys dug vegetables, and fifth-grade girls helped sort vegetables. (Denver Public Library.)

CHAPTER SIXTEEN
Economic and Ethnic Diversity

Economic Diversity

At age seventeen, Charles Boettcher left Germany for America. He was not alone. Germans were the single largest foreign-born group settling in Colorado before 1900. He hopped off the Union Pacific train at Cheyenne, Wyoming, for a visit with his brother, Herman, who ran a hardware store. Herman put his little brother to work in the store, paying him $2 a week and letting him sleep under the counter at night.

When Colorado began to grow in the 1870s, the Boettcher brothers decided to open branch stores there. Charles built the two-story brick store that still stands at Pearl and Broadway in Boulder. A few years later, Charles moved to Leadville and started another hardware store. By 1890, he had moved to Denver to start still another branch business.

Boettcher was smart. He put his money into many different businesses. He had seen his friends put all their money into one mine, one business, or one railroad. When hard times came, as in 1893 and 1929, they lost everything. For Boettcher, however, if one enterprise failed, he still had the others. Boettcher's approach became Colorado's best example of economic diversity. He created the biggest and richest business empire in Colorado history.

Boettcher loved work more than play, but his wife, Fannie, finally talked him into taking a vacation in Germany. Charles soon got bored with travel and took his family on a tour of sugar beet farms. There he saw how the Germans grew the beets and made sugar out of them. Then, according to one story, he made

Charles Boettcher came from Germany as a teenager. He became Colorado's best example of a well-diversified businessperson. His multiple investments in sugar, cement, electric power, transportation, ranching, and a dynamite factory helped him to ride out economic ups and downs. (Thomas J. Noel Collection.)

Charles Boettcher avoided risky investments in mining but sold supplies to miners and others in this Leadville branch of his hardware company. His slogan was "Hardware. Hard Goods. Hard Cash." (Colorado Historical Society.)

Fannie empty her suitcases so he could fill them with sugar beet seed. He took the seeds back to Colorado and, with some friends, started the Great Western Sugar Beet Company in 1900. Soon Great Western had fields and factories all over the state.

When Great Western was building its Loveland plant, Boettcher made an inspection tour. He found that cement for the new plant had been brought from Germany. His engineers told him they had tried American-made cement, but it was not as strong. Charles Boettcher was upset. Why pay such high prices and freight fares from Europe when all the materials needed to make cement — lime, silica, and alumina — were available in Colorado? Within a matter of months, he had set up his own cement company. It evolved into one of Colorado's largest firms — Ideal Basic Industries.

Boettcher invested in railroads, streetcars, the Public Service Company, Capitol Life Insurance Company, meatpacking, cattle ranching, a dynamite factory, and dozens of other firms. The Crash of 1929, which bankrupted some of Colorado's millionaires, did not destroy Boettcher's empire. Although some of his various businesses sank during the depression, others rose in value.

One of Boettcher's purchases was Denver's grand old hotel, the Brown Palace, where he lived until his death in 1948. Although he owned the hotel, Charles refused to buy his soft drinks there. "Too expensive," he said, and walked across the street to a public pop machine.

Boettcher made his millions in Colorado and he and his son, Claude, decided to return some of it to Coloradans. They created the Boettcher Foundation, which has given more than $100 million to Coloradans for college scholarships, hospitals, museums, and other worthy causes. Claude Boettcher's house in Denver was donated to the state as the Governor's Mansion. The family's summer home on Lookout Mountain now houses the Jefferson County Nature Center. The Boettcher Foundation also has given over a million dollars to the Colorado Historical Society, which has museums in Denver, Georgetown, Fort Garland, Fort Vasquez, Leadville, Montrose, Pueblo, and Trinidad.

Boettcher and his partners made the Great Western Sugar Company one of Colorado's largest employers. Migrant laborers from Russia, Germany, Japan, and Mexico were among the thousands who worked in sugar beet fields. (Library of Congress.)

Charles Boettcher is just one example of how smart business-people brought new jobs into Colorado by keeping the economy diverse. Coloradans learned the hard way that relying on only one source of income is dangerous. Mining collapsed in the 1890s, and farming failed in the 1930s. Thanks to the efforts of Boettcher and others like him, Coloradans now work at a wide variety of jobs.

New Businesses

Since 1950, Colorado has attracted many new businesses. Kodak, the camera and film makers, built a $100 million plant at Windsor near Greeley in the 1970s. Martin Marietta, an aerospace firm, moved to Littleton in 1955. By the 1980s, Martin Marietta had 7,500 employees who have built Titan missiles and space satellites and helped put Americans on the moon. The Storage Technology Corporation of Louisville became Colorado's fastest-growing industry in the 1960s. It was founded by four former IBM employees who set up the business in a tiny office above a Boulder restaurant. By 1980,

Martin Marietta, an aerospace firm, made Titan missiles at its plant near Littleton. (Martin Marietta Astronautics.)

Storage Technology had over 7,000 employees designing and selling computer systems.

King Soopers grocery stores are another example of how small Colorado businesses have flourished. In 1946, Lloyd J. King came back to Denver after serving in the navy during World War II. He converted a small meat market in Arvada into the first King Soopers store. By 1980, his company had become

Aspen, a dying silver town, opened a ski lift in the 1930s and emerged as a major winter resort. The many empty lots in this 1950s view from Aspen Mountain have filled up with million-dollar homes and resorts. (Amon Carter Museum.)

one of Colorado's leading employers, with stores throughout the state.

Jesse Shwayder, whose Jewish family left Poland for Central City, started making Samsonite luggage in Denver in 1910. With the increase in travel and tourism, Samsonite Corporation has added factories in ten other countries and sells its suitcases all over the globe. When someone asked Shwayder why he didn't move his headquarters to a bigger city, he said, "I'd rather make a dollar in Denver than three dollars in New York."

Tourism, another major industry, has become a year-round moneymaker. In the old days, tourists came to Colorado only during the summer. Now winter and spring skiing bring millions of guests to "Ski Country, U.S.A.," and fall aspen tours lure visitors during September and October. In the 1940s, an advertising campaign urged tourists to "spend one more day in Colorado." In the 1970s, the average tourist stayed about eight days. By the 1990s, skiing was attracting more than 10 million skiers a year.

Ethnic Diversity

Visitors to Colorado have found an ethnically diverse population as well as a diverse economy. Native American peoples were joined first by Hispanics and then by European Americans. Later these Coloradans were joined by African Americans and Asian Americans.

Hispanics

Spanish-surnamed people were the first Europeans to explore and settle in Colorado. They gave the state its name. Yet despite their proud heritage and their position as Colorado's largest ethnic group, they sometimes have been treated as second-class citizens by the Anglo (English-speaking) majority.

Since the 1960s, Hispanics have been fighting hard to improve their lives in Colorado. Among the more militant Chicanos has been Rodolfo "Corky" Gonzales, who was born in Denver in 1928. As a young man, Gonzales was a professional boxer. Since the 1960s, however, he has been fighting for *La Raza* (the Hispanic people). Gonzales is also a poet. He wrote about the experiences of his people in "I Am Joaquin":

> Here I stand,
> poor in money,
> arrogant with pride,
> bold with machismo,
> rich in courage and
> wealthy in spirit and faith.
>
> My knees are caked with mud.
> My hands calloused from the hoe.

Margarita Garcia tempts a passerby with sweets at La Popular, 2012 Larimer Street in Denver. Mexican food has become a favorite of many Coloradans. Salsa has replaced ketchup as the best-selling sauce. (Photo by Roger Whitacre.)

I have made the Anglo rich,
yet equality is but a word —
the Treaty of Hidalgo has been broken
and is but another treacherous promise.

Hispanics helped create Colorado. Nine Hispanics served in the early state legislature, representing southern Colorado. Later, when Spanish-surnamed people began to leave southern Colorado and settle in the north, they lost political representation. Today about 75 percent of the state's Hispanics live in the Denver, Pueblo, Greeley, and Colorado Springs areas. In 1990, 107,382 Spanish-surnamed people lived in Denver, forming more than one-fifth of the city's population. Statewide, some

310,000 Spanish-surnamed Coloradans make up about 15 percent of the population.

Among many successful Hispanic professional and businesspeople is Cecil J. Hernandez. In the 1950s he started a one-man cabinet company in Denver. By 1980, Hernandez's Mastercraft Cabinet Company had become the largest minority-owned business in Colorado, with two shops in Denver, one in Loveland, and another in Phoenix, Arizona. Mastercraft cabinets are sold all over the West.

Hispanics are learning the keys to economic and political opportunity — getting an education, registering to vote, and voting. Some of the first Hispanics to fight for their rights lived in Center, in the San Luis Valley, where they ran for positions on the town council and the school board. Elsewhere in the valley, people worked to bridge cultural gaps. For example, the Cultural Resource Center at Alamosa provided bilingual and bicultural materials for schools. During the 1980s, Hispanics served as mayors of Pueblo and of Denver. As Colorado's largest and fastest-growing minority, Hispanics look forward to more political and economic gains.

African Americans

Most of Colorado's 110,000 black residents live in Denver. This African American community is one of the most prosperous and best educated in America, with an income higher than the average for all Americans. Sixty-eight percent of Denver's blacks own their own homes, and almost half own two cars. The average black in Denver has had at least one year of college.

African Americans have had to struggle to do well. For years they were concentrated in the old Five Points neighborhood just northeast of downtown Denver. In the 1950s, however, some blacks began to move across Colorado Boulevard into the Park Hill neighborhood, which has beautiful, tree-shaded homes. Whites who were afraid of these new people tried to sell their houses. Sometimes many houses on a block would have "For Sale" signs at one time. Because blacks and whites did not know or trust each other, they were afraid to live near each other.

Church groups in Park Hill decided to do something. They helped set up what has become the Greater Park Hill Community, Inc. This group introduced black newcomers to the white residents. They held block parties, gave picnics, put out a newspaper, and helped people to realize that whites and blacks could live in the same block, go to the same schools, use the same playgrounds, and pray in the same churches.

Park Hill has become a success story. Blacks call it "Struggle Hill" because of their struggle to get there. Whites call it proof that Americans can rise above the racial prejudices of the past. Nationally, Park Hill is called one of the best-integrated neighborhoods in the United States. In Denver, where the majority of the residents are white, the election of an Hispanic and then a black mayor in recent years suggests that it is one of America's more tolerant big cities.

Japanese Coloradans

Few Japanese people came to Colorado before 1900. After 1900, they came to work in the sugar beet fields of Charles Boettcher and others. Most of these newcomers settled near sugar beet farms in the Arkansas and South Platte river valleys.

Wages were low, but the Japanese workers carefully saved their money. Entire families spent the day planting, weeding, and harvesting sugar beets, but early in the morning and late at night they also tended their own vegetable patches. Slowly, many Japanese saved enough cash to buy their own farms or to move into towns and start small businesses.

Their hopes for acceptance were shattered in 1941. Japan bombed Pearl Harbor in Hawaii, the Pacific base for the United States Navy. As a result, the United States declared war on Japan and entered World War II. At that time nearly 3,000 Japanese Americans were living in Colorado. Their number was soon to grow because the U.S. government, in a wartime panic, rounded up all the Japanese people in California, Oregon, and Washington. Although these people were American citizens, some people thought they would help Japan attack the United States.

The Japanese Americans were sent to relocation camps away from the West Coast. One camp, Amache, was built near the little town of Granada along the Arkansas River in southeastern Colorado. Tiny babies and very old ladies were among the 10,331 Japanese Americans imprisoned in this remote corner of southeastern Colorado. Overnight, Amache became one of the largest towns in Colorado, but it lasted only a little over three years.

These Japanese Americans and their parents, like Native Americans a century earlier, were forced onto reservations. (Thomas J. Noel Collection.)

To prove their loyalty to the United States, many of the men at Amache volunteered to fight in World War II. The Japanese American combat troops earned more medals for bravery than any other group fighting in World War II. Many of them proved their loyalty with their lives. Others at Amache worked for the Red Cross or for the farm program, which produced 3.3 million pounds of vegetables in 1944.

Some Coloradans wanted to lock up the Japanese people in Colorado with those from the West Coast in the Amache concentration camp. Governor Ralph Carr, however, pointed out that they were loyal Americans, just like the German Americans who were loyal to the United States and not to the German leader, Adolf Hitler. Governor Carr refused to jail Japanese Coloradans, and after the war the Japanese honored the governor who had defended them. They put a statue of Governor Carr in Sakura Square, the center of Denver's Japan Town.

Prejudice and Ignorance

The illegal imprisonment of Japanese American citizens during World War II is a reminder that ignorance and prejudice are an ongoing threat. Prejudice based on ignorance has led some Coloradans to think they are better than other residents. Such discrimination was aimed at the first Coloradans — the Native Americans. They welcomed newcomers only to be driven out of Colorado by the whites or killed. Only the two small Ute reservations in the southwest corner of Colorado remain Indian territory today.

Terrible treatment also chased Chinese workers away from many early mining camps and from Denver, where anti-Chinese feelings led to a major race riot in 1880. Because the Chinese workers worked for low wages and supposedly took jobs away from whites, they were beaten and, in some cases, hanged — simply because of their race.

Prejudice reached an all-time high in Colorado during the 1920s. Exploiting ignorance and fear, the Ku Klux Klan signed up one of every eleven Coloradans. The Klan is a group of people who believe that whites of northern European background are superior to other races and ethnic groups. With this large membership, the Klan became powerful enough to elect a governor of Colorado, a mayor of Denver, and a U.S. senator.

Dr. John Galen Locke, a Denver physician, presided as Grand Dragon, or leader, of the Colorado Klan. Led by Locke, Klan members paraded in their spooky white sheets with hoods to hide their faces. While attacking Native Americans and Hispanic Americans who had been in Colorado for generations, the KKK bragged that its members were "100 percent American." The Klan attacked Jews, Catholics, Hispanics, and newcomers from Europe, as well as African Americans.

The KKK nightmare soon ended, and the Klan was only a skeleton organization by 1930. Yet ignorance and prejudice still haunt Colorado. In 1992 and 1993, for instance, Klan members tried to disrupt the Martin Luther King holiday festivities in Denver. Fortunately, most people ignored this effort to introduce violence. Why ruin a peaceful parade to honor the Reverend King, a black minister who preached nonviolent resistance to ignorance and prejudice? Prejudice, as King noted, is prejudging people you do not know.

A Diverse State

All Coloradans trace their roots to foreign lands. So we are many people — Indian, Hispanic, African American, and Asian American, but also French and English, German and Irish. Some of us are Jews from Russia, others are Moslems from the Middle East. Italians, Greeks, and Slavs have settled in the Highest State, as have Swiss and Scandinavians. People have come to Colorado from all corners of the world.

Southeast Asians have been among the latest immigrants. They started coming in the 1970s, fleeing wars in Vietnam, Laos, and Cambodia. After getting used to a land with both snow and cactus and with large, crowded cities as well as wide-open, empty spaces, many of these people have come to like Colorado. By studying hard in school and working hard in jobs, many are doing well in America. These Asian Americans, like early immigrants, usually have found that Coloradans are big-hearted, friendly people. Most Coloradans realize that different people, like different jobs, make our state richer and more interesting.

QUESTIONS

1. Why did Charles Boettcher start many different kinds of businesses?
2. What are the advantages of a diversified economy?
3. What different kinds of jobs are done in your county? Would you say it has a diversified economy?
4. Can you trace the different ethnic and national groups in your family? What ethnic groups live in your town?
5. Was the U.S. government justified in locking up the Japanese at Camp Amache near Granada, Colorado, during World War II?
6. What makes Denver's Park Hill neighborhood special?

ACTIVITIES

1. Take a tour of the biggest factories in your county. Ask the president of the factory if the company has diversified over the years.
2. Visit your town hall or chamber of commerce and ask the officials what the biggest tourist attractions are in your community.
3. Take a bus tour of the richest and the poorest neighborhoods in your area. What differences do you see?
4. Ask your parents about the countries from which your ancestors came. Does your family use any foods, songs, or traditions from the old country?
5. Organize a class trip to one of the ethnic restaurants in your area. Have everyone order a different food item so class members can sample different dishes.
6. Celebrate diversity in your class by asking classmates to share stories, traditions, foods, clothing, or other unique parts of their heritage. Place colored dots on a world map

showing the place of origin of each class member's family. Connect those places with string to a Colorado map.

Books You and Your Teacher Might Enjoy

Geraldine Bean. *Charles Boettcher: A Study in Pioneer Western Enterprise.* Boulder: Westview Press, 1976. This book is a sharp profile of Colorado's most successful businessman and industrialist.

Robert A. Goldberg. *Hooded Empire: The Ku Klux Klan in Colorado.* Urbana: University of Illinois Press, 1981. An excellent history of the racist group, which rose to power briefly in Denver, Pueblo, Colorado Springs, Canon City, and Grand Junction.

Bill Hosokowa. *Nisei: The Quiet Americans.* Niwot: University Press of Colorado, 1992. One of several books on Japanese Americans by a former editor of the *Denver Post*, who spent World War II in a Wyoming relocation camp.

Stephen J. Leonard and Thomas J. Noel. *Denver: Mining Camp to Metropolis.* Niwot: University Press of Colorado, 1990. The Mile High City's economic and ethnic diversity is emphasized in this detailed history.

Jose de Oñis. *The Hispanic Contribution to the State of Colorado.* Boulder: Westview Press, 1976. This anthology covers topics ranging from religion and language to land grants to political leaders.

Did You Know?

Metro Denver is Colorado's melting pot. In 1990, its population was:

79 percent white

12 percent Hispanic

5 percent African American

3 percent Asian

1 percent American Indian

Richthofen Castle, 1887, just after completion in Denver's Montclair neighborhood.
(Thomas J. Noel Collection.)

CHAPTER SEVENTEEN
Conserving Colorado

While the United States celebrated its two-hundredth birthday in 1976, Colorado observed its hundredth anniversary as a state. For many Coloradans, 1976 was a good time to look back at the first 100 years and think about their history.

The biggest change was in the number of people. In 1876 there were about 100,000 Coloradans. In 1976 there were over 2 million. In 1876, many Indians still lived in Colorado. In 1976, about 13,000 were left, mostly on two small Ute reservations in the southwestern corner of the state. About 4,000 other Native Americans lived in Denver.

The 1858–1859 gold rush had brought more than 40,000 fortune seekers into Colorado. These newcomers — miners and townspeople, farmers and ranchers — went to work like beavers. They built dams and ditches to provide water for their mines, towns, farms, and factories. The settlers changed the natural flow of waterways to serve people wherever they wanted to work and live.

Many early Coloradans did not like the mountains. To them, the Rockies were only the waste rock that hid gold and silver, coal and oil, marble and granite. The mountains were blasted and dug and tunneled for mines, wagon roads, railroads, and auto roads.

Nature's Revenge

Nature gave a few warning signs. After trees were cut down, the snow, with no trees to shade it and hold it back, melted quickly. It ran off the mountains in a torrent and flooded towns. The Arkansas River flooded Pueblo in 1921, killing 100 people with a wall of water. The angry Arkansas carried away horses, wagons, autos, and even railroad cars as if they were toys. After such floods, Coloradans built more dams. Even dams do not always hold, however. Castlewood Dam broke in 1933, and Cherry Creek flooded Denver. Colorado's waterways have continued to break through dams and channels. In 1976, nearly twelve inches of rain fell in four hours in the Big Thompson River Canyon. The river rose nineteen feet above its normal level and roared down the canyon from Estes Park to Loveland. This was the worst flood in Colorado history, killing 145 people and destroying 418 homes and 52 businesses.

In 1982, another flood left Coloradans feeling uneasy because so many towns lie below dammed-up water. Lawn Lake Dam burst in Rocky Mountain National Park. The roaring flood did not stop until it had buried the main street of Estes Park in mud and water. Some people thought the answer was to build bigger and better dams. Others argued that Colorado already had too many dams. We should live in harmony with nature, they said, rather than trying to rearrange waterways and the landscape. These conservationists argued that modern Coloradans should try to live more like Native Americans did, without altering and polluting the land. In other words, we should try to conserve, or protect, the natural state of the land.

Conservation or Development?

The fight between conservationists and developers is not new. Remember Enos Mills and his fight to create Rocky Mountain National Park? President Theodore Roosevelt also fought to preserve parts of Colorado as national parks and forests. Mills and Roosevelt argued that parts of the western wilderness should be preserved for future generations. Mountains, Mills said, would make Colorado a tourist attraction. Why keep tearing down the mountains, chopping and burning the forests, and polluting and diverting the streams? Mills urged Coloradans to enjoy the high country. Ski the snowy slopes and fish the clear streams. Hike into virgin blue spruce forests and camp under the stars. Why not look for wildflowers instead of gold, and hunt with a camera instead of a gun?

*A huddle of high-rises at the corner of Seventeenth Street and Broadway in
downtown Denver reflects Colorado's recent boom decades.
(Photo by Roger Whitacre.)*

The Arkansas River flood of 1921 swept railroad cars through Pueblo as if they were toys. (Pueblo Library District.)

During the 1960s and 1970s Coloradans became concerned that Colorado's rapid growth would damage the state's environment. They worried about real estate developers who were looking for "unspoiled" areas where they could build resorts, summer homes, suburbs, and shopping centers. During the past forty years, thousands of new subdivisions and shopping centers have sprung up all over Colorado.

Fears that Colorado would be overdeveloped led to a historic turning point in the early 1970s, when many leaders wanted Colorado to host the 1976 Winter Olympics. Those who favored holding this world-famous international sporting competition believed it would bring people and money to Colorado from all over the globe. Others thought there were already enough winter resorts and development in the mountains. The Olympic Games would mean more traffic jams, more "NO TRESPASSING" signs, and less chance to find peace and quiet in the high country. Still others asked who would pay for the Olympics. Slowly people began to suspect that Colorado taxpayers would pay the bills while a few developers made the profits.

Taxpayers organized a revolt after Colorado politicians and businesspeople said that the Olympics would be held at all costs. A group of citizens drew up a petition forbidding the state to spend any more money on the 1976 Winter Olympics. State officials already had spent some funds planning and promoting the event. More than 76,000 voters signed the petition, and the question was placed on the ballot in the fall of 1972. Two out of every three voters said no to the Winter Olympics. Rather than support the Olympics, many Coloradans encouraged the federal government to set aside wilderness areas. In these areas, development and all motorized traffic are outlawed; you go into a wilderness area only on foot. By 1995, Colorado would have forty-eight wilderness areas — 1.2 million acres of land left in a wild state.

Politically, the 1976 Winter Olympics revolt started a new era. Many elected officials lost their jobs during the next few years, including the governor, both U.S. senators, and three U.S. representatives. Most of these politicians lost to candidates who promised to do more to protect the environment and to control growth.

Historic Preservation

Centennial celebrations in 1976 made Coloradans more aware of their history. People began to look around their communities for pioneer railroad stations, stores, hotels, schools, homes, and churches. Many of these historic structures were gone. During the postwar boom, thousands of old buildings had been knocked down. In Denver, dynamite was used to blow away buildings until people complained about the dust and the danger.

Finally, some people began to worry about the numbers of historic buildings that were being demolished. They considered many old structures to be an important part of a community's heritage. Such buildings, they believed, should be preserved. Often they were converted into museums.

In Denver, concerned residents formed a group called Historic Denver, Inc., in 1970. It had grown into one of the largest preservation societies in the United States by the 1980s. Among Historic Denver's accomplishments has been the saving of the Molly Brown House in Denver's Capitol Hill neighborhood. "Unsinkable" Molly Brown's house is now a museum drawing

Natural disasters can lead to good things. After the 1982 Estes Park flood, that town restored natural plants to the banks of the Big Thompson River and created this riverwalk. (Photo by Thomas J. Noel.)

thousands of visitors each year. Families also come to Denver to see the United States Mint, the Colorado History Museum, the Denver Art Museum, the Children's Museum, the Denver Museum of Natural History, the Denver Zoo, and restored

Colorado History Museums

Fort Sedgwick Depot

Phillips County
Heigenbothom House

Wray

Hahn's Peak Schoolhouse

North Park Pioneer

Overland Trail

Burlington Old Town

Fort Collins

Pioneer Schoolhouse

Lincoln County

Cheyenne Wells Old Jail

Kit Carson Depot

Steamboat Springs Tread of Pioneers

Museum of Northwest Colorado
Hayden Heritage

Fort Morgan

Washington County Schoolhouse

Greeley Centennial Village
Greeley

Estes Park

Loveland

Lamar Big Timbers

Kit Carson Museum

Rocky Ford

Bent's Old Fort

Hot Sulpher Springs Schoolhouse

Meeker Officer Quarters

Kauffman House

Lyons Schoolhouse

Comanche Crossing

Platteville Pioneer
Fort Vasquez
Longmont Pioneer

Palmer Lake

Nederland
Gillaspie House

Gilpin County Schoolhouse
Gold Mine
Underhill House

Lebanon Mine
Silver Plume Schoolhouse
Dillon Schoolhouse
Frisco Historic Park
Summit County Mining Sites

Hamill House

Montezuma
Schoolhouse

Hiwan Homestead

SEE
DENVER
METRO
MAP
PAGE 310

Hornbeck Homestead
Ute Pass Museum

May Natural History

Cripple Creek Depot

McAlister House
Pioneer
Hall of Presidents

Rifle Creek

Glenwood Springs

Florence Pioneer

El Pueblo

Fort Francisco

Dexter Cabin
Heritage

Healy House
South Park City

Wheeler House

Canon City

Marble Schoolhouse

Museum of Western Colorado

Rock Creek School

Buena Vista Heritage

Silver Cliff

Baca House Bloom Mansion

Delta County

Salida

Gunnison County

Saguache County

Montrose

Rio Grande County

Fort Garland

Rimrock Schoolhouse

Ouray County

Telluride Miner's Hospital

San Juan County Jail

Mineral County Depot

Four Corners

Animas School

Pagosa Springs

10 0 10 20 30 40 50 Miles

Colorado's Rockies offer a wild environment that lures millions of tourists every year to attractions such as "We Drive . . . You Look" jeep tours of the silvery San Juan Mountains. (Photo by Jerry Haines.)

historic neighborhoods such as Auraria (the oldest part of Denver), Capitol Hill, Five Points, and Highlands.

Grand Junction

Other cities across the state also began to preserve their old downtowns. Grand Junction in 1962 remodeled its Main Street into a pedestrian mall with lots of room for walkers, window shoppers, sculptures, and landscaping. The J. C. Penney Store was recycled as the Dinosaur Valley Museum. Other old stores also found popular new uses.

Thanks to such improvements, Grand Junction is the largest community in western Colorado. In 1993, it became a city of 100,000 and also led the entire state in job growth. Many families tired of big-city problems moved to this friendly town surrounded by scenic playgrounds such as Grand Mesa, the Colorado National Monument, and the Gunnison and Colorado Rivers with their awesome whitewater canyons.

Grand Junction's Main Street Mall inspired other towns. The Pearl Street Mall in Boulder, Main Street in Littleton, Main Avenue in Durango, Main Street in Sterling, Old Town in Fort Collins, Pitkin Place in Pueblo, and the Corazon de Trinidad in Trinidad are among other restored main streets.

Mining-Town Restoration

Georgetown, Colorado's first silver city, has been the state's star for historic preservation. Since 1970, this little town snuggled in a mountain valley has boasted that not one of its 200 historic buildings has been destroyed. Georgetown set up one of Colorado's first historic districts. In historic districts, homes, businesses, churches, schools, and other older buildings are protected and new developments are discouraged. The Georgetown Society, the local preservation group, raised money to repair old houses. When a developer started to build new condominiums on the Guanella Pass Road, this tiny town of around 900 people committed over $500,000 to buy out the developer in order to preserve Georgetown's historic charm.

Historic districts became a popular way to prevent handsome old neighborhoods from being torn down and replaced by parking lots and ugly new uses.

Like Georgetown, other famous old mining towns have restored structures from their past to improve their quality of life and attract tourists. Breckenridge, Crested Butte, Lake City, Leadville, Morrison, Ouray, Silverton, and Telluride are among Colorado's National Registered Historic Districts. They strive to keep the flavor of the old days. Antique buildings have been restored and turned into new restaurants, hotels, art galleries, homes, shops, and museums.

To make a living, many busted mining towns turned to "white gold" — snow. Skiing has now passed mining, and even ranching, to become the major source of paychecks on the Western Slope. Scandinavian miners from Sweden, Norway, and

After an iceberg sank the ocean liner Titanic, *Molly Brown rowed away to fame and the nickname "Unsinkable." Historic Denver rescued her house from the wrecking ball and made it into a favorite tourist stop at 1340 Pennsylvania Street in Denver. (Thomas J. Noel Collection.)*

Littleton's Main Street, the setting for this 1950s hula hoop contest, retains many of its friendly little old-time businesses. (Photo by John Grissinger. Littleton Historical Museum.)

Colorado Historic Districts

Fort Collins Old Town & Laurel School

McGregor Ranch
Rocky Mtn. Nat. Park Beaver Meadows
Fort Morgan Sherman Street

Lyons
Longmont
West Side East Side
Lafayette Coal Mining

Holzwarth Ranch

Boulder Downtown
University Quadrangle
Walker Ranch
Denver, Northwestern & Pacific Railroad
Central City Black Hawk
Idaho Springs Downtown
Georgetown–Silver Plume
Golden 12th Street
Lakewood Jewish Consumptive Relief Society
Morrison
Evans Ranch
Evergreen Episcopal Center

Breckenridge

Estabrook

North Fork

Leadville
Leadville Fish Hatchery
Twin Lakes
Interlaken Resort

Grand Junction North 7th Street

Redstone
Independence Ghost Town
Ashcroft Ghost Town

Crested Butte

St. Elmo

Salida Downtown

Manitou Springs
Colorado Springs North End
Old Colorado City
Cripple Creek Victor

Canon City Downtown

La Junta San Juan Avenue

Pueblo Union Avenue
Pitkin Place

Ouray Lake City

Telluride

Silverton

Durango–Silverton Narrow Gauge Railroad

Durango Main Avenue & 3rd Avenue

Mesa Verde Nat'l Park Hdqts.

Plaza de San Luis

Cokedale Corazon de Trinidad

10   0   10   20   30   40   50 Miles

Georgetown's grand old Hotel de Paris is one of the many antiques in the town's historic district that tickle the fancy of tourists. (Historic Georgetown.)

Finland showed other Coloradans how to ski as far back as the 1880s. Carl Howelson, a Norwegian stonemason, set up ski jump hills and races at Hot Sulphur Springs and Steamboat Springs in the early 1900s. During the 1920s and 1930s, the Colorado Mountain Club organized ski trips to Berthoud Pass, near where the Winter Park Ski Area opened in 1938.

Aspen opened a ski hill with a primitive ski lift in 1937. By the 1960s, skiing had made Aspen one of the richest and most popular places in Colorado. Other mining towns, such as Breckenridge, Crested Butte, Keystone, and Telluride, opened ski areas in the 1960s and 1970s. Vail, a town founded in 1962 as a winter sports area, has become the largest and most popular ski resort in North America. Thanks to ski areas open from November to April, Coloradans can enjoy the mountains year-round.

Fort Collins has revived its Municipal Railway to take people from downtown to City Park. (Photo by Thomas J. Noel.)

Return of the Railroads

Until the 1940s, most Coloradans used trains instead of cars to travel the Highest State. Once, more than 100 railroads operated in Colorado. By the 1990s, there were only five major lines left: AMTRAK, Burlington Northern, Denver & Rio Grande Western (D&RGW), Santa Fe, and Union Pacific.

The most famous Colorado passenger train is a narrow-gauge line (a railroad track only 3 feet wide instead of the standard 4 feet, 8ʃ inches) built by the D&RGW between Durango and Silverton. More than 2 million people from all over the world have ridden this old-fashioned steam train. Its popularity inspired the states of Colorado and New Mexico to reestablish another old passenger train between Antonito, Colorado, and Chama, New Mexico. Other popular train rides take passengers up Pikes Peak; between Victor and Cripple Creek; between Denver and Salt Lake City on the AMTRAK Zephyr; and up to Fremont Pass on the Leadville, Colorado & Southern. In 1982, the Boettcher Foundation gave the Colorado Historical Society $1 million to restore the Georgetown–Silver Plume railroad loop for passenger service.

Steamboat Springs celebrates its major industries, ranching and skiing, with the local sport of skiing behind horses. (Colorado Historical Society.)

Fort Collins reopened its Municipal Railway Service from City Park to downtown during the 1980s. Streetcars, which had been abandoned in Denver in the 1950s, returned in 1994 with the opening of light rail passenger service. The first rail link connected the Auraria Higher Education Center with downtown and the historic Five Points neighborhood in northeast Denver. Many Coloradans hope that the long, expensive trip to Denver International Airport soon can be made aboard the trains. Rail alternatives to automobiles may enable your children to tour more of Colorado the way your grandparents did — by rail.

Your Future

Colorado's people have been industrious, but also reckless and destructive. Not until the 1970s did many Coloradans realize that they were damaging the mountains and plains and polluting the fresh air and the clean water. Colorado, once a health resort for the nation, now suffers from too much pollution and, some say, too many people. How can we brag about Colorado when it has some of the dirtiest air in America and it is no longer safe to drink from mountain streams?

What will Colorado be like in 2076, our state's two-hundredth anniversary? Coal and oil, sought by modern miners, cannot be replaced. Will future Coloradans find coal and oil ghost towns? A shortage of water may have driven the Indians out of their great cities at Mesa Verde. Some people think the same problem may also cause our biggest cities to dry up and become deserted.

Yet Coloradans always have been a hopeful people. After celebrating our centennial in 1976, many of us became more interested in preserving the state's history and conserving its natural resources. Perhaps you will not be around in 2076, but your children will be. And they will be looking for the same things we are: blue skies and clear water, unspoiled mountains to play in, and well-preserved towns to live in. In 2076, they will judge how well we have conserved Colorado.

QUESTIONS

1. Discuss several of the problems faced by Coloradans between 1876 and 1976. What measures have people taken to solve these problems since 1976?
2. What is the basic dispute between conservationists and people who are in favor of development?
3. What are some of the consequences of rearranging natural waterways for the convenience of humans?
4. Why did many Colorado citizens oppose the state hosting the 1976 Winter Olympics?
5. List the narrow-gauge railroads that you can ride in Colorado today.
6. What are the good things about your community that you would like to pass on to your children?

ACTIVITIES

1. Look up your town's newspapers for Colorado Day (August 1, 1976). What projects was your community doing to celebrate Colorado's hundredth birthday?
2. Ask your Chamber of Commerce for guides to historic sites in your community. See if they have a walking tour

available. If not, draw a map and make your own walking tour to include the most important, most historic, and most architecturally interesting buildings in your town or neighborhood. What are some of the new uses for these old buildings?

3. Look up your town's newspapers for November 1972. See what people said in editorials and letters to the editor about holding the 1976 Winter Olympics in Colorado. Hold a class debate on the issue.

4. Ask your local Chamber of Commerce what developments are being planned for your county in the coming years. See if the officials will give a talk to your class on this topic. Prepare questions relating to water sources, conservation of the environment, and other issues you think are important.

5. Telephone your city or county planning office. Ask them if someone can visit your class to talk about your town's future.

Books You and Your Teacher Might Enjoy

Colorado Railroad Museum. *The Colorado Rail Annual.* Golden: Colorado Railroad Museum, 1962–present. This is one of many lavishly illustrated publications on railroading from the Golden museum.

Abbott Fay. *Ski Tracks in the Rockies: A Century of Colorado Skiing.* Evergreen, CO: Cordillera Press, 1984. An entertaining, well-illustrated history of how skiing became a major Colorado industry.

Mark S. Foster. "Colorado's Defeat of the 1976 Winter Olympics," *Colorado Magazine* 53, Spring 1976, pp. 163–186.

David McComb. *Big Thompson: Profile of a Natural Disaster.* Boulder: Pruett Publishing, 1980. This book shows how terrible a flood can be.

Did You Know?

San Juan County, with only about 500 people and one town — Silverton — is Colorado's least-populated county.

The Eisenhower Tunnel is 8,941 feet long and cost nearly $1,100 per inch to build.

More tourists come to Colorado from Texas than from anywhere else in the world.

Almost 900 Colorado buildings and 90 historic districts are on the National Register of Historic Places.

Colorado's oldest well-preserved buildings are the pit houses at Mesa Verde.

Among both locals and out-of-towners, the most popular cultural attraction has been the Denver Museum of Natural History. (Photo by Glenn Cuerden.)

CHAPTER EIGHTEEN
Boom and Bust

Colorado's ups and downs have been as high as the state's 14,000-foot mountains and as low as its river canyons. Colorado history is a tale of boom and bust.

For centuries, Spanish- and English-speaking peoples avoided the state with its high mountains and its semidesert lowlands. It took a gold rush to lure European Americans to Colorado. The first big boom came with the 1858–1859 gold strike, which started a large-scale hunt for natural resources. After thirty years of gold and silver rushes, the searchers switched to coal, molybdenum, uranium, and oil. But all of these natural resources — and the buyers for them — were limited. Each mineral boom ended in a bust.

The oil crash of the mid-1980s reminded modern-day Coloradans of this boom-and-bust cycle. The lesson was underlined in 1982 when the price of oil dropped from $40 to $9 per barrel. Suddenly, the petroleum industry dried up. Thousands of geologists, oil-field workers, and others lost their jobs. Exxon and other giant international firms dropped their billion-dollar plans to mine oil shale (rock containing oil deposits) in western Colorado. By the mid-1980s, Colorado was losing people. In Denver, one-third of the downtown offices were empty. Fortune seekers left for greener fields, such as California.

Just as busts follow booms, however, a boom is likely to follow a bust. The oil bust lasted until the 1990s, when a new boom began. Coloradans learned, as they had during the 1890s, to create new and different jobs. Tourists did not stop coming to Colorado. Cable television, a major new business with national headquarters in metro Denver, became the brightest new source of paychecks.

*DIA (Denver International Airport) opened in 1995, giving Colorado
one of the world's largest and most modern travel hubs. Because
Colorado is relatively isolated and has such rugged landscape, transportation has been a major concern ever since Coloradans struggled to attract
railroads in the 1870s. (Thomas J. Noel Collection.)*

Compared to many other areas, Colorado's homes with their big yards were inexpensive. They attracted people from crowded, high-priced areas such as California and New York. Families from all over the United States, Mexico, and Canada joined a new rush to Colorado, making it one of the fastest-growing states during the 1990s. The population reached 3.3 million in 1990 and may climb to 4 million by the year 2000.

Good times returned to the Highest State. In 1993, World Youth Day brought Pope John Paul II and more than 200,000 teenagers to Colorado from every country in the world. In 1992–1993, 10 million skiers came to ski Colorado's slopes. This record-breaking number gave a big boost to the ski industry. Gamblers were thrilled when casinos opened in 1991 in Central City, Black Hawk, and Cripple Creek and on the Southern Ute and Ute Mountain Reservations. Coloradans voted to allow gambling partly because several million dollars in gambling taxes are used each year to restore historic sites.

The Mile High City

To greet newcomers, Denver opened the giant new Denver International Airport in 1995. The passenger terminal has a tent-like top that brings sunshine in during the day. At night, the glowing translucent roof can be seen from many miles away.

After people land at the airport, they find plenty of things to do in Denver, the biggest city in the Rocky Mountain West. Visitors can tour the Denver Zoo, the Denver Botanic Gardens, and the U.S. Mint. They can see the wild animal dioramas at the Denver Museum of Natural History, the gold-domed capitol, the totem poles at the Denver Art Museum, and the Colorado History Museum's awesome diorama of 1860s Denver, complete with tiny dogs and cats. They can watch the Denver Broncos,

This 1907 photo shows the Colorado State Capitol before the dome was gold-plated. (Photo by Jackson Thode Collection.)

During their first season in 1993, the Colorado Rockies set a major league record by attracting 4,483,350 fans. In 1995 the Rockies moved to Coors Field in lower downtown Denver. (Colorado Rockies.)

the Denver Nuggets, and the Colorado Rockies, the most popular team in the history of professional baseball. In their first season, 1993, the Rockies averaged more than 50,000 fans for each home game.

National League baseball is the latest lure of metro Denver, which is home to about 2 million of Colorado's 3.5 million residents. While many American cities are suffering from decay, poverty, and crime, Denver uses its history to keep its neighborhoods strong and attractive. For example, Denver's old Lower Downtown district ("LoDo") around the railroad station was made into a historic district. This 1988 plan saved many old brick and stone landmarks from being torn down for parking lots or high-rise towers. Building owners are given tax breaks to repair their landmarks and give them new life as restaurants, apartments, and offices. LoDo, once a dirty skid row, became a hot spot to shop, eat, look at art, and hang out.

Mayor Federico Peña

Among the million newcomers to metro Denver since the 1950s was a Hispanic law school graduate from Texas, Federico Peña.

Federico Peña, one of Denver's most energetic mayors, brought the Mile High City a new airport, convention center, library, and major league baseball team during the 1980s. (Federico Peña Collection.)

Peña became a state legislator and then, in a surprising upset, won election as mayor of Denver in 1982. His election typified the growing status of Hispanics, who comprise about one-fifth of the city's population.

Peña proved to be one of the more energetic and visionary mayors in the Mile High City's history. He helped persuade Denver voters to spend $242 million to fix Denver's streets, parks, parkways, and government buildings. During Peña's two terms, some 30,000 trees were planted throughout the city. The South Platte River and Cherry Creek valleys were transformed from trash-strewn dumps to greenways and parks with paths for biking, jogging, walking, and in-line skating.

Denver also built a $126 million Colorado Convention Center, added $199 million in expansions to the Denver Public Schools, began a project to build a $100 million new downtown Denver Public Library, and began the restoration of many branch libraries. Mayor Peña persuaded Denverites to replace Stapleton Airport with the $5 billion Denver International Airport. Metro Denver also voted for a sales tax to pay for Coors Field for a major league baseball team, the Colorado Rockies. In his two terms as mayor, Peña helped make Denver a big league city. Impressed with what Mayor Peña had done in Denver, President Bill Clinton asked him to come to Washington, D.C., in 1993 as secretary of transportation.

Mayor Wellington Webb

Denver next elected its first black mayor, Wellington Webb. Like so many others, Webb had come to Denver as a child for the climate cure. Doctors told him that his asthma would be helped by moving to dry, sunny Colorado. The climate cure worked for Wellington Webb. He grew into a six-foot, four-inch basketball star at Denver's Manual High School and then played at Greeley's University of Northern Colorado (UNC). Webb graduated from UNC and became a high school teacher. He also joined the civil rights crusade for equal rights for all races and won election in 1972 to the state legislature. In 1991 he ran a low-budget campaign to become mayor of Denver.

Wilma and Wellington Webb, shown here in front of Denver's East High School, were both state legislators before his election as mayor of Denver in 1991. Mayor Webb, a former high school teacher, made education a top priority. (Photo by Steve Groer. Rocky Mountain News.)

Rather than buy expensive television ads, he walked through all seventy-three Denver neighborhoods in his size 12 sneakers to talk to people.

"Denver is still a friendly city," Mayor Webb reports. "Most people still look you in the eyes and say hello. My election and that of Mayor Peña show that Denverites give everyone a chance, regardless of their skin color. My goal is to keep this a friendly, safe, and exciting city."

Denver Suburbs

Besides the core City and County of Denver, the Denver metropolitan area includes Adams, Arapahoe, Boulder, Jefferson, and Douglas Counties. In these suburban counties, communities on

A spiderweb of freeways around Denver has captured giant developments like this one at the junction of Denver Tech Center Boulevard and I-225. (Photo by Jim Krebs.)

the edge of the metropolitan area are growing much faster than Denver, which has a stable population of around 470,000.

In the 1990s, most Coloradans live in suburban communities, not in rural areas or in core cities. Besides Aurora and Lakewood, Denver's suburbs include two dozen fast-growing towns. One of the oldest suburbs, Arvada, is now the sixth-largest city in Colorado. Boulder, the home of the University of Colorado, is the eighth-largest city. Westminster, between Boulder and Denver, is the ninth-largest community, with more than 75,000 residents.

Aurora

Aurora is Denver's largest suburb. To celebrate its evolution from a tiny farm town to a major city, Aurora built a big new city center during the 1980s. Along with large modern government

buildings, the Aurora City Center includes the Aurora History Museum. The nearby Delaney Round Barn and the Gully Homestead are reminders of Aurora's 1891 origins as a farm and ranch town. Another relic of Aurora's early days is the Plains Conservation Center, where you can still see antelope, deer, and rattlesnakes and visit a sod house and an old one–room schoolhouse.

Aurora, named for the Greek goddess of the dawn, is waking up to a bright future. Denver International Airport, which is closer to Aurora than to Denver, has caused a real estate boom. Aurora received more good news in 1993: The U.S. Army agreed to recycle the Rocky Mountain Arsenal into a wildlife refuge. This action would finally clean up the toxic site, where poisonous weapons had been made since World War II. Aurora has annexed (added) enough land to make it the largest city in Colorado in terms of area. In population,

Light rail is a fast, cheap, and clean alternative to automobiles. It began running in Denver in 1994. The Regional Transportation District (RTD) hopes to expand this rail service to Denver's many suburbs. (Photo by Thomas J. Noel.)

Delaney Round Barn, a relic of Aurora's agricultural past, is now the centerpiece of a historic park next to Aurora's City Center. (Aurora History Museum.)

230,000 Aurorans make it Colorado's third-largest city, behind Denver and Colorado Springs.

Lakewood

Colorado's fourth-largest city is Lakewood, on the west side of Denver. It was founded in 1889 by railroad builder and *Rocky Mountain News* owner William A. Loveland. Like Aurora, Lakewood for many years remained a small farm and ranch town. When the federal government built a large weapons plant in Lakewood during World War II, the town began to boom. After the war, the arms plant became the Federal Center with 8,000 employees working for thirty federal agencies.

Despite explosive growth, Lakewood saved some of its historic buildings. The city showcases its past in the Historical Belmar Village and Museum, a collection of old farm and ranch buildings and equipment. The Jewish Consumptive Relief Society (JCRS) once housed victims of tuberculosis, asthma, and other lung diseases. Now it is a campus of handsome old hospital buildings, and the synagogue has been converted to a museum. The JCRS complex is a reminder that more people came to Colorado seeking health than gold and silver. Several hundred thousand people left the humid, gray eastern states for a sunnier life in Colorado.

Rapid growth is not always good. More people mean more cars and more air pollution. More people also mean more crime. Coloradans in the 1990s finally passed laws to keep handguns out of the hands of teenagers, who have been responsible for a record number of murders since 1990. Partly because crime and violence threaten family life and the home, many more women became keenly interested in politics. They hoped to help find answers to Colorado's problems.

A Woman's Place

By the 1990s, 35 of the 100 senators and representatives of the Colorado Legislature were women. Many towns have women mayors and city council members. Until her retirement in 1996, Colorado's only congresswoman, Representative Patricia Schroeder, was the senior member of our state's six representatives in Washington, D.C. Since 1972, Representative Schroeder had been regularly reelected and had become the most powerful woman in Congress. Along with many other issues, she championed women's and family issues and also crusaded for controls on handguns and automatic weapons.

Colorado women are still dreaming of the day when one of their sex will occupy the governor's seat or one of the two U.S. Senate seats. During the 1980s, Nancy Dick became Colorado's first lieutenant governor. Mary Estill Buchanan became secretary of state and was followed in that position by Natalie Meyer. In 1990, Gail Norton became the first woman to be elected state attorney general. Women have enjoyed political power in Colorado since 1893. That year Colorado men became the first in the world to vote for full women's suffrage, or voting rights.

A Triumph for Native Americans

In recent years ethnic minorities slowly have gained political power. Ben Nighthorse Campbell, a Native American, started his life in an orphan's home and did time in a home for juvenile criminals before rising to the U.S. Senate. Campbell's story is a

Coloradan Ben Nighthorse Campbell, a Northern Cheyenne shown here leading a motorcycle rally, became a U.S. senator in 1991. He is the only Native American member of Congress. (Ben Nighthorse Campbell Collection.)

reminder that Native Americans, despite past persecutions, are once again a growing population. Campbell, who is part Cheyenne, became a successful rancher and a well-known jewelry maker. After moving to Ignacio on the Southern Ute Reservation, he won election in 1986 to the U.S. House of Representatives. In 1992 Representative Campbell was elected to the U.S. Senate, the first Native American to sit there. In Washington, Campbell has delighted easterners by wearing his ponytail, face paint, and Native American costume while riding in parades on horseback.

"We need more average Americans in politics," said Senator Campbell. "I'm the only guy I know in the U.S. Senate who has been on all three sides of the law. I was on the bad side in juvenile hall, then a cop on the good side. Then, I was in the middle as a counselor in a prison and running a halfway house. That was hard work, but politics is even harder on you and your family. It takes at least eighty hours a week of your time."

Rural Colorado

Coloradans living in rural communities on the eastern plains and
Western Slope have had their own boom-and-bust cycles and
small-town urban problems. They have worked hard to improve
their towns and schools.

For example, during the 1980s the small town of Brush in
northeastern Colorado was facing decline and set out to make a
comeback. Town leaders made an effort to attract new businesses
and industries and improve the main street business district.
Main street merchants reopened their stores, housing construction increased, and unemployment went down. When the Brush
High School Beetdiggers won the state class 3A football champi-
onship in 1992, town pride soared. Karval, a community of
fewer than 100 people south of Limon, graduated a high school
class of two in May 1993. The two seniors adopted a motto:
"Quality, not quantity — that's what's important." You might
not think living in a town that small would be fun. One of the
seniors observed, however, "People here are friendly. Small isn't
always bad." There were only ninety students in the entire
school from kindergarten through high school. Karval, as one
student noted, is a "tree-filled cluster of houses and abandoned
old buildings." There are other towns like Karval throughout
Colorado.

Colorado's Future

Among the hardest-working politicians is Governor Roy
Romer, who grew up in the farm town of Holly in southeastern
Colorado. He is the father of seven children and a businessman
who made a million dollars before going into politics. Romer
worked overtime to get to the top and be elected governor in
1986. "I work sixteen hours a day," Governor Romer explained.
"I usually get up about 5:30 in the morning, and I go to bed
about 11:30 each night." Coloradans reelected the governor in
1990 and 1994 (even though he was caught catnapping in his car
between meetings!).

Governor Romer echoed the feelings of many Coloradans
when he said, "I think that the things most important to our
state's future are education and environment." Education has

The University of Colorado at Boulder is the state's oldest public center of higher education. (Photo by J. Martin Natrig.)

been a top priority with Coloradans, who have one of the country's highest educational levels. Many realize that higher education is often a ticket to a better job and a better life. The University of Colorado has campuses at Boulder, Colorado Springs, and Denver. It is the largest school in the state, with about 45,000 students. Colorado State University at Fort Collins, the University of Northern Colorado at Greeley, and the University of Southern Colorado at Pueblo also attract many local and out-of-state students.

The Utes, who have lived in Colorado for hundreds of years, survive despite tremendous changes to the mountains, plains, and canyon lands that they now share with three million other Coloradans.
(The Durango Herald.)

Twenty-five other Colorado communities have four-year or junior colleges. These schools range from the huge Metropolitan State College in Denver to tiny Western State College in Gunnison. The University of Denver, founded in 1864, is the state's oldest college. The Community College of Aurora, founded in the 1980s, is the youngest. A terrific range of educational possibilities provides numerous options for high school graduates.

Colorado's roomy, crisp, sunny environment has lured many to the state. Locals and tourists like to explore Colorado's high plains, mountains, and canyonlands. Despite the huge growth in population and development since the gold rush days, the natural environment still overwhelms the built environment. Even in the crowded Front Range strip along I-25 between Pueblo and Fort Collins, the distant Rockies dominate the western skyline. If you drive an hour to the east of I-25, the vast high plains seem to swallow you up.

These mountains and plains, as well as the people who built the communities we live in today, make Colorado special. The more you explore Colorado and learn its history, the more you will enjoy the Highest State.

By the 1990s, Coloradans could look back on a history more colorful and dramatic than any television show or movie. You will have to discover this drama for yourself, however, by traveling around the state, by reading, and by asking older people to tell their stories to you.

QUESTIONS

1. What has been the most important new industry in 1990s Colorado?
2. List the four largest cities in Colorado in terms of population.
3. What problems have rural communities had to face in the 1990s?
4. What factors contributed to the growth of Aurora and Lakewood?
5. How long have women been able to vote in Colorado?
6. Which college or university is closest to your home?

ACTIVITIES

1. Telephone your mayor or town manager and ask who the women leaders of your community are. Interview them and ask them what role they think women should play in politics.
2. Make a list of Colorado's U.S. senators and representatives.
3. Imagine you work for your community's tourist bureau. Write and illustrate (with photos or drawings) a brochure that would encourage people to visit your area. Be sure to mention the interesting sites and facts.
4. Interview your parents (and/or grandparents) and write a history of your family's life in Colorado.

Books You and Your Teacher Might Enjoy

LeRoy R. and Ann Hafen. *The Colorado Story: A History of Your State and Mine.* Denver: Old West Publishing Company, 1953. (A revised edition, *Our State: Colorado, a History of Progress,* was published in 1966 and reprinted in 1975 by Old West.) This fine text was the forerunner of the book now in your hands. To see how Colorado history was taught between the 1950s and 1970s, take a look at the Hafens' textbook.

Lakewood, Colorado: An Illustrated Biography. Lakewood: Lakewood's Twenty-Fifth Birthday Commission, 1994. With lively stories and lots of photos, this book tells about Colorado's fourth-largest city.

Stephen J. Leonard and Thomas J. Noel. *Denver: Mining Camp to Metropolis.* Niwot: University Press of Colorado, 1990. This overview of the five-county metropolis includes many maps and pictures focusing on twentieth-century Denver and its suburbs.

Steven F. Mehls, Carol J. Drake, and James E. Fell, Jr. *Aurora: Gateway to the Rockies.* Evergreen, CO: Cordillera Press, 1985. Here is the story of the tiny farm and ranch town that grew into Colorado's largest city in terms of square miles.

Robert Michael Pyle. *The Thunder Tree: Lessons from an Urban Wildland.* Boston: Houghton Mifflin, 1993. A naturalist tells tales of his boyhood growing up in Aurora alongside the Highline Canal.

Did You Know?

Denver is both the largest (in population) and smallest (in size) of Colorado's counties.

One-third of Colorado is owned by the federal government and set aside mostly for recreation.

Colorado has a higher percentage of college graduates — about 25 percent — than any other state.

Denver is called the Mile High City because its elevation is 5,280 feet — one mile high.

Denver International Airport covers fifty-three square miles, making it the largest airport in the United States in terms of land.

State Capitol building in Denver. (Photo by Roger Whitacre.)

Appendix: Colorado Governors

Jefferson Territory
Robert W. Steele, 1859–1861

Colorado Territory
William Gilpin, 1861–1862

John Evans, 1862–1865

Alexander Cummings, 1865–1867

A. Cameron Hunt, 1867–1869

Edward McCook, 1869–1873

Samuel H. Elbert, 1873–1874

Edward McCook, 1874–1875

John L. Routt, 1875–1876

State of Colorado
John L. Routt, 1876–1879

Frederick W. Pitkin, 1879–1883

James B. Grant, 1883–1885

Benjamin H. Eaton, 1885–1887

Alva Adams, 1887–1889

Job A. Cooper, 1889–1891

John L. Routt, 1891–1893

Davis H. Waite, 1893–1895

Albert W. McIntire, 1895–1897

Alva Adams, 1897–1899

Charles S. Thomas, 1899–1901

James B. Orman, 1901–1903

James H. Peabody, 1903–1905

Alva Adams, 1905

Jesse F. McDonald, 1905–1907

Henry A. Buchtel, 1907–1909

John F. Shafroth, 1909–1913

Elias M. Ammons, 1913–1915

George A. Carlson, 1915–1917

Julius C. Gunter, 1917–1919

Oliver H. Shoup, 1919–1923

William E. Sweet, 1923–1925

Clarence J. Morley, 1925–1927

William H. Adams, 1927–1933

Edwin C. Johnson, 1933–1937

Ray Talbot, 1937

Teller Ammons, 1937–1939

Ralph Carr, 1939–1943

John Vivian, 1943–1947

Lee Knous, 1947–1949

Walter Johnson, 1949–1951

Dan Thornton, 1951–1955

Edwin C. Johnson, 1955–1957

Stephen McNichols, 1957–1963

John A. Love, 1963–1973

John Vanderhoof, 1973–1975

Richard D. Lamm, 1975–1987

Roy Romer, 1987–

Annotated Bibliography

General Works

Abbott, Carl, Stephen J. Leonard, and David McComb. *Colorado: A History of the Centennial State*. Niwot: Univ. Press of Colorado, 1994, rev. ed. 394 pp. Index, illus., endnotes, bib. essay, maps. A fine overview particularly strong on urban and environmental history.

Bauer, William H., J. L. Ozment, and J. H. Willard. *Colorado Postal History: The Post Offices*. Denver: J-B Pub. Co., 1971; 1989 rev. and expanded ed. 248 pp. Bib., maps, illus. Valuable reference guide listing each post office (and its name changes). For each post office, this book lists county, dates of construction, abandonment, and very brief remarks. Great for tracking ghost towns.

Caughey, Bruce, and Dean Winstanley. *The Colorado Guide*. Golden, Colorado: Fulcrum Pub. Co., 1991, rev. ed. 628 pp. Index, illus. Historic and recreational attractions are spotlighted in this most comprehensive guide to Colorado.

Colorado Magazine. Denver: Colorado Historical Society, 1923–1980. Quarterly. Indexes. This is the best single source on Colorado history, with articles by hundreds of historians on thousands of topics. *Colorado Magazine* was preceded by the *Sons of Colorado* magazine (1906–1907) and by *The Trail* (1908–1920). In 1981 *Colorado Magazine* was replaced by two journals: a scholarly annual, *Essays and Monographs in Colorado History,* and a lavishly illustrated popular magazine, *Colorado Heritage.*

Ellis, Richard N., and Duane A. Smith. *Colorado: A History in Photographs*. Niwot: Univ. Press of Colorado, 1991. 266 pp. Index, illus. Crisp text and many heretofore unpublished photos make this a gem.

Friggens, Myriam. *Tales, Trails, and Tommy Knockers: Stories from Colorado's Past*. Boulder, Colorado: Johnson Pub. Co., 1979. 144 pp. Bib., illus. Especially good for younger readers.

Gehres, Eleanor M., Sandra Dallas, Maxine Benson, and Stanley Cuba, eds. *The Colorado Book*. Golden, Colorado: Fulcrum Pub. Co., 1993. 414 pp. Index, illus. A wonderful sampler of the best that has been written about Colorado, with brief excerpts from fiction, nonfiction, poetry, exploration. The illustrations are examples of the best art depicting the Highest State.

Hafen, LeRoy R., ed. *Colorado and Its People*. New York: Lewis Historical Pub. Co., 1948. 4 vols. Footnotes, illus., index. Of the multivolume state histories (Baker and Hafen, Byers, Hall and Stone), this is the most comprehensive and authoritative, although Baker and Hafen's 1927 five-volume *History of Colorado* should also be consulted.

Lamm, Richard D., and Duane A. Smith. *Pioneers & Politicians: 10 Colorado Governors in Profile.* Boulder, Colorado: Pruett Pub. Co., 1984. 187 pp. Index, essay on sources, illus. Fascinating vignettes of Colorado's best and worst governors by a former governor and Colorado's most prolific historian.

Lorch, Robert S. *Colorado's Government.* Niwot: Univ. Press of Colorado, 1976, 5th ed. 1991. 328 pp. Index, illus., maps. The definitive reference book.

Mangan, Terry William. *Colorado on Glass: Colorado's First Half-Century as Seen by the Camera.* Denver: Sundance, 1975. 406 pp. Illus., footnotes, bib., index. This is a crackerjack collection of photographs, with information on the men and women who took them.

Noel, Thomas J., Paul F. Mahoney, and Richard E. Stevens. *Historical Atlas of Colorado.* Norman: Univ. of Oklahoma Press, 1994. Maps, bib., index. Maps and brief overviews survey major developments in Colorado, from Indian battlegrounds to historic and hospitable landmarks, from transportation systems to literary landmarks.

Ubbelohde, Carl, Maxine Benson, and Duane A. Smith. *A Colorado History.* Boulder, Colorado: Pruett Pub. Co., 1972, 9th ed. 1993. 421 pp. Index, suggested reading, illus. An up-to-date, clearly written, one-volume overview.

The WPA Guide to 1930s Colorado, with introduction by T. J. Noel. Lawrence: Univ. Press of Kansas, 1987. 511 pp. Illus., maps, bib. A reprint of the 1941 *Guide to the Highest State,* the best guidebook ever created for Colorado. This book was compiled by an army of unemployed researchers and writers hired by the WPA's Federal Writers' Project.

Wynar, Bohdan S., ed. *Colorado Bibliography.* Littleton, Colorado: Libraries Unlimited, 1980. 565 pp. Author and title indexes. The only comprehensive bibliography of Colorado history, culture, geography, politics, economics, education, and other topics. Includes 9,182 books and booklets "of permanent and scholarly value."

The Highest State

Griffiths, Mel, and Lynnell Rubright. *Colorado: A Geography.* Boulder, Colorado: Westview Press, 1983. 325 pp. Index, illus., maps, bib., endnotes. This book surveys the geography that has shaped history in the Highest State.

Michener, James A. *Centennial.* New York: Random House, 1974. 909 pp. An exhaustive, fictionalized history of the South Platte Valley of northeastern Colorado. Michener has chapters on the prehistoric period, Indians, trappers, miners, cowboys, hunters, sheep ranchers, sugar beets, and Hispanics.

The First Coloradans

Cassells, E. Steve. *The Archaeology of Colorado.* Boulder, Colorado: Johnson Books, 1983. 325 pp. Bib., illus., index. The best overview and introduction to prehistoric Coloradans.

Smith, Duane A. *Mesa Verde National Park: Shadows of the Centuries.* Lawrence: Univ. Press of Kansas, 1988. 254 pp. Index, bib., endnotes, illus. This book recounts the long struggle to create the first U.S. national park to preserve Native American architecture.

Watson, Don. *Indians of the Mesa Verde.* Mesa Verde Museum, 1961. 188 pp. Illus. A small paperback combining poetic style with scholarly research portrays Colorado cliff dwellers.

Indians of Colorado

Bent, George. *Life of George Bent Written from His Letters by George Hyde.* Norman: Univ. of Oklahoma Press, 1968. 389 pp. Illus., index, bib., footnotes. George was the son of William Bent of Bent's Fort and his Cheyenne wife, Owl Woman. He chose to live with his mother's people. This is a firsthand account of Cheyenne history and culture, including the tribe's losses at the Sand Creek Massacre.

Coel, Margaret. *Chief Left Hand: Southern Arapaho.* Norman: Univ. of Oklahoma Press, 1981. 338 pp. Index, bib., footnotes, illus. A biography of the Arapaho leader who welcomed whites to Colorado only to be slaughtered by them a few years later at Sand Creek.

Hughes, J. Donald. *American Indians in Colorado.* Boulder: Pruett Pub. Co., 1977. 143 pp. Index, bibliography, notes, illus., maps. A splendid introduction and overview.

Explorers, Trappers, and Traders

Beckwourth, James P. *The Life and Adventures of James P. Beckwourth.* Univ. of Nebraska Press, 1972. 649 pp. Index. This new edition of the old classic, with introduction and notes by Delmont Oswald, is the best so far. Beckwourth was an African American, an Indian chief among the Crow, a mountain man, a Colorado pioneer, and the champion of all western liars. In this edition, Oswald does an admirable job of trying to sort out fact and fiction.

Conrad, H. L., ed. *Uncle Dick Wootton: The Pioneer Frontiersman of the Rocky Mountain Region.* Chicago: R. R. Connelley & Sons, 1957. 465 pp. Illus., index. Readable reminiscences of the energetic mountain man and pioneer whose load of Taos Lightning ignited Denver's first Christmas party.

Ruxton, Frederick. *Life in the Far West,* LeRoy Hafen, ed. Norman: Univ. of Oklahoma Press, 1950. 252 pp. Uproarious, somewhat fictionalized account by a young British adventurer who came to Colorado and went native in 1838. Excellent on the culture of the mountain men and Native Americans.

Up the Rio Grande

Bolton, Herbert E. *Pageant in the Wilderness: The Story of the Escalante Expedition to the Interior Basin, 1776.* Salt Lake City: Utah Historical Society, 1951. 265 pp. Index, bib., footnotes, illus. Fine account by the dean of Southwest historians of the first recorded exploration of Colorado.

Deutsch, Sarah. *No Separate Refuge: Culture, Class, and Gender on an Anglo-Hispanic Frontier in the American Southwest, 1880–1940.* New York: Oxford Univ. Press, 1987. 356 pp. Index, notes, bib., illus. Although difficult to read, this book tackles an important topic.

The Dominguez-Escalante Journal, trans. by Fray Angelico Chavez. Provo, Utah: Brigham Young Univ. Press, 1976. 203 pp. Bib., illus., map. Father Chavez has provided a lively English translation of the first detailed report on Colorado.

Horgan, Paul. *Great River: The Rio Grande in North American History.* New York: Rinehart and Co., 1954. 2 vols. 1,020 pp. Maps, source notes, bib., index. A definitive, brilliant, and poetic account by one of the greatest of all Southwestern writers.

Simmons, Virginia McConnell. *The San Luis Valley: Land of the Six-Armed Cross.* Boulder, Colorado: Pruett Pub. Co., 1979. 193 pp. Index, illus., maps, endnotes. Poetically written account of the south-central Colorado Valley where Spanish-surnamed people first settled.

Tushar, Olibama López. *The People of El Valle: A History of the Spanish Colonials in the San Luis Valley.* Pueblo, Colorado: El Escritorio, 1992. 228 pp. Index, bib., appendices, illus. Fine insights from a descendant of pioneer settlers in the San Luis Valley.

The Longest Civil War

Hoig, Stan. *The Sand Creek Massacre.* Norman: University of Oklahoma Press, 1958. 217 pp. Index, illus., footnotes, bib. The best book so far of a dozen works on this controversial tragedy.

Rockwell, Wilson. *The Utes: A Forgotten People.* Denver: Sage Books, 1956. 307 pp. Illus. Rancher Wilson Rockwell wrote a good book about the Native American tribe he and other Western Slopers displaced.

Smith, Duane A. *The Birth of Colorado: A Civil War Perspective.* Norman: Univ. of Oklahoma Press, 1989. 268 pp. Index, bib. essay, illus. This is a terrific account of Colorado's infancy.

Miners

Backus, Harriet Fish. *Tomboy Bride.* Boulder, Colorado: Pruett Pub. Co., 1979. 273 pp. Photos. The wife of a mining engineer chronicles their cold, lonely, isolated life with warm memories and rich descriptions of Colorado's silvery San Juans.

Ellis, Anne. *Life of an Ordinary Woman.* Boston: Houghton Mifflin, 1931. 264 pp. Photos. Reprint 1981 by Univ. of Nebraska Press with introduction by Elliott West. A crackerjack account of mining town life by an extraordinary woman.

Fell, James E., Jr. *Ores to Metals: The Rocky Mountain Smelting Industry.* Lincoln: Univ. of Nebraska Press, 1979. 341 pp. Index, endnotes, bib. illus. An important, readable book on the neglected, unromantic, but crucial subject of ore processing, which made paydirt pay off.

Gulliford, Andrew. *Boomtown Blues: Colorado Oil Shale, 1885–1985.* Niwot: Univ. Press of Colorado, 1989. 302 pp. Index, bib., endnotes, illus. A good updating of the boom-and-bust story that makes admirable use of oral history.

Hollister, Ovando J. *The Mines of Colorado.* New York: Promontory Press, 1974 reprint. 450 pp. The classic first book on Colorado mining was written in 1867 by a colorful journalist and indefatigable booster.

Smith, Duane A. *Colorado Mining: A Photographic History.* Albuquerque: Univ. of New Mexico, 1977. 176 pp. Illus. This title and the two that follow are three of the best works by the leading expert on the history of Colorado mining.

————. *Horace Tabor: His Life and Legend.* Niwot: University Press of Colorado, 1973. 395 pp. Index, endnotes, illus.

————. *Rocky Mountain Mining Camps: The Urban Frontier.* Bloomington: Univ. of Indiana Press, 1967. 304 pp. Index, endnotes, bib., illus. This classic overview explains how mining camps urbanized the Rockies.

Wolle, Muriel S. *Stampede to Timberline.* Denver: Sage Books, 1948, centennial ed., 1975. 544 pp. Drawings, maps, index. Wolle's graceful illustrations and writing style make this the best — as well as the first — book on Colorado's mining ghost towns.

Townspeople

Bird, Isabella. *A Lady's Life in the Rocky Mountains.* London: John Murray, 1879. Reprint 1960 by Univ. of Oklahoma Press with introduction by Daniel Boorstin. 249 pp. Drawings. This tiny, eccentric English world traveler left a memorable but not flattering picture of Colorado in 1873. "The great braggart city spread out brown and treeless upon a brown and treeless plain," she calls Denver, and the South Platte she found "shriveled into a narrow stream with a shingly bed six times too large for it, and fringed by shriveled cottonwoods."

Coel, Margaret. *Goin' Railroading: A Century on the Colorado High Iron.* Boulder, Colorado: Pruett Pub. Co., 1985. 312 pp. Index, bib., chapter notes, illus., maps, charts. Superb railroadiana and oral history based on Coel's interviews with her father.

Crofutt, George A. *Crofutt's Grip Sack Guide of Colorado: A Complete Encyclopedia of the State.* Golden, Colorado: Cubar Associates, 1966. Reprint of 1885 edition. 264 pp. Maps, photos, drawings. Although a booster guide designed to lure tourists and investors, this marvelously illustrated book serves as a fascinating town-by-town guide for the 1880s.

Foster, Mark S. *Henry M. Porter: Rocky Mountain Empire Builder.* Niwot: Univ. Press of Colorado, 1991. 184 pp. Index, endnotes, bib., illus. A good look at one of the business tycoons of Denver.

Simonin, Louis L. *The Rocky Mountain West in 1867,* trans. by Wilson O. Clough. Lincoln: Univ. of Nebraska Press, 1966. 170 pp. Index, footnotes, illus. A witty, unique look at early Colorado through the letters of a young French mining engineer who found pioneer Colorado society as fascinating as the minerals.

Wilkins, Tivis E. *Colorado Railroads: Chronological Development.* Boulder, Colorado: Pruett Pub. Co., 1974. 309 pp. Index, bib., maps, illus. A most useful reference guide to the building and abandonment of some 100 Colorado railroads. Arranged by year, this book lists the miles of track involved, plus brief, basic information.

Railroads, Coal, and Oil

Simmons, Virginia McConnell. *The Upper Arkansas: A Mountain River Valley.* Boulder, Colorado: Pruett Pub. Co., 1990. 353 pp. Index, suggested readings. From Leadville to Pueblo, the Upper Arkansas nourished miners, farmers, and ranchers.

Whiteside, James. *Regulating Danger: The Struggle for Mine Safety in the Rocky Mountain Coal Industry.* Lincoln: Univ. of Nebraska Press, 1990. 265 pp. Index, illus., endnotes, bib. essay. Looks at the darker side of coal mining.

Cowboys and Farmers

Babb, Sonora. *An Owl on Every Post.* New York: McCall, 1970. 217 pp. A sensitive account of the author's girlhood in 1913 in a bleak sod house on the "grey desert" of eastern Colorado.

Borland, Hal. *Country Editor's Boy.* Philadelphia: J. B. Lippincott Co., 1970. 313 pp. A distinguished and prolific writer recalls his boyhood from 1915 to 1918 in Flagler, Colorado. Borland, who became a nature writer and editorialist for the *New York Times,* has written two dozen other works, fiction and nonfiction, often capturing the strange, lonesome beauty of the high plains.

Eberhart, Perry. *Ghosts of the Colorado Plains.* Athens, Ohio: Swallow Press, 1986. 252 pp. Index, illus. One of the few efforts to portray the hundreds of high plains communities that have expired with far less fanfare than mountain ghost towns.

Moody, Ralph. *Little Britches: Father and I Were Ranchers.* New York: W. W. Norton & Co., 1950. 260 pp. Drawings. Classic account of growing up on a Colorado ranch.

Steinel, Alvin T. *History of Agriculture in Colorado, 1858–1926.* Fort Collins, Colorado: The State Agriculture College, 1926. 659 pp. Illus., footnotes, index. The definitive history, which is surprisingly readable as well as encyclopedic and authoritative.

Western Slopers

Vandenbusche, Duane, and Duane A. Smith. *A Land Alone: Colorado's Western Slope.* Boulder, Colorado: Pruett Pub. Co., 1981. 337 pp. Maps, photos, endnotes, bib., index. Professor Vandenbusche of Western State College at Gunnison and Professor Smith of Fort Lewis College in Durango have produced the definitive history of western Colorado.

Waters, Frank. *The Colorado.* New York: Rinehart & Co., 1946. 400 pp. Index, bib., illus. A good account by a literary giant.

Hard Times

French, Emily. *The Diary of a Hard-Worked Woman,* Janet LeCompte, ed. Lincoln: Univ. of Nebraska Press, 1987. 166 pp. Index. Extraordinary insight into the life of a divorced washerwoman that will dispel any romantic notions about "the good old days."

Reformers

Haywood, William D. *Big Bill Haywood's Book.* New York: International Publishers, 1938. 368 pp. Uproarious autobiography of the one-eyed, heavy-drinking socialist union organizer who used to terrorize the Oxford Hotel bar and the Mining Exchange Building before moving to Russia in 1919. Big Bill was the star promoter of The Western Federation of Miners and the Industrial Workers of the World (the IWW, or Wobblies).

Larsen, Charles. *The Good Fight: The Life and Times of Ben B. Lindsey.* Chicago: Quadrangle Books, 1972. 307 pp. Index, endnotes. The best biography of Colorado's foremost reformer and muckraker.

McGovern, Eugene, and Leonard F. Guttridge. *The Great Coal Field War.* Boston: Houghton Mifflin, 1972. 383 pp. Maps, bib., index. A prolabor account of southern Colorado's 1914 Ludlow Massacre, the most deadly confrontation in the history of the U.S. labor movement. Based on Senator McGovern's Ph.D. dissertation at Northwestern University.

Noel, Thomas J., and Barbara S. Norgren. *Denver: The City Beautiful and Its Architects.* Denver: Historic Denver, 1994. 248 pp. Index, illus., maps, sources, glossary of architectural terms. Learn about the types and styles of buildings common in Colorado and about leading Colorado architects.

Papanikolas, Zeeze. *Buried Unsung: Louis Tikas and the Ludlow Massacre,* with foreword by Wallace Stegner. Salt Lake City: Univ. of Utah Press, 1982. 331 pp. Index, bib., notes, illus. A beautifully written reconstruction of the life of a Greek labor organizer.

Sinclair, Upton. *The Coal War.* New York: Macmillan, 1917. Reprint 1976 by Colorado Associated Univ. Press with an introduction by John Graham. 417 pp. An account of the Ludlow Massacre by the Pulitzer Prize–winning novelist.

Suggs, George G., Jr. *Colorado's War on Militant Unionism: James H. Peabody and the Western Federation of Miners.* Detroit, MI: Wayne State Univ. Press, 1972. 242 pp. Index, bib., notes. Best account of the labor wars that shook up turn-of-the-century Colorado.

The Automobile Age

Noel, Thomas J. "Paving the Way to Colorado: The Evolution of Auto Tourism," *Journal of the West,* July 1987, pp. 42–49.

Depression, Recovery, and Growth

Leonard, Stephen J. *Trials and Triumphs: A Colorado Portrait of the Great Depression, With FSA Photographs.* Niwot: Univ. Press of Colorado, 1993. 313 pp. Index, bib., endnotes, illus. A gorgeously illustrated history, rich in anecdote and detail. Easily the best book on the 1930s by one of Colorado's most erudite scholars.

Economic and Ethnic Diversity

Bean, Geraldine. *Charles Boettcher: A Study in Pioneer Western Enterprise.* Boulder, Colorado: Westview Press, 1976. 220 pp. Photos, footnotes, bib. Biography of the founder of Great Western Sugar Beet Company, Ideal Basic Cement Company, Capitol Life Insurance Company, and numerous other enterprises, as well as Colorado's greatest philanthropic foundation.

Goldberg, Robert Alan. *Hooded Empire: The Ku Klux Klan in Colorado.* Urbana: Univ. of Illinois Press, 1981. 255 pp. Index, endnotes, bib. The best study of the 1920s KKK nightmare in Colorado comes to some surprising conclusions.

Gonzales, Rodolfo. *I Am Joaquin/Yo Soy Joaquin.* New York: Bantam Books, 1967. 122 pp. Illus. Poetic insight into Chicano life by the militant founder of Colorado's La Raza Party.

Lovelace, Walter B. *Jesse Shwayder and the Golden Rule.* Denver: Shwayder Bros., 1960. 65 pp. Illus. This Jewish pioneer founded Denver's world-famous Samsonite luggage company.

Noel, Thomas J. *Denver: Rocky Mountain Gold.* Tulsa, Oklahoma: Continental Heritage, 1980. 256 pp. Index, bib., illus. A lavishly illustrated history with some color sections, this book includes brief accounts of many leading Colorado businesses and institutions.

Conserving Colorado

Benson, Maxine. *Martha Maxwell: Rocky Mountain Naturalist.* Lincoln: Univ. of Nebraska Press, 1986. 335 pp. Index, endnotes, bib., illus. A look at the woman who first attempted to capture and preserve Colorado wildlife.

Dallas, Sandra. *No More Than Five in a Bed: Colorado Hotels in the Old Days.* Norman: Univ. of Oklahoma Press, 1967. 208 pp. Illus., bib., index. Well-illustrated accounts of thirty-seven early Colorado hotels, resorts, spas, and watering spots. As many of these great Victorian havens are still around, this book by one of Colorado's best writers can be used as a guide for current-day vacationing.

McCarthy, G. Michael. *Hour of Trial: The Conservation Conflict in Colorado and the West, 1891–1907.* Norman: Univ. of Oklahoma Press, 1977. 327 pp. Maps, illus., footnotes, bib., index. This book on the early Colorado conservation movement foreshadows the great developer-versus-conservationist debates of recent decades.

Mills, Enos Abijah. *The Adventures of a Nature Guide.* New York: Doubleday, Page & Co., 1923. 271 pp. Illus. Enos Mills (1870–1922) was the pioneer conservationist of Colorado. He settled near Longs Peak as a boy, climbed it hundreds of times, rode avalanches, fathered Rocky Mountain National Park, and instigated and led the crusade to preserve the Colorado wilderness. Mills spent weeks at a time — even in winter — roaming the Colorado high country alone, then recording his experiences in his numerous articles and books. Largely forgotten today, Mills is long overdue for resurrection. See also *In Beaver World* (1913), *Waiting for the Wilderness* (1932), *Bird Memories of the Rockies* (1931), *Rocky Mountain National Park* (1924), *Watched by Wild Animals* (1922), *Your National Parks* (1917), and *Wild Life of the Rockies* (1909). In addition, see the biography by his devoted daughter, Ester Burness Mills, and Hildegarde Hawthorne, *Enos Mills of the Rockies* (Boston: Houghton Mifflin, 1935, 260 pp.).

Ormes, Robert. *Tracking Ghost Railroads in Colorado.* Colorado Springs, CO: Century One Press, 1975. 156 pp. Maps, photos, index. An ambitious, fascinating effort to pinpoint the roadbeds of Colorado's many dead railroads. Numerous photos and helpful maps make this an excellent guide for hikers and cross-country skiers as well as researchers.

Busts and Booms

Baron, Bob, et al. *Colorado Rockies: The Inaugural Season.* Golden, Colorado: Fulcrum Pub. Co., 1993. 180 pp. Illus. A lavish color portrait jammed with trivia.

Colorado Guide: Landscapes, Cityscapes, Escapes!! Golden, Colorado: Fulcrum Pub. Co., 1989; 1991 rev. ed. 614 pp. Index, illus. The best guide since the WPA guide, this book offers not only eating, drinking, sleeping, and playing tips but also some historical perspective and suggested readings.

Leonard, Stephen J., and T. J. Noel. *Denver: Mining Camp to Metropolis.* Niwot: Univ. Press of Colorado, 1990. 544 pp. Index, bib., endnotes, illus., maps. The most recent detailed history emphasizing the ups and downs of the mile-high metropolitan area. Almost three-fourths of the book is devoted to the twentieth century, with full-chapter coverage of Adams, Arapahoe, Boulder, and Jefferson Counties.

Index

Note: Page numbers in italics refer to illustrations.

About the Authors

Thomas J. Noel is professor of history at the University of Colorado at Denver. He is the author or co-author of many books on Colorado including *Denver: Mining Camp to Metropolis*. Duane A. Smith, professor of history at Fort Lewis College in Durango, is the author or co-author of numerous books on Colorado and the West including *Colorado: A History in Photographs*.

Both scholars completed their masters and doctorate degrees in history at the University of Colorado at Boulder. Both have chaired their towns' historic preservation commissions and have been sheriff of their towns' Westerners' Posse. They also conduct tours, give talks, are active with their local libraries and museums, and serve on the National Register of Colorado Review Board.